WRITERS ON WRITING
VOL. 1 TO 4 OMNIBUS

**EDITED BY
JOE MYNHARDT**

Crystal Lake Publishing
www.CrystalLakePub.com

Copyright 2016 Crystal Lake Publishing

All Rights Reserved

ISBN: 978-1-68418-759-1

Cover Design:
Ben Baldwin—http://benbaldwin.co.uk/

Interior Layout:
Lori Michelle—www.theauthorsalley.com

Proofread by:
Paula Limbaugh
Nancy Scuri
Robert Teun
Nancy Holder
Amanda Shore
Hasse Chacon
Guy Medley

This is a work of fiction. Names, characters, businesses, places, events and incidents are either the products of the author's imagination or used in a fictitious manner. Any resemblance to actual persons, living or dead, or actual events is purely coincidental.

No part of this publication may be reproduced, stored in a retrieval system, or transmitted in any form or by any means, without the prior permission in writing of the publisher, nor be otherwise circulated in any form of binding or cover than that in which it is published and without a similar condition including this condition being imposed on the subsequent purchaser.

OTHER NON-FICTION BOOKS BY CRYSTAL LAKE PUBLISHING

Horror 101: The Way Forward

Horror 201: The Silver Scream Vol.1 and *Vol.2*

Modern Mythmakers: 35 interviews with Horror and Science Fiction Writers and Filmmakers

COPYRIGHT ACKNOWLEDGEMENTS

"The Infrastructure of the Gods: 11 Signposts for Going all the Way" copyright © 2015 by Brian Hodge

"The Writer's Purgatory: Between Finishing the First Draft and Submitting the Manuscript" copyright © 2015 by Monique Snyman

"Why Rejection is Still Important" copyright © 2015 by Kevin Lucia

"Real Writers Steal Time" copyright © 2015 by Mercedes M. Yardley

"What Right Do I Have to Write" copyright © 2015 by Jasper Bark

"Go Pace Yourself" copyright © 2015 by Jack Ketchum

"A Little Infusion of Magic" copyright © 2015 by Dave-Brendon de Burgh

"Never Look Away: Confronting Your Fears in Fiction" copyright © 2015 by Todd Keisling

"Once More With Feeling" copyright © 2015 by Tim Waggoner

"Embracing Your Inner Shitness" copyright © 2015 by James Everington

"The Forgotten Art of Short Story" copyright © 2015 by Mark Allan Gunnells

"Well, That Escalated Quickly: Adventures in Teaching Creative Writing copyright © 2015 by Lucy A. Snyder

"Submit (to psychology) for Acceptance copyright © 2015 by Daniel I. Russell

"Character Building: How Not to be a Stalker" copyright © 2015 by Theresa Derwin

"Heroes and Villains" copyright © 2015 by Paul Kane

"Do Your Worst" copyright © 2015 by Jonathan Winn

"Creating Effective Characters" copyright © 2010 by Hal Bodner

"Fictional Emotions; Emotional Fictions" copyright © 2016 by James Everington

"Home Sweet Home" copyright © 2016 by Ben Eads

"You" copyright © 2016 by Kealan Patrick Burke

"How about them free books, eh? (the art of becoming a book reviewer)" copyright © 2016 by Nerine Dorman

"Treating Fiction like a Relationship" copyright © 2016 by Jonathan Janz

"Blunt Force Trauma: How to Write Killer Poetry" copyright © 2016 Stephanie M. Wytovich

"Happy Little Trees" copyright © 2016 Michael Knost

"In Lieu of Patience Bring Diversity" copyright © 2016 Kenneth W. Cain

"Networking is Scary, but Essential" copyright © 2016 Doug Murano

"Are You In The Mood?" copyright © 2016 Sheldon Higdon

"What if Every Novel is a Horror Novel?" copyright © 2016 Steve Diamond

"Description: You Can't Win so Why Play" copyright © 2016 Patrick Freivald

"Long Night's Journey Into . . . This? A First-Time Novelist's Odyssey" copyright © 2016 William Gorman

"I Am Setting" copyright © 2016 J.S. Breukelaar

"Finding Your Voice" copyright © 2016 Lynda E. Rucker

TABLE OF CONTENTS

Writers on Writing Vol. 1

The Infrastructure of the Gods: 11 Signposts for Going all the Way by Brian Hodge 3

The Writer's Purgatory: Between Finishing the First Draft and Submitting the Manuscript by Monique Snyman 13

Why Rejection is Still Important by Kevin Lucia 25

Real Writers Steal Time by Mercedes M. Yardley 29

What Right Do I Have to Write by Jasper Bark 35

Go Pace Yourself by Jack Ketchum 44

A Little Infusion of Magic by Dave-Brendon de Burgh.............................48

Never Look Away: Confronting Your Fears in Fiction by Todd Keisling 55

Once More with Feeling by Tim Waggoner 60

Writers on Writing Vol. 2

The Infrastructure of the Gods: 11 Signposts for Going all the Way by Brian Hodge 73

Embracing Your Inner Shitness by James Everington...............................83

The Forgotten Art of Short Story by Mark Allan Gunnells...93

Well, That Escalated Quickly: Adventures in Teaching Creative Writing by Lucy A. Snyder 101

Submit (to psychology) for Acceptance by Daniel I. Russell...113

Character Building: How Not to be a Stalker by Theresa Derwin 120

Heroes and Villains by Paul Kane 127

Do Your Worst by Jonathan Winn 135

Writers on Writing Vol. 3

Creating Effective Characters by Hal Bodner 149

Fictional Emotions; Emotional Fictions by James Everington 168

Home Sweet Home by Ben Eads 178

You by Kealan Patrick Burke 184

How about them free books, eh? (the art of becoming a book reviewer) by Nerine Dorman 189

Treating Fiction like a Relationship by Jonathan Janz 203

Writers on Writing Vol. 4

Blunt Force Trauma: How to Write Killer Poetry by Stephanie M. Wytovich 217

Happy Little Trees by Michael Knost 225

In Lieu of Patience Bring Diversity by Kenneth W. Cain 229

Networking is Scary, but Essential by Doug Murano 236

Are You In The Mood? by Sheldon Higdon 245

What if Every Novel is a Horror Novel? by Steve Diamond 254

Description: You Can't Win so Why Play by Patrick Freivald 259

Long Night's Journey Into . . . This? A First-Time Novelist's Odyssey by William Gorman 268

I Am Setting by J.S. Breukelaar 277

Finding Your Voice by Lynda E. Rucker 290

WRITERS ON WRITING
VOL. 1

THE INFRASTRUCTURE OF THE GODS:
11 Signposts for Going all the Way

BRIAN HODGE

"If you're going to try, go all the way. Otherwise don't even start."—Charles Bukowski

IT'S NEVER BEEN easier to call yourself a published writer. All it takes is one working finger. Lose the other nine and you're still good, as long as you have that last digit to click the publish button. And there you go. Victory dance. Technically, you're published. If that's all you wanted, mission accomplished.

Oh. So you want more.

Readers, then—do you have those? How about raving fans waiting for your next release? Do you have editors and publishers asking to work with you?

If that's your vision, then you're in this for the long haul. You want to go all the way. It doesn't matter if you're inclined toward self-releasing, traditional publication, or a hybrid of the two. It doesn't matter whether you have your eye on the small press or the major houses or both. Getting anywhere is an epic

WRITERS ON WRITING

journey, slow and uphill and demanding so much work and commitment it makes an ironman triathlon seem like a warm-up. It never ends. You never stop learning. Some days you'll want to quit.

You don't blunder your way through the long haul. Navigating it requires relying on what I think of as your personal infrastructure: a framework of good habits, work ethics, mindsets, and codes of conduct, that helps you leverage small steps into big leaps without letting yourself derail too badly in the process. And when you do derail, your infrastructure makes it that much easier to reorient and resume.

You see it all the time: people claiming they want to accomplish something, then going about it as if their top priority is to sabotage themselves at every turn. They seem to have never examined what they insist they want to do, and figured out the best way to make it happen. What to do, what to avoid, how to keep from quitting when it gets hard? Not a clue.

If you're serious about this writing path, here are some of the most vital things to focus on. Some I've learned on my own. Some came from observing the successful and catastrophic examples of others.

It's not the alpha and omega of advice. Nothing ever can be.

But it's a start.

(1) The Most Important Word You Can Tattoo On Your Brain

If a van were to screech up beside me and six commandos jumped out, yanked a black hood over my head, shove me inside, drive me to an undisclosed

VOLUME 1

location, tie me to a chair, yank the hood off, put a gun to my skull, and order me to tell them the single most crucial word to live and work by, I'd have that word ready:

Consistency.

Consistency is, ultimately, what fills pages, then bookshelves. Consistency is what leads to *better*, and gets stuff done over time.

So consistently show up to do the work. Consistently put in the time and effort. Consistently endeavor to improve. Consistently strive to get beyond your influences and develop your own voice. Consistently make each day's work its own reward.

Consistency is less about one day's quantity than long-term frequency. Because it adds up and it's sustainable.

"A small daily task, if it be really daily, will beat the labors of a spasmodic Hercules," said Anthony Trollope.

And how did that work out for him? He produced 47 novels and 16 other books, many of which he wrote while working as a high level official in the postal systems in England and Ireland.

(2) The Way of the Cave Bear

There's a hardline out there that goes something like this: *If you're a real writer, you should be able to do it anytime, anywhere.*

If you can, more power to you. And move along to Section 3, please—there's nothing for you here.

But if things aren't that automatic, don't think something is wrong with you. Don't try to crowbar

WRITERS ON WRITING

yourself into fitting somebody else's image of how you should work. Their judgment is meaningless.

Studies on creativity generally conclude that it thrives best when space is made for it, on a regular schedule. That's what showing up is all about.

Creators tend to be creatures of habit. Your extracurricular assignment is to get your paws on Mason Curry's compulsively readable book, *Daily Rituals: How Artists Work*. Here you'll find the structured routines that enabled dozens of writers, visual artists, composers, even a few scientists and philosophers, to build their bodies of work.

Whether you know it or not, there are probably optimal conditions that help you get the most done with the least amount of resistance. This computer or legal pad. That desk or coffee shop. A particular time of day. Loud music or pin-drop silence.

Pay attention to what works. Do more of that. Isolate. Shut the door. Pop in those ear buds. Don't take assumptions for granted, and realize rhythms can change. I used to be an afternoon/evening writer, after easing into the day. Later I morphed into a morning writer, but only after a lot of stubborn arguments with myself about why afternoons no longer seemed as conducive, and trying to force them into submission.

Whatever it may be, identify your groove, your routine, and stick to it as best you can. It helps when the muse knows when and where to meet you halfway.

And once you're there, starve your distractions of oxygen until they convulse and turn blue. You know what they are. Going online is the worst, a black hole free fall. Turn off your Wi-Fi card, if you have to, or unplug from your modem. Delete that game that

VOLUME 1

yammers to be played. Whatever. The sybaritic ancient Roman in you who lives for instant gratification will always grab for the toys. You have to drown that fucker in his bath on a daily basis.

(3) There Are No Shortcuts

It could only happen now, in this monstrous age of narcissism and raging self-esteem entitlement. There are specimens out there calling themselves writers who feel they're owed eyes on their work simply because it's there. Never mind the typos and grammatical wreckage and continuity errors and the grasp of storytelling so tenuous it would shame a seventh-grader. *I wrote it. So you should read it. Because I wrote it.*

There may be a statistically significant correlation here with devotees of the first-draft-only-draft ethos. Because that first draft is more pure or spontaneous or something.

It gets better. There are specimens out there calling themselves writers who don't even write. To them, just *thinking* about the hypothetical work is enough. *It's in my head. How dare anyone question the way I choose to self-identify.*

Thinking about writing isn't writing. Planning to write isn't writing. Neither is talking about it, posting about it, or complaining how hard it is.

These may be part of the process. But only writing is writing.

And quality takes time. Sometimes quality takes slow, painstaking effort.

The surprising thing about *Daily Rituals* is how

little it took for many of the writers therein to consider it a productive day. A few hundred words. A thousand words. A page or three or five.

In contrast, you can see people online pushing formulas to kick your daily word count into the stratosphere. 5000 words a day. 10,000 words a day. Do your novel in a weekend. The trap here is being so desperately concerned about spraying words like a garden hose that you completely lose sight of whether they're remotely the *right* words.

Yes, there's a case to be made for getting a first draft banged out as quickly as possible. And explosive creative marathons happen. They just tend to be an exhilarating exception rather than a daily rule.

Most professionals recognize that creative energy is not an inexhaustible resource, and once you hit a point of rapidly diminishing returns, you're not doing the work any favors. It's better to disengage and recharge.

(4) Embrace the Grind

This is a phrase that comes from the worlds of collegiate wrestling and combat sports. It refers to all those endless, grueling, repetitive acts of daily training discipline that help grapplers and fighters hone their abilities and improve, little by little.

With writing, the grind is the rewriting process. Polishing. Cutting fat. Tearing things apart and putting them back together again, only better. For me, this is where the magic happens.

If you can fall in love with it, so much the better.

Way way back in the long ago, when all I had to my

VOLUME 1

byline was a few short story credits, with a pair of novels underway, I lucked into spending a couple days around an idol of mine, Robert R. McCammon. I was surprised when he said he disliked the revision process. He would do it, of course. He's a pro, then and now. He just didn't like it, because, he explained, once the story or novel was out of him, further work on it felt like beating a dead horse.

I told him that's not how I was finding it. That I enjoyed rewriting, even loved it, because, once that first draft was down, I was finally able to hold the whole squirming thing in both hands and grasp what it really was. I could see its shortcomings and potential, and start working it into the best shape I was capable of.

"That'll serve you well," McCammon told me.

And I believe it has.

(5) Murder Jealousy In Its Crib

Like every other category of human, writers are an envious lot. There's always somebody out there enjoying the success we want. Flaunting it by their mere existence, the swine: sales figures, audience size, skill level, story acceptances, film rights, book contracts, glowing reviews. Name it, and somebody out there has more of it than we have and *oh my god they don't deserve it, not like I do, I hate them, we hates them all, we swears it on the Precious*.

People achieve what they achieve. They reap what they reap. Merit may not always have much to do with it, and nobody's going to check in for your approval. You can either live with that, or let it eat you alive.

WRITERS ON WRITING

A beautiful example of the right attitude? Once upon a time, Kathe Koja and I were two of the authors being published in a well-received line of books from Bantam Doubleday Dell, called Dell Abyss. At one of numerous convention panels we were on, someone asked if we didn't absolutely *hate* Danielle Steel, because our mutual publisher probably spent more promoting a single one of her books than they did our entire line.

Kathe wasn't having it. I've never forgotten her instantaneous response: "I love Danielle Steel. She pays my advances."

Kathe understood the big picture. That the profits from a mega selling glitzy romance writer—whom our tribe was supposed to scorn—have to go somewhere, and we were beneficiaries of that.

Bottom line, publishing is not a zero-sum game. Somebody else's success does not come at the expense of your own. If anything, it's proof of what's possible, because somebody just did it.

(6) OK, One Exception

The one arena where somebody else's win might mean your loss? Magazines and anthologies. There's only a certain amount of space; budgets allow for a set word count or number of slots.

Cue the conspiracy theorists. They love this one.

Spend enough time hanging around the right Internet forums and convention party suite corners, and eventually you'll encounter one or more someones complaining that tables of contents always feature the same names. *Game's rigged can't get a break mutter*

VOLUME 1

mutter asshole over there he only gets in because he's blowing mumble mumble pass the Jägermeister. The chief bone of contention isn't that they're necessarily sick of reading these authors. Rather, it's that some of those ToC slots rightfully belong to them.

Fact: Newcomers continue to break in, same as they ever have. It isn't easy, same as it never was.

Fact: The complaint isn't inaccurate. You *do* see a lot of familiar names cropping up a lot.

Confession: Some people probably see me as one of them. I'm closing on 120 pieces of short fiction. Most have been published more than once. As I write this, I've had three new ones come out in the past month alone. And I've never blown anybody. Nobody's even asked.

Whatever faults the system may have, it isn't a cabal. There's no velvet rope, and nobody trying to keep newcomers on the wrong side of it. To insist otherwise is to ignore the fact that every repeat offender in those tables of contents started in the same place: with zero publishing credits, toiling in anonymity. They earned their frequent flyer miles by delivering. By being too good for somebody to ignore, then doing business like a professional, and not stopping.

If there's one question veteran editor Stephen Jones hears a lot at conventions, it's this: "How can I get into one of your anthologies?"

His usual answer: "Write better stories."

That's all he wants. That's all any editor wants.

You have no control over what other writers do. Or what editors decide. Or the degree to which readers gravitate toward titles because of the names they know

WRITERS ON WRITING

and trust.

You do, however, have complete jurisdiction over your own quality control. That's your job here: to win over editors in order to get into a place where you can win over readers.

Complaining is easy. Hard work isn't. Choose your focus wisely.

And that should be plenty to take on board for now. We'll conclude with the final five signposts in Writers on Writing Vol. 2, later in this omnibus.

THE WRITER'S PURGATORY: BETWEEN FINISHING THE FIRST DRAFT AND SUBMITTING THE MANUSCRIPT

MONIQUE SNYMAN

"Editing might be a bloody trade, but knives aren't the exclusive property of butchers. Surgeons use them too."—Blake Morrison

THERE ARE NUMEROUS misconceptions about writing, but none are more common—or deceptive—than an author thinking their work is done after typing that final sentence. Regardless of your genre of choice, the fact remains that every author eventually finds themselves in writer's purgatory. This in-between state of completing the first draft and submitting the text at hand is a grueling experience for most, but it doesn't have to be.

As with all trades, honing your writing skills will take time, and being able to distinguish certain writing problems—in order to fix the text before submitting—may help you avoid the slush pile.

WRITERS ON WRITING

SELF-EDIT LIKE A PRO

Self-editing can be a daunting task, especially if you're not naturally unbiased when it comes to your own writing. Editors don't always have time to give feedback in their rejection letters, which leaves authors with very little information as to what they did wrong. As a result, authors may find themselves in a perpetual loop of write-submit-reject. It's a terrible cycle, but it is avoidable. The author's best chance in bettering themselves is thus to determine his/her own shortcomings.

Dialogue and Punctuation

There *is* a difference between a dialogue tag and an action tag, but many writers don't implement the proper punctuation distinguishing the two from one another.

Dialogue Tag: *"Harriet made the decision for us," said Reese.*

Action Tag: *"Harriet made the decision for us." Reese waved a hand through the air, dismissing the matter at once.*

Notice that the dialogue tag ends with a comma, while the action tag ends with a period. Of course, there are advanced techniques in regards to this point, but this is the simplest way to understand—and correct—your text. If you are unsure as to how to punctuate your dialogue, search the almighty Google for further instructions.

VOLUME 1

Other Concerns

Ellipses—Many editors prefer their ellipses a certain way, but it is universally acceptable (unless the publisher's in-house rules say otherwise) to use the ellipse as follows:

"Annie did it . . . I think."

As you can see the ellipse is preceded and succeeded by a space. If the sentence ends on an ellipse, though, do not follow it with another period or a space. It should look like this:

"I think Annie did it . . . "

The Oxford Comma/Harvard Comma/Serial Comma—If you don't know how to use this comma, leave it out. Your editor will put it in *if* they feel it necessary. It is commonly used before the word 'and' at the end of a list: *"I've taken Harriet, Reese, and Annie to the theatre."* However, many new authors tend to go overboard by placing a comma in front of every 'and'. Therefore, if you are unsure as to its proper usage, rather leave it out.

Coordinating Conjunctions—There's been a lot of debate on whether it is proper to start a sentence with a coordinating conjunction ('but', 'and', 'or', 'for', 'so', and 'yet'). Some editors approve of its use, others do not. As an author, however, you won't know an editor's view of these things. Therefore, it might be best to avoid using them as much as possible.

Present Participles—*NEVER* begin a sentence with a present participle. Present participles are '-ing' words, and are considered a trap for new authors who have not learned the ins-and-outs of writing yet. Sometimes they cannot be avoided, true, but *ALWAYS* try to at least halve the number of present participles in your manuscript with each rewrite.

Adverbs—Adverbs are '-ly' words, often found at the end of a dialogue tag:

"Joe stumbled and fell," Reese mocked gleefully.

Again, they cannot always be avoided, but as Stephen King says: *"I believe the road to hell is paved with adverbs, and I will shout it from the rooftops."*

Spaces—NEVER USE A DOUBLE SPACE BETWEEN SENTENCES. It's a single space, always.

Passive Tense to Active Tense—This might be the most important, albeit most difficult, part of self-editing . . . Change your tenses from passive tense to active tense *before* you even contemplate submitting your manuscript. Active tense can be achieved by rewriting any—preferably *all*—sentences with a 'was' in it. 'Was'es' and 'were's' are bad for crisp, clean sentence constructions.

Passive Tense: *"Lily was crying when the children were laughing at her art project."*

Active Tense: *"Lily cried when the children laughed at her art project."*

See the difference? It's snappier and to the point when active tense is implemented. Of course, sometimes it's not as easy as removing a 'was' or a 'were', but this makes for a fine starting point in your self-editing journey.

Point-of-View Shifts

Shifting point-of-views occurs mainly in texts written in third-person. Often, authors shift perspectives between characters to create an omnipresent situation

VOLUME 1

for the reader. More often than not, though, the reader is left in a state of confusion. A general rule to follow, *if* the author wishes to write multiple points-of-view, is to stick to one viewpoint per scene and to clearly define the shifts with scene breaks. However, it should be noted that even by implementing these practices, shifting too often can hinder the reader's experience.

Filler Words

Sometimes a filler word is necessary to get a point across, but don't fall into the trap of using a filler word because you're too lazy to pick up a dictionary or to construct a proper sentence. Filler words includes, but is not limited to: 'thought', 'felt', 'saw', 'very', 'tiny', 'little', 'that', 'really', 'there was', 'there were', 'like', 'just'. Rework sentences with filler words in them and your manuscript will already look cleaner to an editor.

Pet Phrases

Pet Phrases are like filler words, except you don't often realise you're using them. It's one of those personal writing problems that often give the reader a sense of déjà vu. Pet phrases lead to redundancy, leading to frustrated editors, which often means your manuscript will be dumped into a slush pile. To avoid the slush pile, you will have to search for your personal pet phrases, which may (or may not) look like the following examples:
"Rolled her eyes."
"Grinned like a fool."
"Heart raced."

WRITERS ON WRITING

There are many phrases like these in your manuscript, you just have to weed them out as best you can or rework them to sound different.

Clichés

Clichés can sometimes make or break your whole story. A cliché becomes a cliché when a word, sentence, idea, or expression is overused to such an extent that it's become trite and irritating. Yes, clichés are irritating. Ergo, they should be avoided. If, however, they cannot be escaped, try to make the cliché your own. For example: *"Ah, to be young and foolish . . . "* can be changed to something like: *"What I'd give to be sparkly-eyed and naïve again."*

Redundancy

I'm sure many authors hate their editors, especially when they receive their edited manuscript—crimson dripping from the pages like blood flowing from a wound. Therefore, let it be known that nothing pisses off an editor like continued redundancy. Every redundant sentence will get scratched out, and a snarky comment will possibly accompany the reason as to *why* it's been omitted. Also, if you're new to the game and you've decided not to self-edit (bad judgment on your part), be prepared for your 90,000 word novel to be cut down to ±50,000 words instead. It's unfortunately what you get for trying to over-explain something that could've been said in one sentence.

Once you've self-edited to such an extent that

VOLUME 1

you're considering a short stay at a psychiatric facility, go through your manuscript one last time. Only then will you be ready to take the next step.

PROOF-READERS TO THE RESCUE

When searching for beta-readers, scratch family and close friends' names off the list. Not only will they be too biased to give you necessary critical feedback, but you might not want your mother to read an especially spicy scene in your story. Besides, the best proof-readers are other writers. Join a writers' group if you can, or enroll in a creative writing class. Here, you will learn about other problems in your manuscript that would've otherwise gone unnoticed. It is important, however, to return the favor. This common courtesy will help you connect with other professionals, which may be invaluable for your career as an author.

A good beta-reader will tear you a new one.

If you can survive a critical beta-reader, whilst keeping their suggestions of improvement in mind, you can survive a tame editor.

Remember, you don't *need* to alter everything your beta-readers suggest changing. It is still *your* story at the end of the day. That said, make sure to listen to beta-readers when common themes pop up in regards to characterization, confusing scenes, restructuring of plot-lines, etcetera.

TO SELF-PUBLISH OR NOT TO SELF-PUBLISH, THAT IS THE QUESTION?

You've written your novel, self-edited it until you've

WRITERS ON WRITING

reached borderline insanity, sent it out to proofreaders, and somehow survived their abuse. Now what? Well, after you've cleaned up your manuscript as best you can, it's time to decide if you want to go old school with a traditional publisher or if you're going to follow the trend by self-publishing your novel.

I'm not going to go into detail about self-publishing, mostly because there are a lot of sources available on the internet that will help you on your journey to becoming a successful self-published author. I will, however, say that many big-name authors—Beatrix Potter, Virginia Woolf, and James Joyce—were originally self-published. Impressive, huh?

That said, not *everyone* can win the lotto either.

Some authors are not skilled enough to take on a project as large as self-publication. After all, the amount of work that goes into getting a book on the shelves is ridiculously complex. You have to do, or outsource, the work of a whole publishing team. This includes: editing, text formatting, cover design, and marketing. Not to mention, you need to understand copywriting, know how to buy ISBNs, understand how your country is going to tax you, etcetera. The time spent on self-promotion, or on finding adequate people/companies to do these things on your behalf, is also wasted. Time you could have used to write your next book.

Self-publishing can be downright hellish, especially if your returns aren't what you expected.

Traditional publishing isn't much easier to deal with. Not only will you have to wait weeks, sometimes months, to get a reply from a submission editor, but

VOLUME 1

the publishing process can take years to complete. The upside, however, is that you will at least have a team of professionals backing your book—*if* you're successful in grabbing their attention in the first place. Unfortunately, the publisher usually has the last say in every single matter in the publishing process. Think you can design your own cover? Think again. Want to change the formatting of your book to something more whimsical? Fat chance! Granted, a traditional publisher knows what sells, and even if they don't know, you're out of luck in trying to change their minds.

Either way, there are advantages and disadvantages to both self-publishing and traditional publishing. It's up to you to research your options and to decide what choice you'll be willing to live with.

BEWARE VANITY PUBLISHERS

Now is a good time to touch on the subject of vanity publishers.

What is a vanity publisher?

Vanity publishers are publishing houses that publishes books in return for payment from the author. They are vampires, preying on desperate authors and sucking the joy out of writing. They seldom put any work into their editing services, outsource their cover art designs to inexperienced (and cheap) graphic designers, and hardly ever market the author's works. Vanity publishers go out of their way to gush over your work until you've paid them exorbitant amounts of money to get it published, and then they couldn't care less what happens next.

WRITERS ON WRITING

How do you tell a vanity publisher from a real publisher?

A real publisher is a picky bastard that won't spare your feelings when it comes to what's wrong with your book. A vanity publisher, on the other hand, will make it sound like you're the next Stephen King—and all you have to do to get your book professionally published is to "contribute towards the cost of publication".

How can I avoid vanity publishers?

Vanity publishers advertise their services everywhere on the internet, they're sneaky that way. But in order to avoid them (and any other unethical publishers), make sure that you do your research beforehand by checking out some writer forums online. Also, read your contract carefully. You don't want to sign away your life savings unnecessarily. Money should always move toward the author, otherwise it's vanity publishing.

PLANNING YOUR SUBMISSION

If you've read this far, I take it you've decided to submit your manuscript to a traditional publisher and/or agent. Congratulations, you've reached the trickiest part of your journey through writer's purgatory! If you think self-editing was a dreadful ordeal, you're in for a big surprise. Nope, self-editing is a cakewalk in comparison to planning a successful submission. Sorry to burst your bubble, my dearest fellow writers.

This step comes with a nifty checklist, to keep you on track:

Search for an appropriate publisher for your

VOLUME 1

manuscript. Keep the genre of your book in mind during your search, and make sure the publisher is interested in publishing that particular genre before you do anything else.

Study the publisher's in-house writing rules. Most publishers have an online presence. *If* they are accepting submissions they'll likely have their preferred writing style on their website. Adhere to these rules or you'll automatically end up in the slush pile. If the preferred writing style is not displayed on the website, then your best bet is to follow a standard manuscript format. Google it if you're unsure how a standard manuscript format looks.

Research how to write a book proposal. Writing a book proposal that comprises of no more than 1 page, is catchy enough to grab the submission editor's attention, informative enough to give the publisher an idea as to whether it will sell or not, and shows off your skills as an author, is almost impossible to achieve. Almost, being the operative word. With practice, you too can bewitch a submission editor with your skills, but it's not going to happen overnight. Prepare for that.

Write and rewrite your synopsis until it can be seen as literary genius by itself. A synopsis isn't supposed to be tricky, especially seeing as you wrote the book, but many authors seem to struggle with this part, too. Reread your manuscript, until you've got a good idea what you want to say in the synopsis (I find making notes along the way helpful), then go crazy. If it helps, search for examples on the internet to help you along the way.

How to write an author biography. Keep it short

WRITERS ON WRITING

and sweet. Write it in third-person. Don't be arrogant. Don't be timid. Just be who you are in everyday life. That *should* be enough.

Send the whole submission packet to your trusted writer friends. Your writer friends will come in handy now, especially when it comes to picking up those last few mistakes in your text. Those tiny errors may not look like much to you, but submission editors are unforgiving. One spelling mistake can earn you a rejection letter. Simple.

Only when you are sure do you send the submission. If you can make the manuscript better, do. If you've done all you can, send it.

IN CONCLUSION

Prepare yourself for a rejection letter. It happens even to the best writers, but it's not the end of the world. Learn from your mistakes, correct them, and try again.

Remember not to get impatient. When you send email after email requesting a decision for your manuscript, many submission editors will feel inclined to send a rejection letter just to get you off their back.

Lastly, sit back and contemplate your next project while you wait for a decision. Not every idea is a winner, deal with it. Besides, if you are a true writer, you'll never stop trying to tell that story brewing in your mind.

WHY REJECTION IS STILL IMPORTANT

KEVIN LUCIA

MY FIRST REJECTION nearly ended my career.

Picture this: Young Writer, excited about submitting his first short story to a new publication offering sizable cash awards. Young Writer has labored over said story. He's also spoken to the editor several times through the magic of MySpace and feels confident of his success.

To his dismay, Young Writer receives not the glowing acceptance he's expecting, but a rejection, and an acute critique of his story. In several paragraphs, the editor has dismantled the story Young Writer spent hours crafting.

Understandably, Young Writer takes umbrage with this merciless rejection. How dare the editor reject what he's worked so hard on? Those three pages of first-person italics the editor so harshly mocked? Anyone can see that's supposed to be internal monologue! And the main character is NOT a lame version of Blade, *obviously*. He's a *white* guy who

WRITERS ON WRITING

drives a *Mustang*, not a *Charger*, and only has *one* samurai sword, not *two*. And the "cheesy" vampire dialogue? He's evil and ancient! He's *supposed* to sound that way!

Young Writer angrily clicks his mouse and hovers the cursor over his email's *delete* icon. He's had it with the editor. Obviously this guy doesn't know good fiction when he sees it, and this publication obviously isn't the place for Young Writer's powerful and action-packed stories.

But, before he clicks *delete*, he notices the editor's parting comment at the end of the rejection. It reads something like this: "There's too much wrong with this story . . . but there's also *something* here, something strong in your voice. TRY AGAIN."

Young Writer debates. Obviously, the editor doesn't "get" this story. What's the likelihood he'll "get" another? However, a thought pops up. Young Writer takes a moment and does a hard thing: he wonders if the editor is at least *partly right* in his scathing critique, realizing that, indeed, maybe three pages of first person italics is a bit much. And honestly, the vampires do sound kind of lame.

Then, Young Writer thinks of all the times he's had to absorb harsh criticism to improve at something. He thinks of a college basketball career, and how he would've never improved if his coach hadn't harped on him constantly about bad habits. He remembers how he kept getting C+ grades on his college essays freshman year until one of his instructors really tore his academic writing apart. He remembers how he lost his first teaching job because he was too stubborn to learn from his mistakes.

VOLUME 1

Then, Young Writer asks himself a question that will change everything thereafter: *How badly do you want this? How badly do you want to be published?*

Young Writer sucks it up. He scraps his beloved story and starts a new one from scratch, with no vampires or supernatural vampire hunters, no samurai swords or cool *Mustangs* and with as few italics as he can manage (although probably still too many, because Young Writer really likes italics, as he *still* does). He tries his best to address all of Editor's critiques, and finds that most of them, indeed, make his writing easier to read. And, surprisingly, Young Writer discovers he likes his second story much more than the first.

Young Writer's story is accepted. It receives Editor's Choice honors and garners Young Writer a large cash reward, his first time out of the gate. And none of it would've happened had he not sucked it up and listened to the editor's critiques.

The moral of the story?

Rejection and critique is one of the most necessary things for a young writer (or any writer, for that matter) to endure in order to improve and grow, even with the ease of self-publishing today. Whether a writer plans on submitting to traditional publishers or self-publishing, there *must* be a knowledgeable voice along the way which pulls no punches and spares no blows. Every writer needs this; young writers need it even *more*. To help them develop. Grow a thick skin. Remind them the publishing universe doesn't revolve around them. Help them push their own boundaries.

I still have a long way to go in developing myself. But I feel very blessed that my first story (as I'm sure

WRITERS ON WRITING

you guessed I was Young Writer) was so soundly rejected. It proved to be a pivotal moment. It's shaped my career. It helped me understand how important it is to step outside of myself and accept critique which is, in the end, only intended to make my story better. It made me amendable to critique, which has aided my growth as a writer.

I recently completed my final edits for my next book, *Through a Mirror, Darkly*. As always, the interaction between my editor and I was complimentary, thoughtful, and edifying. I've enjoyed working with numerous editors, and have always found their insight and critique to be helpful. And I believe that's possible only because I was so soundly rejected that first time, and I sucked it up and listened to Editor's final bit of advice: TRY AGAIN. Which is, in the end, the best and only response to rejection.

REAL WRITERS STEAL TIME

MERCEDES M. YARDLEY

I ALWAYS THOUGHT the ideal life of a writer closely mirrored that of Henry David Thoreau. One wakes with the sun to the sounds of nature. After a breakfast of strong coffee, pencil shavings, and whimsy, one wanders down to the river for an invigorating bath. Then the writer writes. For several hours, burning candles (even during the day!) this writer pens works of wonder and imagination. Then the writer breaks and ambles along a winding path in the woods, lost in reverie and, perhaps, lost in the woods themselves. Then it's back to the cabin for a dinner of bear hide and wood bark. More words. Darkness falls and the candles are actually useful this time. Then into bed to dream the most wondrous and literary of dreams.

Writers apparently don't pay bills in my mind. They exist on sunlight and ozone. Writers live alone, off the grid, and I have no idea why I think they only eat wood. Apparently writers are also beavers.

The key concept to this is that I believed writers were mystical creatures created out of hope and time.

WRITERS ON WRITING

They had hours and hours of time dedicated simply to their art. As a fledgling writer, this distressed me. The one thing I didn't have was time! I was a writer deep in my soul and always had been, but I was dissuaded by the terrible fact that I could never feasibly snack on twigs and write for days. I didn't even have hours.

I'm ashamed to say this kept me from writing, and it murdered my soul. Because I didn't have long blocks of time to dedicate to my craft, I figured I was just a wannabe and would never achieve my dreams. Real writers put their art above all else. Real writers know how to sacrifice. I was just human, and my chance of turning into a real writer seemed as far away as turning into a unicorn.

Then I met real writers, and my perspective changed. They had jobs. They had families. They worked as hotel clerks and telemarketers and checked for radiation in dangerous areas. They threw birthday parties for their children, went to PTA meetings, and wrote while the rest of the house slept.

Real writers have lives. Real writers write, but that isn't all they do. And real writers seem to have a penchant for cake and tacos, not simply wood shavings. How could this be? If I was wrong about what a real writer was, could I be wrong about something else?

I'm going to share a secret with you. It's something that took me nearly a decade of dedicated writing to figure out, and I wish I had learned it sooner because it has changed my life. This wonderful and amazing secret?

Novels are built word by word, sentence by sentence. You can put these pieces together in brief stolen moments of time.

VOLUME 1

That's it. That's the secret. It's really all you need to know.

Life is full of little moments that can be harnessed to create your work. Think of cupping your hands together while somebody fills them with water. The water will leak out through your fingers, draining from your hands no matter how tightly you cup them. This is exactly how time works. Time dribbles from your day just as water dribbles from your fingers. The trick is to recognize some of these precious seconds of "wasted" time and to use them.

How do we find some of these unused gems of time? We search for them.

Always have your manuscript available.

Leave your laptop open and your computer turned on. Carry a notebook or voice recorder with you. You don't ever want to be in a position where you can squeeze in five minutes of work and you're lacking your materials. Prepare now, and eventually this will become second nature.

Utilize nonwriting time for your writing purposes.

You've probably heard that the best ideas occur in the shower. They also occur any time your body is moving and you have a second to think. Think about your work while vacuuming. Ponder it on your commute. If you're in a carpool, brainstorm with the other passengers sharing the ride with you. Hairdressers love to throw out plot ideas. Work out a line or two of

WRITERS ON WRITING

dialogue while doing the dishes, and as soon as you're finished, zip on over to your manuscript (which is already open and up on your computer, as told in step one) and jot it down. Your wheels will be turning even when you can't physically write it down at the moment.

Time yourself.

This is one of my most effective tips. In fact, I'm timing myself as we speak.

Setting a timer for five, ten, fifteen, or twenty minutes is a fantastic tool to help you take your work seriously. Since you know that you only have ten minutes to write, it forces you to stop playing around on the Internet. Ten minutes? Your loved ones can leave you alone for ten minutes. Your cat won't starve in ten minutes. You can pay attention for that long, so do. Write as fast as you can until your timer goes off. This isn't the time to search for the perfect word or do any editing whatsoever. This is your time to vomit your words on the page and get them down. You can always edit later. What starts as ten minutes might easily stretch to 30, and that's even better!

But in case you still have difficulty focusing, we have tip number four.

Block distractions.

Or at least do your very best. You might not be able to block air-raid sirens or the zombie apocalypse, but you can block Facebook temporarily. Tell your children that they can wait ten minutes for you to finish your writing unless there's blood. Use programs like Self-

VOLUME 1

Restraint or Self-Control to block access from your favorite Internet sites until your writing is done. I admire a good, clean inbox or clever Pinterest post as much as the next person, but not during writing time. Block it until you reach your goal, and then unblock it when you're finished. You might be surprised how often you unintentionally start checking mail or posts. I was a bit embarrassed to discover how often I zipped over to read the news, often without even realizing it. It was humbling.

Use a program like Dropbox or the Cloud.

Make sure that you can access your work on any device that you have. These programs let you add lines to your manuscript using whatever device is handy, and it can be saved to all of them. Computers, laptops, tablets, and your phone become your new offices. If you're in the waiting room or in line, you can add precious words, lines, and even whole paragraphs to your novel/short story/essay/grocery list/work of art. You'll never be dormant. You'll always be moving forward.

Alternate Responsibilities

Once again, you'll need a handy dandy timer for this one. A great way to keep your momentum is to alternate your responsibilities. Set your time for 10 or 15 minutes and write. Then set your timer again and work on another responsibility. This could be cleaning, meditating, physical activity, preparing a lesson, cooking, or anything that you have to do but are

WRITERS ON WRITING

dragging your feet on. You can do hard things for short amounts of time. Then repeat. Repeat as many times as you need to. Do it once a day. Do it 10 times a day. Whatever fits your schedule. Whatever fits your needs. Remember that this is all about what works for *you,* and what makes you happy. Productivity tends to make us happy. Creating art brings joy.

Here's the ironic part about this whole thing: I struggled mightily to find time to write this essay. I have three kids all home right now. Our backyard chicken is sick (yes, that actually manages to cut into my time. You have no idea how very, um, *intimate* a sick chicken's needs can be). Publishers need things. Schools need things. Dentists and orthodontists need things. I feel vaguely hunted.

But do you know what saved me? The advice and tips I gave above. It would be absolutely lovely to have half an hour to sit and write, but unfortunately that isn't going to happen at the moment. However, I do have five minutes here and forty seconds there. A pink Post-It and a pen in my purse helped me come up with some of the bullet points I wanted to hit. I typed out two lines one-handed while carrying a sleeping toddler in the other arm.

Piece by piece, bit by bit.

Novels (and essays) are built sentence by sentence. Remember this and you can complete whatever you desire.

Best of luck to you, my friend. Now go amaze yourself and the rest of the world. You have something important to say, so say it.

WHAT RIGHT DO I HAVE TO WRITE?

JASPER BARK

It is a truth universally acknowledged, that never has the prospect of cleaning the oven, unblocking the toilet, filing your grandmother's bunions, or bathing a whole colony of lepers looked so tempting as when you have to sit down and start writing.

When people find out you write for a living, many of them will get a misty look in their eye and wistfully confess: "Oh, I've always wanted to write." They don't say "I'm planning to do some writing" or "I'm going to do some writing," it's always something we mean to get around to—some day. And sadly, some day rarely comes for many of us.

It's as though the circumstances are never right for writing. We don't have the time, we don't have the space in our lives, we don't have anywhere we can lock ourselves away to devote ourselves to that great novel. It's common to start fantasizing about starting a new life, where we take ourselves off to the South of France, open a little bistro and then maybe start that novel. Overlooking the whole time, just how time consuming

WRITERS ON WRITING

it would be to relocate to another country and set up a new business. So time consuming it wouldn't be the least bit conducive to the arduous task of writing a novel. We dream of escaping to write a novel because we can't see any place for writing in our current lives.

I'm here to tell you that there *is* a place. The only thing you need to start writing is to sit down and start writing. It really is that simple. Grab a pencil and a notepad, open up your laptop or tablet, pick up a stick and start scratching in the dirt, it doesn't matter, so long as you're putting words together. As soon as you start doing that, more words will come and the ideas will slowly start to flow. But only if you START WRITING!!!

The only thing standing in your way, the only thing stopping you from sitting down and writing is *you* yourself. And *you* are a pretty formidable obstacle to your writing. You always will be. You'll constantly be looking over your own shoulder and tutting at what you write, pointing out your appalling grammar, commenting on the ridiculous plot holes in your story and bemoaning the fact that you ever suspected, even for a moment, that you had any talent for writing.

If you're not doing that to yourself, you'll be whispering in your own ear about how great it would be, right about now, to go and make a sandwich. Okay, so you only had dinner an hour ago, and yes you're finally on a roll, but think about how much you could go for a snack right about now. Or you'll be suggesting that you go check twitter or your Facebook page, cos it's only been five minutes since you last looked and something really important might have happened since then. Think of all the cute cat videos you're

VOLUME 1

missing, can you really afford not to check it? It'll only take a few minutes, and yes those few minutes will probably stretch into a half hour, but at least you're sorta writing aren't you, I mean you're typing words and stuff. Or hey, listen, there's a rerun of the second season of *House* starting in a few minutes, and okay, it's not your favourite series, but it has Hugh Laurie in it and he does a really good American accent for a Brit. He must have put a lot of time and effort into getting his accent that good, so the least you can do is sit down and watch four episodes back to back instead of rudely wasting your time with all this pointless writing.

Unfortunately, no matter how long you write, you will never go away and stop doing this to yourself. One of the most important lessons you'll ever have to learn as a writer is how to get over yourself, and trust me, it's a constant battle.

What it takes, more than anything, is discipline. When you find yourself in the kitchen making a sandwich, put everything back in the fridge, sit back down and write. When you realise you're looking at Facebook for the third time in the last half hour, switch off your router, put it in a cupboard and sit back down and write. When you're flicking through late night channels, because you didn't really like *House* that much after all, get off the couch, unplug your TV then SIT BACK DOWN AND WRITE! You need to be constantly vigilant and permanently aware of all the little tricks you play on yourself to stop yourself writing.

The sort of discipline this requires is the sort of discipline an adult uses when they're put in charge of young children, especially if those young children are

WRITERS ON WRITING

hyperactive and suffer from ADD. That's because the part of you that gets in the way of your writing is a child. A scared and vulnerable child who's terrified of you getting what you most want out of life. That's because you don't think you deserve it.

We all wrestle with issues of entitlement, some of us more than others. Part of getting what we want out of life is learning to accept these issues and working around them to overcome the problems they cause us. We secretly judge ourselves far more harshly than we judge others, and every time we fall short, we punish ourselves. That self-punishment usually involves some form of sabotage, we take the things we most want away from ourselves.

There's no easy way to address this issue. I'm not a therapist, but it's something I've wrestled with myself for many years, and there are a few practical things I've learned that will help you deal with it.

The first thing that's crucial for you to accept, if you're ever going to address your sense of 'negative entitlement,' is that writing is no big deal. Let me just type that again, in full caps, in case you didn't catch it the first time: WRITING IS NO BIG DEAL.

Most people, who don't write themselves, seem to think it's some kind of dream job. It's not. It's occasionally a fun job, but it involves working under nightmare conditions. There's a huge divide between the dream of writing for a living and the actuality.

The dream usually involves sitting on a sunny balcony, overlooking a breathtaking view, with your laptop open while you take a call from Spielberg about your latest blockbuster. This usually segues into the speech you make while accepting the Oscar for the

VOLUME 1

screenplay you wrote based on your latest blockbuster. Finally this is followed by visions of the attractive and nubile young fans who queue around the block, whenever you sign, and are as desperate for you to sign their body parts as the multiple books they've bought.

This couldn't be further from the truth. Even for writers like Stephen King, J. K. Rowling, and James Patterson, who are supposedly living that dream. In fact, if you were to put it to them that they are 'living the dream,' they would probably laugh bitterly in your face. This dream doesn't exist and it never has. It has only ever been a dream.

The reality of writing will be that you'll spend up to a year finishing your first work. It will be a painful process that will involve a lot of soul searching, many dead ends and a lot of wrestling with your inner demons. It will be done in whatever spare time you have outside of your job and other responsibilities. If you have family you'll have to negotiate long absences in order to get the space and time to write.

When you've finished the manuscript you'll have to deal with the feedback of your beta readers and an editor (if you've bitten the bullet and decided to hire one). Then you'll have to revise huge chunks of it. When the MS is in a good enough shape, you'll start sending it out to agents and publishers who will send you a slew of polite rejections, if they bother to reply at all. There's a strong possibility that it won't sell, leaving you with the option to put it to one side and start another book, or to go down the self-publishing route.

When your book finally does come out, either through your own efforts, or those of an independent/mainstream publisher, there's a strong possibility that it won't bother any best seller charts. Not even those incredibly obscure ones that Amazon invents such as Kindle Store > Books > Mystery > Romance > Books only written by YOU! Even on that chart there will still be two people above you, and one of them will undoubtedly be Stephen King. Don't ask me why, I'm not even certain King understands himself.

Then there is the endless wall of feedback you'll have to deal with. The bloggers who will sneer at your work even though they can barely write a legible sentence themselves. The Goodreads reviewers who will dismiss your months of painful effort with a single "meh," and the Amazon reviewers who will give you one star simply because the mailman tore the packaging and ripped the cover when he delivered it. Most of the sales you *do* make will be as a result of people you met on-line or at conventions and other events.

After a few years, and growing sales, you might make enough to take the family on holiday or pay for some much needed home repairs. Your writing career will become a fun and occasionally lucrative hobby, or a secondary career, a bit like running a craft fair stall on the weekends. Many writers who are lucky enough to make enough money to write full time, still decide to go back to full time employment after a few years, because they don't enjoy the hours of isolation and the insecure income. What's more, they find they can get almost as much written doing it part time anyway.

So like I said above. Writing is no big deal. Once you accept that, you can crawl out from under the

VOLUME 1

crushing weight of expectation you're placing on yourself. You'll realise that there's no point punishing yourself by stopping yourself writing, because you're not missing out on anything much, just the simple fun of doing something you enjoy. Writing is, and always will be, its own reward.

This is the next important thing to remember when you get dispirited, discouraged or distracted. Think about how neat it would be to see a finished piece of writing with your name on it. There will be something in the world that wasn't there before, something you can take great pride in. Imagine seeing your story in an anthology that you could show to others, or even seeing your name on a book that contains nothing but your work. If those thoughts don't excite you and fill you with giddy ambition, then why the hell are you bothering to write?

Use this excitement and ambition as an incentive, whenever you feel too tired to write, or when you think you're not in the mood. Dangle the huge possibilities, that come with creating something, in front of you like a carrot. Use them to drive you on when there's a hundred other things you feel like doing. That way you'll stick it out, stay put, and finish the damn thing. And simply finishing the damn thing is a great, great feeling.

The next thing to think about is why you're writing this particular story? What's the juice that's driving it, the love that keeps you coming back to this idea? What is it that you really want to say with this work? The things that cause us to become obsessed with certain stories are not always the stories themselves, but what those stories represent to us. Maybe you're coming to

WRITERS ON WRITING

terms with a loved one abandoning you, or perhaps you need closure on a painful work relationship, the story is your way of addressing that, of saying everything you need to say about it, putting it all down in black and white and getting it straight, because, damn it, it needs to be said.

Maybe it's not even that deep or highfalutin, maybe it's just that you've never seen or read a Kaiju story that really does the genre justice. That shows monsters fighting and ravaging a city in the way you know it could and should be done. Perhaps it's about time you sat down and showed the world how it ought to be done and how goddamned cool it would be if it was finally done properly.

Whatever the case, you should use this enthusiasm, and this need to tell the story, as a spur to goad yourself into action every time you feel your concentration or your determination slipping.

Finally, never lose sight of what it is that makes your writing unique. It's very easy to fall into the trap of wondering why on earth anyone would be interested in reading what you write. We've all asked ourselves why anyone would want to hear what we have to say and whether we have the right to write at all. This can be one of the biggest obstacles to overcome.

We all have something completely original to say though, or we wouldn't be drawn to write. F. Scott Fitzgerald once said, "You don't write because you want to say something, you write because you have something to say." It doesn't have to be something earth-shatteringly different, it doesn't need to revolutionise the whole of fiction, it just has to be something that only you could say.

VOLUME 1

Think about all those witty remarks you've made over the years that had a whole room of people in tears, or were shared endlessly on Twitter. Consider the little rhymes you might have made up to entertain your children or other people's. Remember all the clever little observations you made to close friends and loved ones, the thoughts you gave them that changed the way they viewed a certain thing forever.

None of those things could have come from anyone but you. Wouldn't it be a crying shame if they died with you? If there was no record of them after you were gone? Don't you owe it to the world to make certain they not only live on after you, but that hundreds of people, who you may never meet, get the opportunity to share them, too?

You see, this is what gives you the right to write and this is what entitles you to be an author. This is something very sacred and special that belongs only to you. You should never let the ignorance and incomprehension of others dampen or extinguish that uniqueness and you should never, ever get in the way of it yourself.

This is why you should put this book down this minute and get back to writing. Don't worry about the rest of the essays in here. They'll still be waiting for you when you're done. Right now you need to sit down and start writing because no one else can write the things you can, and you owe it to yourself, and to the world, to get started right away.

Trust your Uncle Jasp on this, you know it makes sense.

GO PACE YOURSELF

JACK KETCHUM

LISTEN TO ME. Listen up.
Listen *hard*.
I'm not going to say this again.
Do it. Try. Come on . . .
You can't, can you?
No way. No way in hell you can hear me.

You can only hear yourself. Your own voice. Your own voice imagini4ng my voice. You're trapped in there.

Am I a man or a woman? You don't know. Not until I tell you. These short sentences seem sort of masculine. But you never know. Maybe I'm just messing with you.

Maybe I'll tell and maybe I won't.
Okay, I want you to do something else for me.
Maybe you can manage this.

I want you to imagine that you're sitting at a desk made of dark hard wood and on that desk is a computer that sometimes stands utterly silent in front of you and sometimes plays little recorded tunes through the speakers on either side should you happen

VOLUME 1

to be on the internet at the time. But now you're working on a story, your fingers tapping away at the keyboard and you've got all the time in the world to finish it up exactly the way you want it to be. This is just what you've always hoped to do for a living and now after all this time you're even getting paid pretty well. Not even the sound of the birds outside or a dog barking far away down the block or the warm air billowing the curtains at the open window beside you can distract you from getting the story exactly right this time.

Imagine that pretty well, did you?
Good.
You've just had a little lesson in pacing.

Writers are full of tricks. Cards up our sleeve, cribbed from everybody from Sophocles to Swierczynski. Unlike magicians we usually don't mind sharing them.

Go back to the beginning of this piece. All those imperatives and short, one-or-two-line sentences. Don't they make you a little nervous? Short sentences or paragraphs do that. They tend to lend a kind of urgency to what you're reading. Forget for a moment that there *are* so many imperatives dragging you in and pushing you on. That's voice. Related, sure, yet another discussion entirely. But the way the eye scans short sentences—and as this section points out, the way the ear hears them, with your own voice inevitably the one that's speaking—rushes you down and through the page, like it or not. That's just the way we perceive things.

The wham, bam, thank you ma'am of reading.

Now go to the second section, the one where I have

WRITERS ON WRITING

you imagining you're a successful writer hotwired to his computer. You're cooking. You're happy. Personally a dog barking down the block *would* distract the hell out of me but that's just me. Look at the length of the lines here.

Longer sentences like these tend to impart a sense of calm, of reflection. They're peaceful. Whereas the first section's jagged as broken glass. The exception to the rule on this is your long rampant run-on—which is actually a bunch of short sentences cobbled breathlessly together. A kind of disguise.

My god look at what this guy's doing, he's telling me about pace and he's fucking with my head at the same time, and I should really pay him something but I don't know what to pay him, I gotta send him something so okay, I'll figure it out eventually, maybe later. Maybe a whole lot later.

It's illusion. But it does rush you through the paragraph.

Now compare the two sections in terms of the number of adjectives in each. In the first section I count three, "short" modifying "sentences," "sort of" modifying "masculine," and "in hell" modifying "no way." In the second section I count well over a dozen. Modifiers slow the eye and ear down, as well. Give you more to ponder maybe, help you relax a bit with a sharper, more specific image in mind. A long line is the recliner chair of fiction.

Finally, consider the number three.

It's a magic number, really.

At least for us writers.

In fact, look at what I just wrote. Just now. These last three lines. Don't you want to know what the hell

VOLUME 1

I'm talking about? Sure you do.

The first section consists of twenty-one lines. And I didn't do this on purpose, honest. I didn't count them when I wrote them. I just did. It's probably ingrained in me by now.

Twenty-one is divisible by three.

Now look at the first few sentences, way up top. Those imperatives. The ones that got you reading this in the first place.

Listen to me. Listen up.

Listen *hard*.

Three.

So consider the number three for a moment. *Beginning, middle, and end.* In a joke, *setup, setup, and punchline.* In a filmscript, *first, second, and third acts.* Until relatively recently, and with the Romans and Shakespeare excepted, also true of most theatrical plays. *Setup, conflict, resolution.*

It's been theorized that the number three is deeply ingrained in the human psyche and that its power lies in that it reflects the basic procreative unit of mother, father, and child. But all I know for sure is that for a writer, threes work. In structure and in the actual writing. Exactly how or why they work I leave for you to ponder. But they punch. They're jagged. They hook.

All you have to do is count the lines in the second section, the relaxing section, to see the difference.

Four.

Nice, fat, round, symmetrical lines. And I swear that I didn't do that on purpose either. I just wrote them, feeling comfy.

It's the pacing.

A LITTLE INFUSION OF MAGIC

DAVE-BRENDON DE BURGH

WHEN YOU BLAME someone for something there is often a negative connotation to it, and though I blame my parents for my love of reading and books in general, believe me when I say it's definitely in a positive way. Not once did they force me to read, or cajole me, or bribe me. All they did was read in front of me.

It was that simple.

While I sat with comics like *Richie Rich*, *Spooky*, *Casper the Friendly Ghost* and *Wendy the Good Little Witch,* they sat with these pictureless, thick square things—and that made me curious. Wondering about what they were reading quickly led to me reading *The Famous Five* and *The Hardy Boys,* and when I read my first openly adult novel (*Pet Sematary*) at the age of nine, everything changed.

It wasn't until much later that I seriously began to consider writing my own tales, and, looking back, I guess that came about as an extension of all the pictures I drew as a youngster. Ask my parents and they probably won't even be able to remember how

VOLUME 1

many pictures I drew and showed them, because there were just too many to remember. I drew the *Teenage Mutant Ninja Turtles*, began flirting with sketching dinosaurs in the time of the *Dino-Riders*, and when my comic-tastes graduated to the likes of *DC*, superheroes took pride of place. My fascination with dinosaurs returned and practically consumed me when *Jurassic Park* hit the big screen, and it was around that time I began writing.

I wrote a story about a group of children who venture into a dark, terrible place after one of their friends is snatched by the monster under his bed; I wrote a tale about a prince, his talking horse, and their quest to save a magical forest; I even flirted with fan fiction. Back then I had no idea what I was doing—I tried to do what I'd read, which is split up the narrative with chapters, include description and dialogue, and add magic, action, gore or whatever else the story needed, as it was needed. I built up such a pile of stories that I began to have trouble keeping everything neat and organized. And not once did I think of submitting anything I'd written anywhere—you see, I went to our local library for books to read. Our family hardly ever bought books. Yet we were book lovers.

Everything changed again when I began working at a bookstore. It was my first introduction to a world in which writers earned money for what they wrote, and it was also a shock to discover how many people read books—which wasn't as many as I had thought. The positives outweighed the negatives, though; I suddenly had access to a wealth of books I hadn't known existed, and I worked with people who loved reading and books as much as I did.

WRITERS ON WRITING

During high school I read and devoured *The Belgariad* by David Eddings, and there's no doubt that my love affair with Fantasy began there, but suddenly I was presented with storytellers such as Robert Jordan, Steven Erikson, and Peter V Brett. I discovered the works of Clive Barker, Joe Donnelly, Richard Laymon and yes, more Stephen King. I fell into thrillers for a while and read novels by Patricia Cornwell, Tami Hoag, and John Sandford. I read more Michael Crichton, devoured Tom Clancy, fell in love with the Vampire Lestat. Having such a massive selection of books around me led me in different directions and showed me the simple, unavoidable truth that *there will never be enough time to read everything I want to read.*

Which is, again, a positive thing.

Typing this, being pointed into the past as I am, I can see the progression of events and choices that led me to being a storyteller, and I've realized not only was I happily lost in a world of stories, but that I was also chasing something, hunting it the way a lioness stalks a wildebeest: quietly, slowly, trying not to make that one misstep which will warn the quarry.

One of the most important things to remember about being a storyteller is this: *write what you love reading.* We're all intelligent folk here, so I'm not going to warn you to take that literally (oh, I just did, didn't I?). When I began to take my writing seriously (writing with the aim to one day publish and perhaps earn some money for what I'd written) I included what I liked and really enjoyed about the novels I'd read—action, drama, blood and guts, big magic, battles, supernatural creatures, assassins, warriors, beautiful

VOLUME 1

landscapes, etc. My dalliance with fan fiction just didn't do it for me—I wanted to create my own worlds and characters and histories. The one genre I felt I could really do this in was Fantasy, and about ten years ago I started writing my first novel.

Now I'm a writer and storyteller. I've had a couple of short stories and a novel published, I'm about to begin writing my third novel, and though I read less than what I would like (there just isn't time, my friends), I read more deeply. I read to learn. I read to savor. I read to question. I read to discover.

And all of this because my parents made me curious about what they were holding and gazing into for such long periods of time.

Even though I'm a book-lover who became a writer I'll always be a book-lover first and foremost—and I'm pretty sure I can cover most storytellers in the world with that same blanket.

I've often thought back and wondered whether I took a wrong turn, somewhere along the road. After all, my initiation into 'grown-up' books was Stephen King. Surely I should be focusing on Horror, not Fantasy. It doesn't bug me for too long, though, that thought.

You see, I think that what you write—and how you came to discover what you love writing—can be compared to getting medication for Depression. Many people don't get the correct medication or dosage from the get-go; their psychiatrist usually has to try at least two or three different kinds of medication before it begins to have the desired effect, and it's unfortunate that the path to finding the correct medication is usually stressful and not dwelled upon afterward (I was one of the lucky ones—got the right meds from the beginning).

If you know that you want to write but perhaps you're a person who would like to try their hand at many different genres, five minutes (perhaps even three, or less) in front of your bookcase will pull you in the right direction. Always write what you love, what excites you, what lodges within you.

Your journey as a writer will have already begun—your job now is learning how to walk that path without breaking your ankle, and, though it's by no means easy, it will be one of the most satisfying 'quests' you'll ever undertake.

Believe me: It took me a while, too.

I played around with many different stories in many different genres before I found that which worked well with what was in my head, and with all those things I've already mentioned that I love. And when I was starting out I didn't finish a damned thing—recently I've gone through boxes in my study and I've found those piles and piles of old tales; now that I've written two novels I almost can't believe I once struggled to finish writing a short story.

I went through periods of *'This is utter crap'* and *'This is so incredible but I don't know how to finish it'* and *'I know I should put this away and write something else but I really like this!'* and even *'What? Is my head completely empty? Can't I write even* one *sentence?'* Hell, I've got about seven years' worth of notes, scribbles, sketches, and fragments which eventually became my first novel. But—and I think this is important to remember—that tale is one I kept returning to, time after time. I *knew* I wanted

VOLUME 1

to finish writing it—I just told myself I didn't know how.

But I *did*. You see? I'd learned what I needed to get started by reading so much. Writers may play with the concepts of magic, enchantment and curses, but *reading* is the ultimate form of magic in our world. Not only do we *learn* as we read but entire worlds and peoples take on vivid life while we are reading. In my opinion, nothing comes close. Sure, I paid for a writing course with Random House, but I know for a fact I learned what I needed to really *understand* about writing from reading. I found my medication in the seeds of my novel.

And here's where I go back to story telling versus writing.

Reading a story, and a lot of stories in the same genre, changes your brain into a sponge. If it's a well-told and -written tale you get lost in it. You take in everything on an almost subliminal level, enjoying each phrase, all the imagery, and every interaction between characters. If what you're reading is badly-told and -written, however, you rail at it. You can pick up practically every mistake, every misstep, every cliché. You *know* what you're reading is crap.

Because you're a *reader*. Because you *allow* yourself to get lost in a good book. That's why it's so important to read as much as you damned well can if you're a writer.

We're constantly learning how to write better and tell stories better. Every story or novel we read is measured against the one before it, *and against what we write*. And ours is one of the most wonderful callings in the world (storytelling and writing *is* a

WRITERS ON WRITING

calling, make no mistake about it), because we truly admire those who *do it well*. Oh, we say out loud 'You bastard!' but we don't mean it. Why? Because we're readers. We love reading something well-written that lives beyond that flat, printed page.

So how would you know whether something was well-written if you didn't read as much as you possibly could? Writing down one word and then another after it and so on and so on *isn't* writing—and yet . . . *It is*.

Not only is our calling wonderful, it is also a territory filled with Catch-22s.

Because to write you *have to write*. Being a storyteller (in whichever genre you love or feel most comfortable writing it) means you exist in two worlds at once—one world encompasses rules, and the other does not; it's where these two worlds meet where the magic lies, and it's that magic which a writer who is also a storyteller can tap into. You could conceivably do it without words and grammar, sure, but then you wouldn't be a writer, would you? And try to capture that magic (or release it, or channel it—choose your phrase) on its own? Again, how would you do it if you didn't know how to write? Any other way, obviously, such as painting, perhaps even being an architect—but *you wouldn't be a writer*.

I've been a reader since I could decipher the words in the speech bubbles of comics, and I've been a writer and a storyteller since that first moment I began to write a story.

One word after another, and so on and so on, with a little infusion of magic.

NEVER LOOK AWAY: CONFRONTING YOUR FEARS IN FICTION

TODD KEISLING

What scares you?

That's such a personal question and one that's rather forward of me to ask when we don't even know each other, so I'll go first.

I'm absolutely *terrified* of snakes. Falling from great heights, failure, cancer, Alzheimer's, and the debilitating effects of depression all come to mind, too. I'm afraid of not doing something that matters, or even worse, that I won't be able to accomplish what I need to with the time that I have in this world.

These are all incredibly personal things. I've probably just outed myself as an extremely phobic and vulnerable individual—and that's part of my point. "What scares you?" is at once an intimate and entirely uncomfortable question for most people because no one likes to talk about what frightens them. Talking about the boogeyman in your closet means *confronting* the boogeyman in your closet, and that's too much for most people.

WRITERS ON WRITING

Let's face it: We're afraid of fear. We're afraid of admitting we're afraid of . . . well, whatever we're afraid of. Our society perceives fear as a weakness—and admitting you're afraid is admitting you're weak. But regardless of how society perceives and deals with fear, one universal fact remains: fear is a part of being human. It's instinctual.

As a horror writer, I'm used to mining my psyche for ways to project my fears into my fiction. The better I can write about what scares me, the more effective the writing will be in engaging the reader. To do this means resisting the urge to look away. Looking away cheats the reader.

This isn't just about horror, though. This goes for every writer in every genre. Tapping into your fears will help you hook the reader and dangle them at your mercy until the last page.

To demonstrate this, I'm going to tell you about the time I had to kill a cat.

***

I'm a cat person. Thing is, people who've read my first novel tend not to believe that statement. Here's why:

He drops to his knees, catching the cat as it tries to escape. He holds the animal steady with one hand, brings down the knife, and exterminates Mr. Precious Paws in a single, violent stroke. Donna can see the feline's eyes, can sense its terror as the poor thing lets out a final, gurgling cry. Blood pours from its middle and its legs twitch in death throes. The knife has gone all the way through, pinning the animal to the floor.

The scene is a simple one: the protagonist's wife is home alone and a strange man comes to her door. He forces his way inside. He's deranged and desperate,

VOLUME 1

and in a moment of fury he murders the family cat. The cat is an innocent bystander. The cat did nothing to deserve such malice, and yet it happens in gory detail.

In the original draft of this story, I left the protagonist (and by proxy, the reader) to discover the aftermath, and the result wasn't nearly as effective. Sure, the way the poor cat dies is a heinous crime, but I initially spared the reader from witnessing the atrocity because I was afraid of witnessing it myself.

The result was a scene that fell flat.

My editor suggested I approach the scene from a different angle to make it come alive on the page. I'd broken one of the cardinal rules: I was telling the reader what happened, not showing.

Showing meant imagining Mr. Precious Paws being eviscerated by a mad man. It meant not looking away.

Mr. Precious Paws was partially based on my cat, Darko. He passed away a few years ago due to feline leukemia. He was a great cat, and the last thing I'd ever want is for someone to hurt him. The scene in question was drawn from a nightmare I'd had years before in which someone broke into my apartment and forced my cat through a paper shredder while I was powerless to stop it from happening. The nightmare was one of those vivid ones where everything's too real, a little too close to home. I could even smell the blood. I still can.

Writing about that nightmare scenario and incorporating it into my fiction was an uncomfortable task, but it worked. To this day, nearly a decade after the book's publication, I still get hate mail from people who take issue with what happened to that fictional cat.

WRITERS ON WRITING

My point in telling you this isn't so that you write to get hate mail, but so that you write to affect the reader. Make them feel something with your words. If you can hook their emotions, they will follow the path you've written for them all the way to the end—even if that path leads them through an abattoir of unspeakable horrors.

All you have to do is be willing to face whatever it is that scares you.

***

Don't be coy. We all have monsters waiting inside our closets or lurking just beneath our beds. I want you to find that monster, whatever it may be, and stare at it. Get a real good look. Don't blink. Note its features: the slime dripping from a grin that's a little too wide and a little too happy to see you, the pus oozing from a festering wound in its forehead, and the light glinting off yellowing, serrated fangs.

Lock eyes with it and do not look away. Ask yourself why you're scared of this thing. What is it about this vile monstrosity that you find so threatening? Is it a fear of what the beast represents? Or is it a fear of what the beast tells you about yourself?

Maybe that's too forward. Let's back up.

When I wrote my first published novel, I wasn't trying to reach other people or entertain them. I wrote it because I was afraid of where my life was going. I was a couple of years out of college, working a dead end job at a law firm. I hated that job, hated that I was stagnating in a back office making copies of legal briefs every day, and I hated that I was slipping into a deep depression because of it.

There was a day when I went to work and no one

VOLUME 1

spoke to me or even acknowledged that I was there, and I had a daydream that I would never leave that godforsaken place. That I'd still be there ten or twenty years down the road, still running legal briefs through a Xerox machine, wondering what happened to my life.

I took that concept and imagined a character who works at a thankless job and has delusions of happiness, a character who's about a decade older than I was at the time, who has similar flaws and goals. I gave him a loving wife, a more successful sibling, and a house cat. I made this character in my image, and then I took a long look at the things that scare me, the things that could threaten the happy little house of cards I'd built for myself.

I'm scared of something happening to my wife. I'm scared that, one day, I'll arrive to find someone's broken into my home. I'm scared that something will happen to my cat, or that I'll never measure up to my potential. I'm scared that I'll be stuck working in a dead-end job my whole life. I'm scared that I'll never do anything that matters, that I'll fade from history without making my mark somehow. I'm scared that my inaction will have repercussions on the lives of those around me. And I'm scared that one day I'll have no choice but to sell out my dreams for a paycheck.

The plot of my first novel was built around each one of these fears. Constructing the story forced me to confront them and examine my life with excruciating objectivity. I wasn't happy, and as I peeled back the reasons for my unhappiness, I found ways to give them flesh in my story. Killing the cat was just a part of it.

My point is, when you understand why you're

WRITERS ON WRITING

afraid of whatever it is that scares you, you can use that knowledge in your fiction. Maybe it's what helps you connect with your protagonist or supporting characters. Maybe it helps you empathize with whatever it is they're going through, and in turn, make their reactions or emotions even more believable to the reader.

Whatever it is, *you must not look away*—even if it means facing some uncomfortable truths about yourself.

Now about that question I asked earlier. I've torn myself open and dissected my fears for you, and I'd like to offer you the same opportunity.

I'll ask again: *What scares you?*

ONCE MORE, WITH FEELING

TIM WAGGONER

ASPIRING WRITERS ARE forever searching for The Secret: the single trick or technique that will elevate their writing from *promising* to *publishable*. Old pros say there is no secret to getting published, that it's simply the result of hard work—reading a lot, writing a lot, getting feedback on your work, learning how to market your work, etc.—and I wouldn't dispute that. But there is one element missing all too often from beginners' fiction, and I'd argue that it's one of the most important aspects of creating successful, compelling stories, and it's as close to The Secret as anyone is likely to get: writing with an emotional core.

Successful stories should entertain, stimulate the imagination, and provide an artistic experience, but they also need to move readers emotionally. At the heart of a story—and there's a reason we call it the *heart*—should lie a strong emotional core. It is, in a very real sense, what a story is ultimately about. For example, on the surface the movie *Back to the Future* appears to be about a teenager who goes back in time

WRITERS ON WRITING

and prevents his parents' meeting, thereby endangering his own existence. He needs to get his parents together, save himself, and then return to his own time. That's the premise and basic plot of the film. But the emotional core of the film—why it moves audiences—is Marty McFly's relationship with his parents and with Doc Brown. He gets to know his parents as teenagers like himself, gaining a new perspective on them. He feels connected to them as a family despite the gulf in years, and because he loves them, he can't stop himself from trying to make their lives better in the past, even at the risk of altering the future in potentially disastrous ways. It's the same for Doc. Marty loves him, and he can't stand the idea of Doc getting killed in the future, so he tries to prevent it, despite Doc's wishes. Simply put, the emotional core of the movie is love of family. Without this core, the movie might've been a fun adventure, but it wouldn't be the much-loved classic it is today. The emotional core is what connects an audience to a story; it's what makes a story *matter* to them.

Here are some things to think about in order to strengthen the emotional core in your stories.

What is the main emotional relationship/connection between characters in the story?

In *Silence of the Lambs,* the main emotional relationship is between Hannibal Lector and Clarice Starling, between predator and potential prey or, if you prefer, between wild animal and hunter. Starling wants to use Lector to catch another killer, and Lector wants to use Starling to amuse himself—*and* escape confinement. But the power dynamic between the two

VOLUME 1

constantly shifts, and it's unclear to the audience, as well as to the characters themselves, how they feel about each other and their roles. This ever-shifting unease—will Starling remain uncorrupted by Lector, can Starling's inherent goodness, if not redeem him, reveal that he at least possesses some small measure of humanity?—is the true mystery that powers the story. And just like *Back to the Future*, it's the emotional core that makes this story a classic, elevating it above a run-of-the-mill thriller.

So consider the characters in your story and decide what connects them. This doesn't mean they have to have a positive relationship. Ahab's relationship to Moby Dick isn't exactly warm and fuzzy. Once you firm up the emotional relationship between the characters—once you've created a strong emotional core—then you can use that relationship as a foundation upon which the rest of your story rests. Or perhaps more accurately, as the seed from which your story will grow.

How is the emotional core reflected in the plot?

In *Jaws*, the emotional core is Sheriff Brody's need to protect the people in his community. This creates conflict in the story because while Brody wants to keep people from being eaten by the shark, he always has a duty to protect the town's economy, and the town depends on the money the summer people pump into it every year. If Brody closes the beaches, he kills the town. If he doesn't close the beaches, more people will die. Brody is trapped in an impossible situation. He cannot protect everyone in every way. He must choose (just to be clear, this economic aspect of the story is more prevalent in the novel than in the film).

WRITERS ON WRITING

In a novel I recently completed, *The Mouth of the Dark,* a middle-aged man's twenty-year-old daughter is missing. The emotional core comes from his need to find her because he believes he's failed her too many times in the past, and he's determined not to fail her again—no matter what. Everything in the plot revolves around this need, and the character does things he would ordinarily never *think* of doing in order to find his daughter. In acting, this is called motivation, but when it comes to creating a story, the emotional core doesn't just motivate your character, it motivates the story's events as well. Write the emotional core of your story at the top of a piece of paper or Word document and list all the ways the core could be expressed in terms of plot events. If you have a plot event that doesn't relate somehow to the core—especially for a short story—don't include it when drafting.

How is the emotional core reflected in the setting?

In both *Moby Dick* and *Jaws,* the sea is the most important part of the setting. Ahab wants revenge and Brody wants to protect his town, but both of those motivations lead these characters to try to control the object of their respective hunts. But the sea is uncontrollable. It's wild and dangerous, and it conceals rather than reveals. Struggling against it during the hunt will test each man and show what lengths he will go to, and what he's willing to sacrifice, to find and kill his quarry.

In *The Wizard of Oz,* the land of Oz appears on the surface to be a beautiful, magical world, a place a little girl (in the book) or a young woman (in the film) would love to remain in forever—especially when she compares it to life in boring Dust-Bowl-era Kansas.

VOLUME 1

But Oz is a confusing, dangerous place of Wicked Witches, deceitful (if ultimately kind-hearted) wizards, Tin Woodsmen created by mechanically replacing the lost body parts of a human man (read the book), creepy-as-hell flying monkeys, and other bizarre elements. It's no wonder that Dorothy ultimately decides that the emotional core of the story—There's no place like home—is a better choice than remaining in a beautiful but chaotic magical land.

Again, write down your emotional core and list all the ways your setting can reflect that core. Is the emotional core of your story Isolation? Think of all the ways your characters could be isolated, both the obvious and not-so-obvious ways. Is the emotional core of your story Sticking by a Friend No Matter What? Think of all the ways your protagonist could be challenged by the setting to continue sticking by his or her friend. For example, two characters are lost in the wilderness and one has a broken leg. What would make it difficult—maybe almost impossible—for the unhurt friend to remain with the injured one, despite his or her resolve to do so? Lack of food and water? Weather? Wolves?

How is the emotional core reflected in the theme?

First, a word about theme. Some writers make conscious decisions about theme while others don't worry about it. If a theme happens to emerge while they're writing, great. If not, no big deal. The important thing is to tell the story as well as you can. But I'd argue that an emotional core *is* the theme, at least with a little tweaking. Ahab wants revenge against Moby Dick, but he can never get revenge. The whale has no idea he hurt Ahab and nothing Ahab

WRITERS ON WRITING

could do to him, including killing him, would ever make the whale sorry for what he did, would ever make him realize that Ahab was the one who killed him. So Ahab can never have the revenge he seeks, and thus the theme: Revenge is ultimately impossible and only leads to self-destruction. In *Back to the Future*, Marty's love for Doc and his family leads to that story's theme: Family connections transcend Time, and these connections define us, bind us, and in the end, might even save us.

Thinking about how the emotional core of your story can grow into a theme allows you to return to the story—to the characters, the plot, the setting—and strengthen the theme, making your story tighter, more focused, and ultimately more impactful for the audience.

How does the emotional core serve as a counterpoint to the plot and setting, and vice versa?

The emotional core, plot, and setting don't have to complement each other. They can serve as counterpoints. A simple example would be a scene depicting a graveside funeral service. The emotional core is sorrow. The clichéd impact of the emotional core on the setting: a gloomy, rainy day. Counterpoint: a sunny day that seems at odds with the emotions the characters are feeling, or a pleasant, but bland day weather-wise, as if nothing important is happening when for the family, something extremely important is taking place: saying a final farewell to their loved one. By playing against the emotional core with the setting, you can actually intensify it.

In the movie *Poltergeist* the emotional core is the fear that your family isn't safe even in their own home.

VOLUME 1

Once the paranormal events in the house increase to a certain point, the family wants to get the hell out of there. The fear should drive them out, but little Carol Anne becomes trapped in a dark dimension adjacent to our world, a dimension only accessible through the house, so the parents must stay (they're good parents, though, so they send Carol Anne's older sister away rather than risk losing her, too). Plot-wise, the characters are forced to do the opposite of what they want to do, what the story's emotional core is driving them to do. It's the plotting power of emotional core counterpoint at its finest.

Each scene can have its own emotional core.

So far, I've been talking about emotional cores that serve as the center of entire stories. But each scene can have its own emotional core, one that may or may not be strongly tied into the overall emotional core. The example of the funeral service I used above can also serve as an example here. Sorrow might be the emotional core of such a scene, while struggling to maintain a marriage in the face of tragedy—such as the loss of a child—might be the overarching emotional core for the whole story. Adding emotional cores to your scenes will make each one of them have an impact on your audience, and they'll build one upon the other, increasing people's emotional investment in your story as it progresses toward its climax.

Emotional cores in short stories versus long stories.

Short stories need to be tighter and more focused than novels (tell us something we don't know, Tim!). Because of this, you'll likely have an important emotional relationship between two characters and no

WRITERS ON WRITING

more. There simply isn't room to develop multiple expressions of the emotional core in a short story. So if your short story is about an elderly man mourning the death of his beloved dog—a man who can connect with animals but who has trouble connecting with people—you won't show multiple people trying to console him and reach out to him emotionally, as you could do in a novel. You'll have only one person fulfill this role. His estranged son. The widow who lives down the street. A neighbor he's never gotten along with but who understands the grief over losing a pet. Two main characters, one emotional core. That's about all a short story can handle.

A novel, however, is another story (see what I did there?). If you want to write a novel about the elderly man who's lost his dog, you can have all of the above characters be a part of it, and you can explore the emotional core on multiple levels and in multiple ways. Some writers claim that there are short story ideas and there are novel ideas, but the two aren't interchangeable. While there might be some truth to this, you can often turn a short story idea into a novel idea—and the other way around—by expanding or narrowing the emotional core. By doing so, I could write about the elderly man at any length and complexity—and so could you.

Which should come first when drafting? The character, the plot, or the emotional core?

Short answer: It doesn't matter as long as everything is in its place when the story is finished and ready to submit to an editor. I suggest starting wherever you feel the most creative energy and potential with a given story. If you're really into the

VOLUME 1

characters, start with them first. If you have an awesome idea for a story, but you're not sure of anything else, work out the idea in detail and add other elements later. If you're a planner, make decisions about your story's emotional core before you begin drafting. If you prefer to write by the seat of your pants, start writing and work on firming up the emotional core in revisions. How you tend to the emotional core doesn't matter. I'd argue that since the emotional core serves as a foundation for your story, the sooner you tend to it, the better, but the most important thing is that you *do* tend to it before you type The End.

Regardless of what kind of fiction you write—entertainment-focused, literary, genre-oriented, experimental, or some blend of these—make sure to write it with a strong emotional core. By doing so you'll not only produce stories that readers will love, but stories they'll remember long after they finish reading. Stories that change them, that make a difference in their lives. Stories that *matter*.

And in the end, aren't those the kind of stories we all want to read and write?

WRITERS ON WRITING
VOL. 2

THE INFRASTRUCTURE OF THE GODS:
11 SIGNPOSTS FOR GOING ALL THE WAY

BRIAN HODGE

THE FIRST HALF of this essay debuted in Writers On Writing Volume 1. It primarily addressed your mental game of work habits and mindsets. You and the words and the empty page, and the self-defeating futility of measuring yourself against other writers—what they've done and how they've done it—rather than trusting yourself to walk your own path in your own timeframe.

That's the whole point of this piece: building a mental and behavioral foundation that serves you, that keeps you in the game for the long haul rather than burning out or sabotaging yourself from the inside.

Here, in the second part, we mainly look at you, the writer, as a social being, in your life and career beyond the page.

(7) Never Pee on Electric Fences or Argue with Readers

WRITERS ON WRITING

In the mood for an evening of cheap, train-wreck entertainment? Go to Goodreads and look out for the writers who've decided to fight the good fight against their readers. Bring popcorn.

Spoiler alert: This never ends well.

You know how many writers come out on top in these exchanges? Exactly none of them. Even George R.R. Martin doesn't look all that good lately, issuing open letters to justify the things that a few vocal *Game of Thrones* readers and viewers have decided merit Berserker-grade outrage levels. He's sitting on a monumental achievement that still needs to be finished. He doesn't need the distractions and doesn't need to stoop.

Yes, criticism hurts, even when it's valid and thoughtful and free of deliberate antagonism. When it's ignorant and ill-informed and mean-spirited and delivered with gleefully vicious malice, it's infuriating. Even all-consuming. It can ruin days of your life, if you let it.

So make a conscious choice to *not* let it. No matter how badly you want to pick up that gauntlet and start swinging, don't. Because you. Will never. Win.

I don't care what they say. I don't care how wrong they get it, or how cruel they are. I don't care how badly they mischaracterize you.

Even adoring readers get it wrong sometimes. As for the ones who treat criticism as a blood sport, they'll never see it your way. Attempting to take them on at their own game is like diving into a latrine pit to punch at phantoms that feed on your efforts at hitting them back.

The world abounds with vicious little trolls. They all can smell blood and come running when they do.

VOLUME 2

Trolls draw nourishment only from attention and other people's anguish. There's an unlimited number of them and only one of you. You will never vanquish them, never get them to admit they were wrong, never bring them to your way of thinking.

The only thing you stand to accomplish is looking as bad as they do, in the eyes of reasonable readers.

It doesn't matter who doesn't get it, who doesn't get you. What matters is who does. So don't alienate the ones who do—and the ones who might—by taking on the ones you'll never win over in the first place.

(8) Rage Goblins, Professional Suicide, and Other Sorry Spectacles

There's a question that often comes to mind when I observe writers in the wild. By which I mean online: "How fucking hard is it to remember Patrick Swayze's Rule #3 from *Road House*: Be nice?"

Insurmountably hard, apparently.

Social media sites are what we make of them: a useful tool, a fun meeting place, or a theater of the grotesque. The magic of the Internet is that it can turn the pastiest basement-dwelling troglodyte into a tiger, and it's largely a consequence-free zone.

Robert E. Howard would've understood: "Civilized men are more discourteous than savages because they know they can be impolite without having their skulls split."

To be sure, being a rude prick will get you noticed. But will it attract readers? Maybe. I don't know. Will it *lose* you readers, or discourage them from ever giving you a try? Count on it.

There's a silly metric that gets dragged out every

WRITERS ON WRITING

U.S. presidential election, about which candidate voters would rather have a beer with. It may be irrelevant nonsense come voting day, but if you don't think a similar thought process actually does go on with a wide cross-section of readers, you haven't been paying attention.

Yes, there's that never-ending debate about separating the artist from the art. Meanwhile, in the pragmatic world, readers have a mile-long buffet of options to choose from, and a lot of them have a professed aversion to sitting down with a writer who comes off like someone they'd cross the street to avoid. They'd rather crack the work of someone who doesn't come with a ton of negative associations.

You know who else might be paying attention? Editors and publishers. Guess what. They don't want to deal with this crap either.

Here's a brief list of strategies and tactics I've seen writers employ to lose readers and alienate peers:

- Relentlessly shilling product without ever engaging with anyone.
- Spamming other people's pages and sites with ads for their work.
- Talking down to everyone like pedantic lecturers convinced they're forced to contend with lowly peons and peabrains.
- Maintaining an ongoing litany of woes, complaints, bitterness, spite, and all-around unrelenting negativity about how much their life sucks.
- Teeing off on one's readers for mistakes in grammar, spelling, or using disliked words and expressions.

VOLUME 2

Think about that last one for a minute. That's the one that gobsmacked me the most. There was no self-serving upside to it. This wasn't a generalized rant. This was a writer angrily singling out individuals for a public scolding. Individuals who, I assume, were there to engage with that writer because they liked her.

Imagine yourself on the receiving end. How eager would you be, after getting a condescending rebuke, to buy that writer's next book, or any other? How eager would you be, merely as an observer to this kind of petty abuse?

And these are established professionals, or at least writers making headway. I can't begin to think of all the aspiring scribes I've seen blow themselves up on the launch pad just by being their odious selves. Racism. Misogyny. Homophobia. Rage issues. Paranoia. Grandiose megalomania. Death or rape threats. Suggesting editors kill themselves because of a rejection.

Here's a handy rule of thumb: If you come off like you need electroshock therapy and Thorazine more than you need a publisher . . . *do I even need to finish this sentence?*

I can think of no greater waste of creative energy than Internet pie fights. People wade into the fray. Hours later, they're exhausted, emotionally depleted, and have jack shit to show for it. Not even pride. They could've channeled that time and passion into doing some good work. But no. They squandered it on goblins.

So, what, then—we're resigned to a steady diet of inspirational quotes and cat videos?

WRITERS ON WRITING

Not necessarily. Really, the thing most readers seem to want out of authors is authenticity. To just be yourself. Unless you're authentically an asshole, in which case, good luck to you. Some authors have definitely made that work for them . . . although it's worth noting they tend to be exceptionally talented assholes.

As for myself, I try to keep things positive; *positive*, however, can take a lot of different forms. I generally steer clear of partisan politics; the climate is too toxic and divisive, and arguing isn't something I find fun, nor do I have time for it. I try to refrain from saying unkind things about people, or treating anyone rudely or disrespectfully. I especially avoid jumping into mob scenes where a bunch of people are dog-piling someone. I don't care if the target has been a complete twat and brought it upon himself; it still reminds me of a ring of kids on a playground using sharp sticks to poke at the emotionally disturbed kid in the middle.

I could call this a code of conduct, but it's not anything that takes effort. I'm not fighting any urges in the interest of maintaining an image. It's just how I am.

Whatever you call it, it bears thinking about. Who are you? Who are you striving to be? What of yourself are you comfortable revealing?

And when in doubt, ask yourself this: If I behaved this way with a savage, would I risk getting my skull split?

(9) Cheerleaders Wanted, Pom-Poms Optional

You may be the one doing the work, but you still can't

VOLUME 2

do this alone. You need people around who believe in you, who support your ambitions, who celebrate the victories and soothe the sting of the setbacks. Family, friends, your significant other. Compatriots in a writing group. It doesn't take many. But they need to be genuine.

If there are other people under the same roof with you, they need to grant you the time and space to show up and do the work. This may not come naturally. The greatest sales job you ever undertake could be to convince them how important this is to you.

If it's someone you love, who loves you back, this opens up the possibility of friction and resentment and hurt feelings. Because this may be time they no longer get to spend with you. So don't take it, or them, for granted. Demonstrable levels of love and appreciation, communication and compromise, can go a long way here. Find a way to give back, to return the favor and be supportive of *their* dreams.

It's not all about you, alone.

And whatever you do, maintain a wide distance from scoffing naysayers, and from people who pretend to support you, but are actually rooting for you to fail. These are vampires in cheerleaders' costumes. They're out there, and their identities might surprise you. Sometimes they're openly snarky about it, and sometimes they're stealth trolls, who squeeze in close to poor-baby you, just so they can slurp up your bad days and pour them over pancakes. Mmm, that's tasty suffering.

(10) Because Who Wants to Feel Like the Love Child of William S. Burroughs and the Crypt Keeper?

WRITERS ON WRITING

Many great works of art and literature have come from a place of mental illness, suicidal depression, and physical decrepitude. But let's not consider these virtues to be cultivated. You're in this for the long haul, remember?

So make an effort to stay healthy. I've seen a lot of miserably unhealthy writers. I've heard their piteous moans. Please stop being miserably unhealthy.

With a minimum of tedious preaching, then:

Don't eat crap. Pounding down buckets of chemical-laden goo is a piss-poor way of expressing your First Amendment Rights. Nutrition journalist Michael Pollan distills his highly regarded tenets to just seven words: "Eat food. Not too much. Mostly plants."

Stay hydrated. Drink plenty of water. I'm not kidding. At even a low level of dehydration, before your desiccating corpus ever tells you you're thirsty, your cognitive faculties could be taking a hit.

And work out. Exercise. You know you should anyway. Never mind the benefits to your overall health and well-being. The benefits to your creative energies could alone merit a long article we don't have time for. But here's a practical one: *It's time spent that more than pays for itself because it buys you even more time.*

A few years ago, the world's coolest billionaire, Richard Branson, was asked how to become more productive. His answer: *work out*. Branson estimated that working out gave him four extra hours of quality productive time per day.

VOLUME 2

(11) Be the Pro *You'd* Like to Work With

Finally, I don't know of any writer who's gotten anywhere who doesn't work with other people in some capacity. Publishing is the same as any industry: working relationships are an infrastructure unto themselves, and can facilitate your success or be your downfall.

I once heard that the ideal writer is one who delivers top-quality work, on time, while being easy to get along with ... but that one might be able to swing it with just two out of three. In other words, you can maybe get away with being a pain in the ass, or habitually late, or not at your best, as long as you have the other two locked down.

But swing for three out of three.

Be the kind of professional that other pros prefer to deal with.

If an editor, publisher, or agent you're approaching has issued guidelines for general contact or a specific project, read and follow them. To the letter. Sometimes they throw in stuff that doesn't seem as if it should matter, just to see who's paying attention. Pros pay attention. Amateurs think it doesn't apply to them.

Deliver on time, and when you can't, be accountable.

Leave as little as possible for proofreaders and copyeditors to do. I've been complimented on the cleanliness of my manuscripts often enough that I can only surmise a lot of writers don't treat this as a priority.

When you have a problem with someone, don't

WRITERS ON WRITING

burn your bridges by airing your grievances in public. Unless circumstances absolutely warrant it—say, you discover you've been dealing with a fraudulent, stone-cold thief about whom others should be warned. In general, though, settle that drama via private channels.

Even there, diplomacy counts, and name-calling never resolves anything. Don't fire off missives in spittle-flecked anger. If you're prone to that, let them sit awhile before sending, chill out, then go back and delete most of the exclamation points and all instances of the word *cocksucker*.

Whether it's been differences of opinion with an editor on revisions, or business matters that needed ironing out, I can't think of more than one conflict I've dealt with that hasn't been resolved to both parties' satisfaction simply by me laying out my point of view clearly, calmly, and logically . . . and listening respectfully to the other person. And we both lived to work together another day.

Communicating to reach someone's heart and elicit a desired response—it's what writing is all about.

And you *are* a writer, aren't you?

EMBRACING YOUR INNER SHITNESS

JAMES EVERINGTON

"The first draft of everything is shit."
—Ernest Hemmingway

HEMMINGWAY WAS RIGHT. My own first drafts, not least of this article, are usually shit (there, I said it). An incomplete list of shit things I typically find on reading through a first draft would include:

- Typos
- Meandering sentences
- Inconsistently named characters
- A spasmodic sense of pace
- Myopic authorial focus
- Complete thematic disunity
- A deep and abiding sense of how shit a writer I can be

This used to trouble me a lot—actually, scratch that, it still does. *As well it should.* Let me say upfront this article isn't going to offer you any get out from the

WRITERS ON WRITING

hard graft of rewriting, editing and generally polishing a story so that it is fit for publication. No quick-wins or silver bullets here. You need to do the hard work if you want to be a writer; doing the hard work is what being a writer *is*.

What I am suggesting is that you do that hard work *at the right time*.

So when is the right time to worry about a shit first draft? Well, when you've *finished* it. Too many beginning writers (and not a few old hands) get trapped rewriting their opening scene or a key chapter trying to perfect it. There are two reasons this is a bad idea:

Firstly, you might never finish that story. It happens to the best of us, especially when we're starting out. But the way you realise you will not finish this particular story is by *trying to finish it*. Not by obsessing over writing a perfectly formed first paragraph. If you're going to fail, fail quickly, so you can move onto the next story; one that hopefully you *will* finish.

Secondly, we all know that stories don't turn out as we expect them to when we start writing. So get to the end and see where your inspiration has taken you. Trying to nail that first chapter is a waste of time unless you know the story it is the first chapter *for*.

So, it's absolutely okay to have written a shit first draft, because the key point is not that it's shit (that can be corrected), it's that you've written it. But to do so you need, just temporarily, not to let your own doubts and insecurities about your writing trouble you.

So with that in mind, here are some tips on how to embrace your own inner shitness as a writer.

VOLUME 2

Think of that shit as draft zero

If the idea that your first draft will be utter rubbish bothers you, think of it as a 'Draft Zero' or 'Pre-Draft' or something. Remember, *no one has to see this*. This isn't the draft you'll send to your beta readers; you don't even have to tell anyone about it. Its only significance is that which you give it, and its only purpose is to give you the raw material for later rewrites.

Write that shit by hand

I write all my first drafts the old fashioned way, pen to paper. Sometimes my second drafts, too. There are many reasons for this: I write faster, I'm less tempted to go back over what I've just written, and it keeps me offline and focused. But the key reason is this: If you write by hand you're going to have to type it up later, which means you'll be rewriting everything. Every. Single. Word. You get a free second swing at *all* of it, so it doesn't matter if you miss first time. You have a safety net so you can relax about crossing the wire. Hell, you can do backflips if you want.

There's a psychological aspect, too: My scrawled and half-illegible handwriting feels a lot more transitory than perfectly formed and spaced words on a computer screen. Which helps me keep clear where I am in my writing process: I'm writing a first draft, which is allowed to be shitty.

Keep up that shit

WRITERS ON WRITING

Build a sense of momentum. Don't, unless you really have to, read over what you've already written when you sit down to write the next day. Because you might spot something shit, and then you'll be tempted to correct it . . . and before you know it, you'll be revising and revising aiming for that one perfect chapter again.

Similarly (and you should know this already) *keep off the internet*. Because if you stop writing to check an email or Facebook status, then when you come back to your story you'll find it harder to pick up where you left off, meaning you will read back what you've just written . . . and then we're back into the spotting shit too early scenario. Before smartphones, writing by hand was the perfect way to keep offline, but nowadays you'll have to be disciplined at all times. Keep off line!

Don't sweat the small shit

Realise half way through your first draft that a character you've called Katherine is now called Catherine? That her favourite food is salami in one scene and sushi in another? Unless it really, really matters to the plot, don't go back and change these things; just make a brief note so you don't forget and press on.

Show The Plan Who's Boss

I'm not going to get into the whole 'plotting versus seat of your pants' debate here—you can find plenty of words written about this topic, but the upshot of it all is find what works for you. What I will say is, if you are a plotter, remember that *you wrote the plan*, not the

VOLUME 2

other way around. If your draft is deviating from the plan, that may be yet another temptation to go back and revise and . . . You know what I'm going to say. Resist that shit.

Finish that shit

As I said, the most important goal you should set yourself is to finish your draft. Don't even think about rewriting any of it before then. Eyes down and focus. Once you have finished, then do all the normal things recommended: take some time away from the project, have a beer, write something different maybe, and come back to your first draft with fresh eyes. You'll spot the shitness in what you've written a lot easier after a break.

Or don't finish

As I said, it happens to us all when we start out writing: We fail to finish stories. But that's okay, an unfinished story can still be valuable to your development as a writer. Take a step back and ask yourself: Why didn't you finish? Was the idea not strong enough? Was it in a new genre where your talents may not be as developed? As the band Rilo Kiley sang, *"All of your failures are training grounds."*

***

"It is perfectly okay to write garbage—as long as you edit brilliantly."—C.J. Cherryh

So you've finished your first draft. Congratulations. You take a few days off, emerge from your house

WRITERS ON WRITING

blinking into the sunlight, go out with friends you've not seen for weeks, catch up on your reading. You deserve it. And then, when you're ready, you take out your first draft and read it through.

Oh god.
It's shit.
It's really, really shit.
What was this Everington guy even talking about, telling me to write a shit first draft? Shit. I mean he even got me to write it by hand, so now I can't bloody read half of it. What a wanker. Shit.

Deep breaths. Don't panic. You've *allowed* yourself to write a shit first draft, remember. And I have more tips.

Don't be overwhelmed by the shitness

If your inner voice is saying something similar to the above at this point (apart from the bits about me being a wanker) then this is what you reply: Seeing so many things wrong with your first draft is a *good* thing. It means you've spotted the things that you need to fix.

Your story might seem like it is irrecoverable at this point, but in my experience once you've got to the end of at least one draft of a story you're far more likely to get it finished. Remember how little you knew about this story when you started out, with nothing but a blank page? Think about how much more you know now, including the things the story *isn't* about.

And remember:

Your second draft can be a little bit shit, too

VOLUME 2

You don't have to fix everything second time round, either. You get as many attempts as you want. Start by making sure you've identified any structural or pacing issues with the story, or characters acting inconsistently, or scenes that just don't work. You don't have to make every sentence sparkle at this point, although polish where you can.

This is partly why I sometimes write my second drafts by hand, too; it reminds me that this isn't the final version, that again no one sees this until I want them to.

Hone your spidey-sense

Various writing books and websites will give you lists of things to check for when revising or editing your work, and these are worthwhile reading and using. But just as significant can be your 'spidey-sense,' if properly honed. Sometimes when you read back what you've written you just *know* something is wrong, without necessarily knowing what or even how you know.

Unfortunately (?), this isn't happening because you've been bitten by a radioactive arachnid. It's happening because if you're a halfway decent writer, you'll have read a lot books. And I mean *a lot* of books. Plot, pacing, style. From childhood you've been absorbing this stuff, often half-consciously and by osmosis. *Reading gives you superpowers*. And that strange, supernatural tingle is the result—your brain is assessing what you've written against all that you've read, and saying 'Nah.' Trust it, and it will help you identify the things wrong with your draft that aren't on any lists.

WRITERS ON WRITING

Remember, not all of it will be shit

Your newly discovered authorial superpowers will also work the opposite way; they'll allow you to see the parts of your shitty first draft that actually aren't that bad. Because you're a *good* writer, remember. And at this stage, faced with a first draft with flaws so big they can be seen from space, it does you good to see the things which you've done well, too.

Underline these bits, too, not just the flaws that need sorting out. These bits which your spidey-sense is shouting "yes, yes, YES!" in response to may be the hints you need when your rewrite is going badly. They may be the lights which will guide you out of a dark, stormy sky to a safe landing. They may tell you what your story is *really* about.

Reverse outline

So maybe your superpowers aren't up to par today, or maybe you're just reluctant to rely on an ill-thought out pop culture reference as the best way to find out what's wrong with your story. Well, reverse outlining might be just what you need here.

It's a technique described in a number of writing guides (I first encountered it in the utterly fantastic *Wonderbook* by Jeff VanderMeer) but the basic idea is simple enough to grasp and easily adaptable to your own personal approach. Essentially, you take what you have written and reverse-engineer an outline from it. For each scene, write down what happens, what new information is conveyed to the reader, how it builds on what happened in previous scenes and what later

VOLUME 2

scenes it enables. You'll have an invaluable tool for seeing at a glance structural problems and inconsistencies in your story. (This hasn't got anything to do with the 'plotter versus pantster' battle mentioned above, by the way. In fact, it's precisely those who do write by the seat of their pants that might benefit most from this technique).

Know Your Weaknesses

I always, always spell 'staring' wrong. For some reason known only to whoever is in charge when I'm writing, I always write 'starring.' Same with 'stared' / 'starred.' Which produces some very odd sentences.

But because I know I'm often shit in this particular and specific way, I've noted it down in a document, along with a load of other things I'm especially prone to. And every story I write, I check against this list. I search for every instance of 'starred' in my writing and delete that extra r. (oddly, the act of adding persistent mistakes to the list is sometimes enough to stop me making them).

***

"Every poem probably has sixty drafts behind it."—Mary Karr

Eventually you'll finish your story and send it out into the big bad world. And you'll get your fair share of rejections, but hopefully your fair share of acceptances, too. You'll see your story all grown up in the pages of a book; you'll see your own name on the spine of a novel.

But always remember: *That story you are so proud of started as a shitty first draft.* That first draft

WRITERS ON WRITING

was a necessary step to getting it published. Which leads me to the final piece of wisdom (thank god) I have to impart:

Accept the shit first draft as part of your writing process

Once you know that all your best stories start off as a first draft that isn't so great, you can learn not to worry about it. Obviously no one writes anything that is deliberately shit, but you'll find it easier to write quickly. Instead of being something to worry about, the completion of a first draft becomes an achievement, a first step on the journey to another volume on your author shelf.
    So go for it.
    Embrace your spidey-sense mutant superpowers.
    Embrace the Hemmingway.
    Embrace your inner shitness.
    Write as if no one is watching (they aren't).
    Write shit.

THE FORGOTTEN ART OF SHORT STORY

MARK ALLAN GUNNELLS

RAY BRADBURY IS one of my favorite writers. In fact, I think he will be remembered as one of America's best storytellers, and I'd wager that many people would agree with that statement. Recently I read his excellent book *The Martian Chronicles*, and it got me to thinking about one of my favorite literary subjects—the short story.

I am very passionate about short fiction. I enjoy novels and novellas, I even enjoy essays and poetry, but short fiction is my true love. As a writer, it's what brings me the most pleasure, and as a reader, I simply love diving into a collection or anthology and discovering those little nuggets of gold.

There was a time when the short story was a well-respected literary art form, and a writer could build a career out of short fiction and be taken seriously. Bradbury is a prime example of this. He is a writer who made his name and earned his reputation primarily through his short fiction. Not that he didn't produce many great longer works, but even some of his most

WRITERS ON WRITING

acclaimed novels—*Dandelion Wine, The Martian Chronicles, From the Dust Returned*—are actually just collections of connected short stories. Once upon a time, short fiction was considered legitimate enough that it alone could make an author.

I don't know that this is the case any longer. The last writer I can remember that really made a name for himself through short stories is Clive Barker. His *Books of Blood* were a phenomenon in the industry, propelled in part by Stephen King's now famous blurb, and almost overnight Barker became a household name. Many novels followed, but initially it was his work in the short form that catapulted him to prominence in the literary world.

Since then, I can name numerous writers producing quality short fiction, but I can't name one who is taken seriously as an author solely on the basis of the short fiction. In fact, I've seen evidence that the short story has developed a reputation as the literary ghetto. You might start out there, but you are always working to move up to a nicer neighborhood.

I've witnessed writers advising newcomers to "cut their teeth" on short fiction but then abandon it for novels when they are ready to get "serious" about writing. I also know writers who say they have given up short fiction as a waste of time, focusing on novels because that's what publishers want. And in fact I do know several publishers that aren't interested in single-authored collections.

In all fairness, this lack of interest on the part of publishers is strictly financial. Collections don't sell the way novels do. The reading public appears to have less interest in the short form than they once did, and I

VOLUME 2

know readers who say with a certain amount of pride that they don't bother with short fiction. In other words, they never travel to the ghetto.

It makes me wonder how Bradbury would have fared in this atmosphere if he were just starting out in the business. Would the short stories we now know as classics fail to find an audience? Would he be advised to stop writing them and focus on novels, which are more fashionable and acceptable? Would books like *Dandelion Wine* and *The Martian Chronicles* have been rejected because they lack narrative cohesion and are really just collections masquerading as novels?

Or would the sheer brilliance of the work shine through, melting the resistance to short fiction that is often prevalent in this modern age? Would he help revitalize the short form and usher in a new era of respectability for it?

I'd like to think the latter would be true, because I don't believe short story writing is the literary ghetto. I believe it is still a vital and important art form that has a lot to offer to the literary community. And I don't think short fiction is dying, merely in a lull. Like most trends in popular culture, literature is a wheel that is ever turning, and fads come and go in a cyclical rhythm. What's popular today may not be popular five years from now, and what's unpopular now may in fact come back into fashion down the road. I've seen it happen with specific subgenres—vampires, zombies, demons, ghosts, etc. I believe it will happen with short stories, as well.

Because I believe this, and because of my deep abiding passion for the short form, I want to spend some time talking about the elements I believe go into

WRITERS ON WRITING

crafting a good short story, and what that particular form has to offer to the reader. Call it Short Story 101.

I don't pretend to be an expert, I'm just someone who loves the short story form and has been working at it for over 20 years. I've published in various magazines and anthologies, as well as released multiple collections with publishers such as Sideshow Press, Bad Moon Books, and Evil Jester Press, and I have several more collections on the horizon, including one with Crystal Lake Publishing. I'm also a voracious reader who devours short fiction like candy.

One thing that I love most about short stories is the fact that structure is less important than in a novel. What I mean by this is that the old cliché of every story has to have a beginning, middle, and end isn't necessarily true for short stories. Not in the traditional sense, in any case. A short story might have a detailed plot, but it may also be just a vignette. A single scene, a moment in time, a conversation. It may have the expected antagonist/protagonist conflict, or it could have a single character dealing with internal demons. It could be told entirely as an inner monologue, or in nothing but dialogue. Because of the brevity of a short story, the rules of structure aren't as rigid and are more easily bent than with a novel. Short stories afford greater opportunities to take risks and experiment with structure.

Short fiction can also pack quite a punch. Not that a novel or novella can't, but again, because of a short's brevity, the power of the piece can be concentrated to deliver a more vicious jab. The power of the emotion, of the horror, of the surprise—compacted into a short story, it can heighten all of these things for the reader.

VOLUME 2

For the writer, short fiction can prove an exhilarating challenge. Structure may be more fluid, but a story still has to feel complete in and of itself, not just a fragment. That doesn't mean you have to wrap everything up with a nice little bow. While some might not agree, I think ambiguity and open endings can work wonderfully in a short story, even more so than in a novel. However, the reader still needs to walk away satisfied that the story has been told in its entirety. Even if the story in question is a vignette with one person sitting alone in a room thinking about a past mistake and has an open ending, when you type "The End" it truly needs to feel like the end. The reader should feel like the tale is finished and not merely a tease. Even with a short story, it isn't fair to cheat the reader.

Characterization is another challenge for the writer of quality short fiction. You do not have the expansive length of a novel to really explore a character and give backstory and develop nuances of personality. That does not give you license to offer up two-dimensional, generic characters without depth or complexity. The trick is trying to provide distinct and fleshed out characters with just a few strategic brush strokes instead of a full portrait.

A good way to pack in a lot of personality for a character is through dialogue. How people talk can reveal a lot about them. What kind of words do they use? Do they curse a lot? Are they sarcastic? How is their grammar? Do they routinely interject words and phrases such as "like" and "you know" into their conversations? Details like this can go a long way toward adding dimension to a character and making

WRITERS ON WRITING

the reader feel like they really know who this person is.

In a short story, it isn't often feasible to provide extensive backstory for a character, but you still want to give a sense that a character has a broader life than just what is represented in the confines of the pages. When I was a younger writer, I would sometimes completely stop the flow of the narrative in a short for a ponderous flashback of a character's past. Sometimes this may work, but often it just interrupts the momentum of the tale and pulls the reader out of the story. You can accomplish backstory by giving small, well-placed pieces of information that suggest the character's past without elaborating on it. Just a mention of a character growing up with an abusive father can be as illuminating as an extensive flashback sequence detailing the abuse. We writers have to trust our readers and understand that they can take bits of information and expand on them in their imaginations, filling in the gaps to form a complete picture.

I also feel the short story offers some unique pleasures for the reader distinct from those of the novel. Not that I'm suggesting the pleasures of a short story are greater than those of a novel, but I am saying I believe they are equal. Certainly not lesser than.

It is not my intention to diminish the immersive experience of a novel, where the reader can spend a large chunk of time in that world with those characters, but there's something to be said for a story you can consume in one sitting. There's something satisfying for the reader when he or she is able to go on an entire journey uninterrupted. There is also a

VOLUME 2

type of magic at play in the short story. When done correctly, it leaves the impression that the reader has received a novel's-worth of entertainment in one single concise short. Like eating a candy bar and feeling as if you've had a four-course meal.

Short stories are also economical for the reader. I'm fond of saying that buying a collection or anthology is like getting a dozen or more fictional worlds for the price of one. I do think a collection provides more bang for the consumer's buck, so to speak.

Short fiction is also a wonderful way to sample a new writer. When I am interested in a writer I've never tried before, I always check first to see if they've released a collection. If so, that's where I start. It gives me not only an idea of their writing style, but by providing a smorgasbord of tales, I can get a glimpse into the breadth of their imagination, the types of subjects that interest them. Within one book, I can experience a variety of genres, plots, characters, themes, and tones. This gives the reader a better understanding of what the writer has to offer more than any one single story could.

Anthologies are also great samplers of different authors. It's impossible for a reader to try every writer publishing on the market, but an anthology can be used to discover authors that otherwise might have been missed. I know for me, I have definitely found a story that impressed me in a given anthology, sometimes by an author I'd never even heard of before, then sought out more work by that writer.

Not all writers are interested in the same things, which is how it should be. It's what makes literature so diverse and interesting. There will be some writers

WRITERS ON WRITING

that genuinely have no interest in the short form, and I'm not suggesting there is anything wrong with that. However, what I would hate to see are writers with a real passion for the short story turning away from it because it is being drilled into their minds that there is no future in it, and I don't want to see writers being shamed for pursuing short fiction as if they are slumming.

If you love short fiction, write it! Don't let anyone dissuade you, because the best writing is that which we are passionate about. Pour your heart and soul into the short stories you write, improve your craft, and research markets that are open to them. There are still publishers that embrace collections and anthologies, and are willing to really promote them. And collections can be financial successful, as well. It really warmed my heart earlier this year to see Neil Gaiman's collection *Trigger Warnings* on the top of the best seller's list.

As I said earlier, trends come in cycles. I do believe the wheel will turn and eventually we'll see short stories celebrated and championed again. The world will never see another like Ray Bradbury or Clive Barker, but there's room for more writers that make a name for themselves with quality short fiction that elevates the form.

That writer could be you. Just believe in yourself and don't give up.

WELL, THAT ESCALATED QUICKLY: ADVENTURES IN TEACHING CREATIVE WRITING

LUCY A. SNYDER

MANY FICTION AUTHORS teach creative writing at some point in their careers. I personally enjoy helping newer writers become better at their crafts. So, to earn the experience and academic credentials necessary to teach at a college level, I'm pursuing a Master of Fine Arts in creative writing at Goddard College. Part of Goddard's degree requirements involve completing a teaching practicum that each MFA student must design and organize on his or her own.

The flexibility of Goddard's teaching practicum presents a double-edged sword. On the one side, there's so much wonderful freedom to lead the kind of course or workshop you've always wanted to try. But on the other side, with so many possibilities, how do you choose?

At first, I considered offering a standard Milford-style critique workshop such as you find in the Clarion

WRITERS ON WRITING

Workshop. I've been in these types of workshops off and on for many years. When they're run properly, they offer plenty of useful experiences for workshop students. But I also realized that it's a workshop format I'm already familiar with, and I'd be acting more as a moderator than as a teacher. The opportunity to engage in more formal teaching/lecturing is something that I've lacked—it was entirely missing from my previous graduate program in journalism—and for the sake of my own growth and experiences, I wanted to try something different.

So, when I was attempting to clarify my practicum plans in September 2014, I initially hit upon the idea of offering a 6-session writing workshop over a long weekend at a science fiction or writers' convention. This plan made sense because I'm well-acquainted with various convention organizers; I discussed my ideas on Facebook and almost immediately the organizers of the writing tracks at Gen Con and Anthocon sent me private messages to offer up space at their events.

However, not even a month later I led a two-hour workshop at the Context convention in Columbus: "Writing Urban Fantasy and Supernatural Horror." I'd led similar workshops before and was confident going in. I didn't expect to be overwhelmed by nerves . . . but I was. I shook, and couldn't stop the trembling in my hands and voice. I was nauseated. My vision started to narrow. I managed to get through the workshop okay—feedback from students was positive overall—but I found it completely exhausting. And that was just two hours.

VOLUME 2

After that, I started seriously doubting the wisdom of trying to do my entire practicum over a long weekend. First, it might be far too much all at once for an introverted, inexperienced teacher such as myself. There would be no easing into things, no real chance to recover, regroup, or refine my teaching techniques. And the convention I was considering as venue happen just once per year. What if I got sick or had a travel snafu? I'd have to scramble to find a different event in a different city with different students. The logistics involved in all that would be difficult, to say the least.

So, I started exploring other options at local venues. I work as a content editor at the International Institute for Innovative Instruction (i4) at Franklin University. My group builds online courses for Franklin and other institutions. The university in general and our supervisors in particular are supportive of our seeking advanced degrees.

After the first residency, one of my supervisors started asking me to "bring back" the knowledge I'd gained at Goddard to i4. Which seemed to be something of a challenge, considering that Franklin (and by extension i4) focuses on business courses—no art or literature—and takes a very technical, structured view of education. But of course I wanted to make my supervisor happy, so I started thinking about what I could offer . . . and the proverbial light bulb went on inside my mind.

I initially pitched my supervisor a writing workshop series for the faculty and staff with a focus on topics that our people can apply to writing games, educational scripts, and case studies: things that would be of some interest to people here at i4. Our

WRITERS ON WRITING

staff members work on educational games and write multimedia scripts, so my supervisor was particularly keen on the gaming session I proposed.

Offering the workshops at i4 had some distinct advantage, but also several challenges. On the plus side, I had good facilities and other resources at my disposal. And I could partly prepare for the sessions at my workplace and not have to worry about trying to get across town during rush hour to another workshop location.

But, because I was leading the sessions at i4, they became tied to my work. The workshops were now something I had to report on to my supervisor and they became a part of my goals for my biannual review. And because I would be offering these workshops to coworkers in a space dedicated to excellence in teaching . . . I felt a bit more pressure to really do an excellent, professional job than if I'd been doing a casual sit-in-a-circle workshop at the local library! There was also a chilling effect with regard to class topics; while a discussion of erotica or extreme horror would have been fine at a science fiction convention, it seemed a bad idea to bring them up in front of my coworkers and supervisor.

Another piece of the challenge of offering the workshops at i4 emerged with regard to scheduling and session planning. I had to tailor the workshops for i4 staff and faculty. Most of them are total beginners when it comes to writing, and furthermore they're very busy folks who typically don't want to stick around campus after 5pm. Because work has to come first and people have deadlines and last-minute meetings, I couldn't count on anyone being able to attend all the

VOLUME 2

courses in sequence, so I'd need to try to make each session stand on its own.

Furthermore, my supervisor said that while I could open the workshops to the general public, I had to schedule the workshops for a time when Franklin staff and faculty were most likely to be free of classes and meetings. That meant Friday mornings.

So I scheduled all the workshops to run from 10am-noon on Fridays, which is a *terrible* time for anyone not affiliated with Franklin. I would have gotten more people from the outside community if I'd been able to schedule evening sessions. Nonetheless, overall attendance was good. The people from outside Franklin who did attend were retirees, schoolteachers, students, contractors, and others with flexible schedules.

Once I knew the time and the place, I needed to figure out the workshop session sequence. I wanted a good logical flow from topic to topic. It made sense to start with the creativity workshop as a way to get staff and faculty interested. It seemed logical to talk about plots and narrative structures before I got into narrative point of view and the finer details of characterization and dialog. And it made sense to cover description before I talked about setting and world building, since so much of the latter relies on the former.

But where to put the game workshop? It didn't fit well with the other sessions, so should I put it at the end, or at the beginning? I opted to put it close to the beginning, right after the creativity workshop, hoping it would act as another "hook" to lure staff into attending future workshops.

WRITERS ON WRITING

Once I had the workshop schedule set and the room reserved, I started advertising them at Franklin and in the community. My main promotional tools were email, Facebook, and the i4 blog. I immediately got some RSVPs from local writers who have begun to sell a few stories here and there, and I realized I'd have even more of a challenge than I'd expected, pedagogically speaking.

How could I ensure a good workshop experience for people who were total beginners but also for those who were experienced writers? Further, how could I best organize the workshops so that they didn't confuse students who had dropped in for a single session but didn't become repetitive for people who attended the entire series?

A bigger question emerged from my promise of making the sessions fun and hands-on. I couldn't count on having the same students from week to week. And Franklin staff wouldn't have much time or patience for homework in a class that didn't count toward a credential. So, what could I have the students do in the way of in-class exercises and activities that would neither overwhelm the dilettantes nor bore the more advanced writers?

Looking at all the questions I'd posed for myself, I started feeling a bit of panic. And heartburn. I knew that I couldn't make the sessions all things for all people. And the lack of homework and lack of students being able to work on more substantial pieces of writing would make it difficult for them to acquire component skills and truly practice them as a way to approach mastery:

Mastery refers to the attainment of a high degree

VOLUME 2

of competence within a particular area. For students to achieve mastery within a domain, whether narrowly or broadly conceived, they need to develop a key set of component skills, practice them to the point where they can be combined fluently and used with a fair degree of automaticity, and know when and where to apply them appropriately. (Ambrose 95)

So, the lack of homework/continuing work was a pedagogical flaw in my series because students didn't get enough chances to try out new forms of writing and receive feedback. If I ever do this series again, I'll remedy this by identifying continuing students early on and offering them optional activities to challenge their skills (as it was, a few people completed short stories as a result of in-class exercises, so those turned out to be more successful than I'd originally anticipated).

Faced with these apparently unavoidable flaws, I decided to be open with my students about the challenges I was wrestling with and take the sessions one at a time. I'd prepare the first session, see how it went, and then create the materials for my next session based on what I'd seen and heard from my students. I decided to try to cover the basics for the beginners in a way that would hopefully also activate prior knowledge and learning in the more advanced students:

Students connect what they learn to what they already know, interpreting incoming information, and even sensory perception, through the lens of their existing knowledge, beliefs, and assumptions. When students can connect what they are learning to accurate and relevant prior knowledge, they learn better and retain more. (Ambrose 15)

WRITERS ON WRITING

The tactic I took—and which evolved as the series went along—was to make the basics as engaging as possible while keeping things simple. I used the same approach I take when I've been asked to write a story containing familiar tropes: I tried to approach things a bit slantways rather than using the most obvious examples. I tried to offer perspectives that people who've attended many writing workshops might not have thought of before. Further, I tried to incorporate personal stories and examples of writing problems and writing success to offer a useful, engaging narrative that writers of all levels could connect to.

I also realized that because I'd be facing a crowd of strangers and coworkers in the first workshop, I could not afford a repeat of my stage fright. It wouldn't merely be a matter of personal embarrassment—it could have lasting negative consequences on my career. And that realization made me even more anxious.

I thought hard, trying to identify the source of my stage fright. I realized that I'd stood up in front of all those perfectly friendly faces and found myself thinking, "What the hell am I doing here?" My mind seemed to have temporarily lost every bit of information I'd intended to convey to my students. And with my shaking hands, my notes were nearly impossible to read.

Clearly, I needed some kind of handy informational prompt, and paper notes weren't going to work. Every single presentation I've attended at Franklin has involved some kind of PowerPoint. I'd long avoided using PowerPoint because it has a reputation for being a vehicle for dull presentations

VOLUME 2

and too often misused. But it this case I thought, why not try? If I completely lost my train of thought, I could at least point to words on the screen and stumble my way through. It wouldn't be ideal, but it would be far better than fleeing the class to go vomit in the ladies' room.

I am extremely glad I opted to go the PowerPoint route. First, having experience using the program is a good professional skill to have, and it was high time I gained it. But more important, the process of putting the slides together for each session really helped me focus and organize my thoughts on each subject. That process enabled me to put together much tighter, more organized, and better-timed sessions than I would have otherwise. The one downside to all that was that putting the slides together took far more time than I anticipated, but now that they're built, I can use them for more workshops in the future.

The original plan was to offer the series in our "smart" classroom in the basement so that we could set up a live webcast. The space has good technology and tables on risers that can't be moved from their positions. The immobility of the furniture concerned me a little—we couldn't sit in a circle so the students could interact face-to-face—and I knew that having that kind of static seating arrangement would impact how students perceived the workshops and would affect their learning:

The seating pattern of the workshop can drive the role the learning facilitator will play. Put simply, the learners' faces go toward the most important element in the room. For this reason, have learners face each other as much as possible, while still having a clear

WRITERS ON WRITING

view of the facilitator. This arrangement keeps the focus on the learners. (Russell 155)

So, knowing that I had to work with immobile, traditional classroom seating, I tried to focus on individual activities and exercises as opposed to small-group activities that would have been more awkward in the space.

The first workshop ("Creative Kickstart") went well—21 students and good reviews on the post-class surveys—but it was utterly exhausting. I wanted to curl up in a dark corner with a blanket afterward but instead had to be at my desk looking functional. After that, I vowed to work on ways to keep the sessions engaging for students but less exhausting for me; my main plan there was to rely more on class discussion, which would be beneficial for the students, as well. I also decided to spend more time on having students share their in-class work, and to take more time after slides to ask students for their thoughts, all of which put more focus on the students and less on me.

But we did have a hitch in that first workshop that meant we had to abandon the "smart" classroom. Two of my students were handicapped, and I discovered to my dismay that although the building has an elevator it doesn't go to the smart classroom's floor (who designs a building with an elevator that doesn't go to all the floors?). Maintenance was supposed to install a chair lift in the stairway but didn't. We managed to get both ladies and their wheelchairs up and down the stairs. However, my supervisors were justifiably worried about ADA issues and my workshops were moved to a space with elevator access and a portable large screen monitor.

VOLUME 2

The second workshop ("Game On!") also went well. I had 13 students, which was a respectable number, and not a terrible thing since there were fewer chairs and tables in the new space. All but two of my students were women; I found myself wondering if men thought a female game writing instructor won't offer a good workshop? That's hard to know. In any case, I'd expected a drop-off in attendance because: (1) a relatively small portion of the people interested in creative writing want to write games, (2) the campus health fair was going on at the same time, and (3) it was bitterly cold that morning. Student feedback was good; I made a tactical error by including a somewhat ambitious writing assignment (make a basic plan for a game) at the end of the session; about half the students (mostly Franklin staff) snuck out then, but the rest seemed to enjoy working on the exercise. The workshop went much better than the first in terms of preserving my energy afterward; we had some very good student discussion, and that helped a great deal.

The workshops after that all went fine; elevator access was the worst logistical problem that arose during the entire series. The students seemed to enjoy themselves, and feedback continued to be positive, although I noticed that Franklin staff (who are surrounded by teaching all the time) were more critical than the people from outside the university. And that's not surprising. Most everyone seemed to appreciate the information they came away with, even if not every in-class exercise I planned engaged people in the way that I'd hoped.

The main problem I encountered was the incredible amount of time planning and preparation

WRITERS ON WRITING

took. For those eight weeks, the workshops felt like a black hole of time sitting in the middle of my schedule. All my other work suffered as a result.

But on the plus side, I learned that no matter how lousy I feel when I wake up in the morning, I can pull up my figurative socks and perform and put on a decent class. I didn't know until this series that I had that ability, but I do now, and knowing that is extremely helpful. I always paid a cost in terms of being exhausted and unfocused after the workshops were over, but I could be "on" as long as necessary for my students.

And now, at the end of it all, I have eight very solid standalone workshops in my back pocket that I can present at conferences and MFA residencies. In fact, I'll be leading two of them—The Plot Thickens and Selling Your Fiction—at StokerCon in Las Vegas in 2016. I hope to see some of you there!

Works Cited:

Ambrose, Susan A. *How Learning Works: Seven Research-Based Principles for Smart Teaching*. San Francisco, CA: Jossey-Bass, 2010. Print.

Russell, Lou, and Martin Morrow. *The Accelerated Learning Fieldbook: Making the Instructional Process Fast, Flexible, and Fun*. San Francisco, CA: Jossey-Bass/Pfeiffer, 1999. Print.

SUBMIT (TO PSYCHOLOGY) FOR ACCEPTANCE

DANIEL I. RUSSELL

NEIL GAIMAN (you might have heard of him) said that, "Writers may be solitary but they also tend to flock together: they like being solitary together."

The stereotypical image of a writer is one of the creative genius, locked away alone, sweating bullets over the blank page and approaching deadline. Such an available heuristic. How many such writers are out there, with manuscripts gathering dust, both real and digital, in desk drawers and hard drives? The inspiration for a story comes from that tantalising relationship between the self and the universe: the places, the sensations, the relationships. The crafting of the story, granted, tends to be a solitary endeavour, and lives up to the idea of the lonesome writer shut away from distraction to get the words on the page. What comes next? What process ensures that manuscript sees the light of day? The writer has to drain that last coffee, lurch away from the screen and stagger into the social world, squinting in the sudden light.

WRITERS ON WRITING

I'm Daniel I. Russell, psychology major and, for the last twelve years or so, horror writer, and psychology major. As I've explored the theories and research in social psychology, I've seen links between these ideas and the experiences of a writer trying to find publishers, trying to develop a reading base, or simply, just trying! Here I'll explain a handful of psychological phenomena with the view that some of you reading this, from new writer to experienced pro, might identify with some of the behaviours. To be aware of ourselves, and know the psychological basis for some of our attitudes, aids in acceptance and transition. Hopefully, a little background knowledge might make the difference between a new writer quitting or pushing on in this sometimes disheartening business.

Let's look at the process for submitting to an anthology/competition/magazine for example, as this can cause the most anxiety. An editor or team may receive hundreds of submissions with only space for a dozen stories. It doesn't take an expert to realise that a handful of writers will be over the moon at the end of the selection process, and that many, many more will feel disappointed, perhaps unfairly treated, often frustrated, angry and pretty damn useless. Here I'm choosing to consider some of the mechanisms in play *before* the rejection/acceptance letter even hits the inbox.

Two constructs that I feel every writer falls prey to are the *Self Serving Bias* and the *False Uniqueness Effect*. We tend to perceive ourselves favourably, justifying our mistakes/weaknesses, taking great pride in our strengths/successes. This is the Self Serving Bias. I used to hate *X Factor*, *American Idol*, all that,

VOLUME 2

back in the day. My partner at the time lapped it up and watched each strain with almost religious fervour. I did, however, have a little time for those early audition episodes. Call me sadistic, but watching some of those people who really *really* think they can sing embarrass themselves? Pure entertainment. I always saw it as a televised, therefore exacerbated and inflated, reality check . . . but sometimes even after the judges laughed in their faces and they became a national joke, some of these people still honestly believed they were great singers. Why?

I guess some individuals have a really strong Self Serving Bias that is hard to overcome, and combined with the False Uniqueness Effect, wherein we underestimate the commonality of our abilities and successes, this convinces them in their minds that they're the next (insert your favourite singer here).

What's this to do with writing? If I write two pieces and only submit one for publication, I have more faith in *that* story. I have to believe that not only is the story good enough for publication but also that the editor will favour it over the other submitted stories. In my years as the submissions editor at *Necrotic Tissue Magazine*, I read through hundreds of stories every submissions period. Some of those, as is the business, were stinkers. You would also tend to see plots replicated, sometimes reading effectively the same basic story ten times over per submissions period (turns out the protagonist was the vampire all along!). Yet each one of these writers had to *believe* that their story was good enough or else why send it in? Even the suggestion that a writer might try their luck and submit anyway doesn't quite fly as luck has no part in

WRITERS ON WRITING

the submissions process. No editor worth the title runs a slush pile like a raffle (although I have known this on rare instances, but I guess that's another article entirely). So from Stephen King to a first timer, the writer must believe at some level that a story is good enough to submit, and thanks to the False Uniqueness Effect, the odds are against you if you believe it's the greatest short story ever written.

We've submitted and, whether you want to think about this term or not, you're now in a competition for one of those few publication spots. *Social comparison* rears its sometimes ugly head here. Social comparison, at its most fundamental, is crucial for self development. We tend to compare upwards rather than downwards. For example, after an acceptance in a token market, a writer is more likely to look towards semi-pro markets next and take notice of the names of other writers who sell there regularly. Not many sit back with their $5 payment and feel contented, as many others were probably rejected, and therefore beaten, in the fight for that $5. Onwards and upwards. Yet climbing the acceptance ladder might require the honing of one's craft, reading more, researching. As a result of comparing upwards, we see where we want to be and hopefully acknowledge the work required to get there.

Social comparison is a double-edged sword. Those perhaps not as confident in their writing, to preserve their self-concept (due to the Self Serving Bias) might reduce the personal importance of acceptance ("I didn't really want to be in the book anyway. I just had a trunk story spare.") or introduce self-handicapping ("I submitted but I won't get in, I was so drunk when I

VOLUME 2

wrote that story . . . "). Do any of these excuses sound familiar? It's nothing to be ashamed of. It's natural! It takes one who is comfortable with their abilities, and more importantly their own self, to accept rejection. However, to regularly *depend* on these 'outs for failure' would be to turn them into habit, which we will look at shortly.

When you receive that wonderful acceptance letter, and after the celebratory champers has been popped, drunk and slept off, how do you attribute that success? Is it due to you being an awesome writer? Was it your kick arse yet literary masterpiece that couldn't have failed? Or perhaps you consider that the editor was kind or that the publication was in need of that certain kind of story for that specific issue? Flipping the coin, think about how you handle rejection. Either your work wasn't up to scratch, or you didn't fit the magazine. Perhaps the slots were saved for friends of the editor, or he simply didn't get what you were trying to do (an Illusion of Transparency, but I digress . . .).

Everyone has a *locus of control*, which is their perception of control, be it intrinsic or extrinsic, and can shift depending on the situation. You can choose to drive under the speed limit so the police don't pull you over, or it doesn't really matter as they'll pull you over anyway if they want to. In writing, an internal locus can be empowering and inspire you to put the hours in, tighten that story, make the next piece better than the last because *you* are in control of *your* career. An external locus tends to be detrimental in this regard. Other people, editors, readers, determine your success, not you. A balance is needed as this reflects reality outside of the self. Yes, an editor makes the call

WRITERS ON WRITING

whether to buy your story (extrinsic), but writing one hell of a yarn will greatly improve your chances (intrinsic).

The continued use of 'outs for failure' can keep the locus of control firmly in the external, and this is dangerous territory, folks. Imagine two young brothers. One hits the other hard on the arm. Now the next time, the brother knows the hit is coming and he tries to avoid it... which proves fruitless. He's pinned down and hit again. This happens sporadically over and over. Eventually, the brother won't even flinch from the blows, having accepted that they will come no matter what he does. This is known as *learned helplessness*, and is a major contributor to depression. I believe it can be summed up in three words: what's the point?

This is common in the writing world, and I feel most of us have been there at some point. I'll admit that I've been there many times over my career (and I'm all for preventative practice, so you know, buy one of my books after finishing this article). For those of you that interact on Facebook and Twitter, rather than solely pimping their wares (for shame!), you can find those fellow writers. Go on there right now and find them! I'm sure they'll be easy to spot. It's the writer's equivalent of a vague FB suicide threat. Those that talk about quitting writing are more likely to go through with it... especially if no one pays any attention, adding to that extrinsic locus of control, heaping on the learned helplessness and possibly losing the writing world some very talented and needed voices.

So what was the point of this article? Going back to my opening statement, I encourage those of you

VOLUME 2

trying to do this on your own to get out there. Be it digitally or even better in person, you will need writing relationships, the supporting, honest kind. It's not all about posting Amazon links or sharing reviews. Those of you that aren't doing so well, and those with a shelf full of awards and published novels . . . both extend a hand. As psychotherapists we're taught to be authentic. I ask for this with your fellow writer. It's a slippery slope. Learned helplessness can be crippling, and can only lead to putting away that pesky manuscript and turning on *X Factor* (if that's even produced any more).

And what can we do within *ourselves*? Consider these psychological constructs. Have a realistic view of your work and continue to write the best story you can. Do not dwell on those rejections and overlooked awards. It might feel like the world is against you but it really isn't. That's just your Self Serving Bias talking!

CHARACTER BUILDING: HOW NOT TO BE A STALKER

THERESA DERWIN

Welcome, dear reader, to Character Building 101: How Not to be a Stalker

We've all done it, as writers. Stared vacantly across a crowded room at an interesting stranger who's just walked into a pub or restaurant and analysed everything about them. From their clothes, to their hair, to their mannerisms, we've nailed that person down for our own literary creations.

Yes, you've thought, that's Bob the serial killer, or Mandy the stockbroker.

But did it ever occur to you that you may look like a stalker if you're caught in your observations?

Indeed, I've been caught a few times in the past, but now experience has taught me how to create characters from the world around me without coming across as a psycho or a pervert.

In this essay I'm going to take you through some basic techniques and exercises to help you create realistic and fleshed out characters for your fiction.

Apologies if some of this is like teaching Grandma

VOLUME 2

to suck eggs, but sometimes it's good to get back to basics. As such, I'm going to start you with the list. This is an old, tried and tested technique that can help you create a believable character. But remember, this info is just for you. Beware of info dumping. The last thing you want to do, is create your character list, then splatter your page with everything about your character.

So, here goes, it's pretty simple. Complete the list below and fill in the missing data to create an overall picture for one of your characters, existing or new. It will help you to understand who that person is and to add depth to the protagonist as a whole.

The List

- Name: (Choose carefully. Make sure you don't repeat names throughout your fiction, that the spelling is consistent and you haven't used alliteration if possible. You can change the name after if it doesn't suit the person. Try using social media and combing friends' names or use the phone book. Baby name items are also useful)
- Age: (How old are they? What year were they born?)
- Height
- Eye colour
- Hair colour and style (old fashioned/modern)
- Occupation (this one is important. Make sure you know a bit about their job before you assign it. No point making Bob a meteorologist if you know nothing about it. Research is key.
- Clothing: see hair, above

WRITERS ON WRITING

Now you've got the physical basics out of the way, it's time to get creative.

- Favourite Food
- Favourite soft Drink
- Tea or coffee (the answer to life and everything)
- Favourite alcoholic drink and units per week (are they a heavy drinker? Could this be a sign of alcoholism, depression or trauma?)
- Qualifications (are they realistic in terms of their career?)
- Star sign (see DOB/age references)
- Religion (there is a whole host of things you can do with your character dependent on religious stance)
- Lives: Where were they born? Have they emigrated? Have they always lived in the city/country?
- Hobbies: Cinema/Sports/Reading. Remember if you are picking a sport, can it relate to your plot? For example, Bob is a rock climber so when he's out he has a fall whilst climbing and needs to be rescued.
- Relationship status
- Books: Favourite author/books. I'll be using this in exercise two.

So, now you have a broad spectrum of data you can use when introducing your characters.

"Bob was devouring his pizza with a couple of beers, when the phone rang, interrupting his night in."

VOLUME 2

The next thing we're going to do, is write a scene somewhere between a Drabble and a Flash piece.

You will choose three things from the list below and write a piece of original fiction based on those objects or characterisations. However, you MUST NOT say what job the person does. You must imply or infer it through the fiction and allow the reader to come to their conclusion.

An example will follow this exercise.

Exercise One: Just Three Things

1. Name
2. Occupation
3. Object: in this case it is an overnight bag. What's in the bag (sorry, having a *Seven* moment there)? What does it tell us about the character?

Example:

Character Profile: Sam

Calloused, yellow fingers worn through hard work, not necessarily age, reached deeper into the black overnight bag, searching. The bag itself was nondescript, no logo, no pattern to make it distinguishable, memorable or easy to recognise. Normalcy was the key here.
    The hand burrowed even deeper into the depths of the bag, pushing aside a selection of navy and black socks and boxer shorts; a single black polo-neck

jumper and a black leather belt. Disgruntled, he pulled the clothing out, tossing it over a broad set of shoulders to Kane on the lush, dark carpet of the hotel room. The clothing had to be got rid of. Though essential for day-to-day existence, they were interfering with his search. And it was imperative that the search continue, that he find what he was looking for.

He needed it. It was his bible, his security blanket, his raison d'être.

Those calloused fingers dug deeper still, bypassing the half open packet of B&H, the gold lighter his mentor had given him when he'd done his first job, and the tightly wrapped roll of notes, secured with an elastic band.

His fingers brushed against the cold, hard metal and he felt a moment of triumph, power and comfort at the thought of what it could achieve in mere seconds. But as comforting as that fleeting touch had been, it wasn't what he was after.

There it was—underneath.

Eagerly he grasped the book, bringing it out into the harsh light of day, its tattered edges curled, yellow and musty with age and frequent reading. There was one page more yellowed, more frayed than the rest. The page he was always drawn to.

This was indeed his bible. His Rule Book, its beautiful pages filled with a myriad of erotic and passionate images.

Deftly stroking one tarnished finger against the cover, Sam traced the words, the title, that gave his life meaning.

Catcher in the Rye.

VOLUME 2

What do you think Sam does for a living based on the above suggestions and references?

Now it's your turn.

Exercise Two: Just Three Things

1. Name:
2. Occupation:
3. Object: Briefcase

Go for it!

***

So, now that you've had a bit of fun with that exercise, I'm going to finish with the stalkerish bit.

Exercise Three: The Pub (Observation)

- Go to a pub, cafe, coffee shop or other public venue.
- You will need an hour at least, copious amounts of coffee and a notepad.
- Look around at the other people in the venuediscreetly please; you are not a stalker.
- What is their name?
- Profession?
- What are they eating/drinking and what does this tell you about them? For example, are there three empty beer bottles on the table before midday?
- Who are they with?
- Why are they here? What happened before?
- Where are they going after?

WRITERS ON WRITING

- Choose about three people and do the same.
- Then using six degrees of separation find a link between two of them.
- Write a story of at least 1,000 words based on your observations.
- When you've completed all of the exercises above, review them and see how you've developed your characters. These exercises can be adjusted to meet almost any requirements.

Good luck, and good writing.

HEROES AND VILLAINS

PAUL KANE

MYSELF AND MY wife—the author and editor Marie O'Regan—run writing workshops all over the country. And, without a doubt, our two most popular ones are 'Monsters' (which I've talked about at great length elsewhere, mainly because of my new collection from Alchemy Press with the same name) and 'Heroes & Villains.' Actually, the two do kind of crossover if you think about it, as many villains in the imaginative genres—Horror, SF and Fantasy—are monsters, as well. Take Smaug the Dragon from *The Hobbit*, played to perfection by Benedict Cumberbatch in the movies; you couldn't ask for a more charismatic antagonist! Then you have the Daleks of *Doctor Who* (or Cybermen, or Weeping Angels, or . . . insert your favourite here), the Klingons of *Star Trek*, not to mention those iconic horror villains, Freddy, Jason, Michael . . . Pinhead—though we'll get back to the Cenobites a bit later on. All of these had a massive impact on me in my formative years, and subsequently my writing when I started to pen my first amateur tales in the '80s.

WRITERS ON WRITING

But it's the relationship between heroes and villains I want to explore in this article, and its use in story. When I think about both these roles, I can't help thinking about the archetypal 'goodies & baddies' from literature, films and TV. One pair that stand out in particular for me are James Bond and Ernst Stavro Blofeld, and it's so nice to see the latter back in the latest film *Spectre*. The characters are, essentially, two sides of the same coin—to put it very simply: good and evil. But things are never that simple, are they? Never black and white, and nor should they be if you want the relationship between your own heroes and villains to be realistic. Both Bond and Blofeld come at things from opposite ends of the spectrum . . . both are representatives of huge organisations, Bond of the British Secret Service and Blofeld of **Sp**ecial **E**xecutive for **C**ounter-intelligence, **T**errorism, *R*evenge and **E**xtortion—in fact he's their leader.

They come into conflict on a number of occasions and each one is trying to stop the other's schemes; Blofeld motivated by money and power; Bond by trying to protect his country (and by extension, the world) and to save lives. Both think they are doing the right thing, and though he is a hero Bond is not averse to using people to get his way, the famous example being his penchant for sleeping with women to get information; he will also sacrifice individuals to save larger numbers of people. On the flip side of this, Blofeld believes the world is run by incompetents, and that it would be in much better hands if he took over. Conflicting viewpoints, especially if grey areas are brought into the mix, make for the best hero and villain rapports. The question is, could one survive without the other?

VOLUME 2

A similar dynamic exists between Robin Hood and the Sheriff of Nottingham, a coupling that I know quite well myself. This goes back centuries, to when Hood's adventures were first written about in traditional ballads. On the face of it, Hood should have been the villain, and the Sheriff the hero. The latter is, after all, in charge of the 'police force' of the land, and Robin is the thief who is robbing people as they make their way through Sherwood Forest and beyond. And that would be true were it not for the fact that the Sheriff does not have the common people's interests at heart, only his own and those of the wealthy. Robin, himself of common birth (depending on which version of the mythology you believe), puts himself in the position of defender of the downtrodden, ordinary folk—stealing not for his own gain, but to give to the poor. In effect, the situation the Sheriff himself creates actually leads to Robin Hood's 'birth,' an origin story that's very familiar indeed.

So, when I came to create my own Robin and Sheriff, for the first Hooded Man book—*Arrowhead*—almost ten years ago now, I had a template to follow. But I also wanted to make these characters mine; create my own unique take on not only the legend, but the hero and villain relationship. I had the setting already, the world of the Afterblight Chronicles, so richly depicted in books like Simon Spurrier's *The Culled*—a world where 90% of the population had died from the A-B virus, leaving only those who had O-Negative blood alive. A post-apocalyptic world where I figured things would probably go back to how they were in Hood's day anyway, with markets and barter systems, dictators trying to take over and run things.

WRITERS ON WRITING

Enter the Frenchman De Falaise, who brings his band of mercenaries through the Channel Tunnel in order to sweep his way up Britain and become—literally—king of the castle. In this instance, Nottingham Castle.

Standing in his way, although he doesn't know it at the beginning of the book, is ex-policeman Robert Stokes, who has lost his wife and son to the virus and retreated to the heart of Sherwood away from everything. Lured out when he sees the injustice of De Falaise's reign, he eventually draws his version of the Merry Men to him. I tried to make my hero and villain fully rounded characters, giving De Falaise redeeming qualities (it wasn't easy, as he is a complete and utter bastard) and Robert very human failings. But the real difference this time is that both are well and truly aware that they are playing their parts in a reworking of an old story, there's just nothing they can do about it. The journey of the heroes and villains of this tale, of course, continued on through two more novels—gathered together in the sellout *Hooded Man* omnibus—and a handful of shorts, which expanded the mythos beyond the original Hood premise and took it somewhere else entirely. The latest novella *Flaming Arrow*, for example gave me the opportunity to catch up with Robert as an older, more grizzled Hood—looking back on his career, his triumphs and failures, and thinking about retiring. All heroes and their villains need an arc, it's what stops things from getting boring and means they progress as realistic characters, reacting to what they've been through, good or bad.

Another standout in terms of the archetypal hero and villain pairing for me has always been Sherlock

VOLUME 2

Holmes and Professor Moriarty, not just in the original Conan Doyle stories but in all the adaptations and reworkings there have been over the years. Holmes is the ultimate detective, and Moriarty the ultimate criminal—the only one who has come close to ever really defeating our hero. Again, their relationship is a complex one and, as seen after the events in "The Final Problem" and "The Empty House"—where it's revealed that Holmes didn't actually lose his own life in order to rid the world of Moriarty—he wrestles with the notion that he will never face such a challenging opponent again. Others come close, but it was also always that curious dichotomy I found the most interesting. For Holmes, it was almost like losing a part of himself when Moriarty died, and I think two characters that are so closely connected but on opposite sides of the 'law' or a 'moral code' are always the most powerful . . . and the most memorable.

It's something I've hopefully explored in my own new novel, *Sherlock Holmes and the Servants of Hell*, only recently revealed by Solaris. Obviously I can't say too much about the book at this stage, as it's not out until July 2016, but I can tell you that I've used the introduction of the Cenobites from Clive Barker's Hellraising universe—told you I would return to them!—not only to bring together some of my own favourite heroes and villains of all time, but to say something about the nature of the usual 'good vs evil' model. The nature of the anti-hero that we feel able to root for. And it's been a very exciting thing to do!

All of which neatly brings me back to the monster as antagonist, something I very consciously pursued in my 2008 novella *RED* and the more recent follow-

WRITERS ON WRITING

up novel from SST Publications, *Blood RED*. As I did with the Hooded Man mythos, I took the original idea of Little Red Riding Hood and not only gave it a modern makeover—the protagonist is now care worker Rachael Daniels, who has to face the rigours of the urban woods, a council estate, to bring one of her clients their medication—I also played with the conventions of who exactly the hero and the villain are. Inspired as much by John W. Campbell's *Who Goes There?* (filmed of course as *The Thing from Another World* and *The Thing*), and Thomas Harris' *The Silence of the Lambs* and *Hannibal*, I created a story in which paranoia prevails and the villain is just as likely to fall in love with the hero as eat her. My wolf is a psychosexual predator unlike any other, able to shapeshift and become anyone—though usually plumps for people's partners because sex and seduction, playing the game, is as important to this creature as the end result.

During the course of the original tale, things twist and turn around at a rate of knots—especially towards the finale—so that you're not entirely sure who's the enemy and who's your friend. It's something I did deliberately to keep the reader on their toes, but also to turn the conventional hero-villain relationship completely on its head. And, from the response I've received, I seem to have done a pretty good job. In *Blood RED*, I took things a step further—but I can't really mention how without giving away the end of the first story. Suffice to say, I found a way to connect both hero and villain that I don't think anyone's *ever* done before, and on a level I'm not sure anyone would ever have wanted to try.

VOLUME 2

So, heroes and villains. One of the reasons our workshop which revolves around this topic is so popular, is that we get people to create their own sets of good guys and bad guys. And we start by getting them to think about the crucial area of what the goals might be for each one . . . For example in something like *Star Wars* the goal of Darth Vader is to rule the known universe on behalf of the Emperor. Luke Skywalker and the rebels are out to stop him, to free the universe forever from the yolk of the Empire—a similar theme to the Robin Hood legend. There's more to it all than that, naturally, and other motivations that come to light during the course of the films, but that's the central struggle of those two characters. Struggle leads to conflict, which is a driving force (if you excuse the use of that word) in narrative; cause leading to effect. The consequence of Vader killing Obi Wan, something that was set in motion in the prequel movies, is that Luke feels he has to avenge his mentor, which sets him on the road to becoming a Jedi himself—but also leaves the way open for him possibly to turn to the Dark Side. And all this stuff is happening in conjunction with, and sometimes as a consequence of, the central goal struggle.

In summary, when creating your own heroes and villains, give them opposing objectives. But also give the hero traits that might make them flawed, whilst at the same time giving the villain characteristics we might be able to warm to; that's what makes a reader or viewer care about the struggle. There's good and bad in everyone, so show how the inner struggles might relate to the outer ones. And don't forget that arc—both heroes and villains should grow and change

WRITERS ON WRITING

as your story goes on, reacting to what happens. If a loved one is killed, that might turn a good man bad—or actually *into* a villain—only for a hero to try and bring them back again to the side of good (just like Luke does eventually with his father).

But the most important thing is to have fun, whether you're creating villains or monsters, heroes or anti-heroes, because if you're not having a good time with it all, neither will your readers . . .

Let battle commence!

DO YOUR WORST

JONATHAN WINN

Oh the sweet, sweet irony.

Having accepted Crystal Lake Publishing's invitation to submit my thoughts to Writers on Writing, Vol. 2, and having decided on a topic I believed would be both entertaining and instructive, I suddenly found myself stuck.

Dumbfounded and confused, I sat there, the pristine white of the page staring back, mocking me. My thoughts on How to Deal with Writer's Block refusing to budge from the useless safety of my head to my more useful fingers hovering over the keyboard. Whatever alleged expertise or experience I was hoping to share frustratingly MIA.

You see what I mean?

Irony.

Obviously I was going to have to roll up my metaphorical sleeves and practice what I was getting ready to preach.

But how?

First things first, I needed to relax. Stop, drop and roll. Take a breath and put things in perspective. Break

WRITERS ON WRITING

down the problem by asking questions. Initiate a dialogue that would help pivot me away from this full-blown panic attack and refocus on the task at hand while also clearing out the static and reminding myself what I'm capable of.

Question #1: Can I write?

Yes. I've proven that time and again. Full-length novels. Short stories. Short story collections. Film scripts. татВ scripts. Blog posts, synopses, blurbs. Essays, emails, love letters. Grocery lists. Random musings on post-it notes. Writing was not the problem. I can write. I can put words on paper, arrange them into sentences, and then paragraphs, and finally something resembling a narrative. I've done it before and will do it again. That's not the worry.

#2: Can I write about this subject?

Yes. I've lived this subject. More times than I'd like to admit. Hell, I'm living it now! I have exercises that work for me. Tactics I've tested time and again. Riddled with battles scars and armed with information and experience, I know how to deal with this.

More importantly, I also have a strong suspicion about what might lie at the root of writer's block, at least for me. And that's something I'd like to talk about. Which is why I accepted Crystal Lake's invitation to share my thoughts.

So, yes, I can write about this.

In fact, I believe a lot of writers can write about this. Because, let's face it, the fear of not being able to fill all that white space with words, words, words, is sometimes, if only briefly, the one thing that links us all together. It's the only thing we writers share,

VOLUME 2

whether we realize it or not. One of the few experiences we've all lived through, fought against and succeeded over.

The temporary inability to put words on paper is a constant and will be written about for decades to come. Might as well toss my two cents on the dog pile, right?

And by answering those two questions, I've broken the cycle, refocused my energy, and have ended up with words on the page.

You see? This, right here, these words, what you've just read, this is how you win, or at least fight, the Battle of Blank Page. By writing! Even if it means sitting down and writing your thoughts and aimless opinions, breaking down the Why and What of your current chaotic state of mind, and then moving on from that to your Story. Putting words on the page is one of many ways to break writer's block. And it's what works for me.

Luckily, my ramblings did double duty by being somewhat informative.

I hope.

But they also clearly showed me progress. Regardless how useful they end up being in the end—that's what edits and rewrites are for—they *visually* moved me away from the seemingly inescapable superiority of all that white to the "yep, I can still do this" celebration of seeing words, words, blessed words.

Never underestimate how important something so simple—cluttering a page—can be when the writer in you is stuck on mute.

So, whenever I'm asked how to break writer's block, I say write. Yes, I'm serious and, yes, I get

WRITERS ON WRITING

laughed at. But it's true. Write. Anything. Everything. Write about how you can't write right now. Write about how bad a writer you are. Write about how you'll never write again. Write about how you're a poser and a fraud and you totally suck. But write it out. Put those words on the page. Hell, if you really want to barge in with guns a'blazin' you can even knock yourself out and write crap.

No, seriously.

But we'll get back to that later.

Once the laughter subsides and people realize I'm serious when I tell them to write their way out of writer's block, I'll ask them what their story's about. Not their concept, but their story. Not the overall arc of what they're saying, but the details. Not the incredible beginning or the amazing end, but the What of how they bridge those two disparate points together.

Most of the time I'm met with a bit of mumbling, perhaps a blank stare. The blush rising in the cheeks as they struggle to quickly coalesce their conceptual macro into a narrative micro.

Almost always they have no clue.

No worries. It's a great square one to begin with.

It's surprising how many writers can effortlessly pitch the macro of what they want their story to be—their unforgettable beginning, their twisty-turny middle, their shockingly awesome end—but when it comes to the micro, all those details, the what of what happens, they get lost. They fumble, they stumble, they falter.

And they fall.

Hello, Writer's Block.

I wrote my first screenplay in 2004. By all accounts, it was an unmitigated disaster. Think of the

VOLUME 2

worst thing you've read and then multiply it by one bazillion and you might come close to how bad that first script was.

But its job wasn't to be perfect or even something worth producing. In fact, its job wasn't even to be readable. Its job was to be the first. To start me on my journey. The point of that first screenplay was to teach me how to tell a story within a structured framework, help me understand how to build characters, and, at the end when I typed FADE TO BLACK, give me the necessary rush of confidence of having done it, of having written, so I could then start the next thing and write even more.

And, that being done, I wrote another script. Then another. And another.

By 2008, though, the screenwriting now feeling more second nature than not, I found myself wanting to expand my horizons a bit. Perhaps even, oh, I don't know, write a book.

You know where this is going, right?

So, in March of 2008, I sat down, popped open a new Word Doc and wrote "Chapter One" of my first full-length novel *Martuk . . . the Holy*. And then Chapter Two. Three, Four, Five and Six soon followed. All the way up Twenty-Eight or Twenty-Nine or something. Just blazing along, cramming that white space with a ton of words. Too many words, probably. But I was writing.

Come January 2009, I didn't just hit the wall, I slammed into it so hard it dang near crumbled. A collision so cataclysmic I'm still shocked it didn't make the news. Or at least a mention in *The Guinness Book of World Records*.

WRITERS ON WRITING

In short, Writer's Block bitch slapped me seven ways to Sunday.

The writer in me, bereft of ideas and out of gas, just stopped. Dead cold. I couldn't write anymore. The story I thought I had wasn't there. I'd sit down, open the Doc and see nothing but silence, emptiness, failure. A blank reminder of my inability to create. A cursor cruelly taunting me with each insistent blink, blink, blink.

When it came to *Martuk,* I had no idea what I was doing anymore.

So, not knowing how to fix it, I swallowed my disappointment, accepted defeat, shrugged my shoulders because, you know, I didn't *really* want to write a book anyway, so, whatever, and went back to writing scripts.

And, man, that felt good. To be working again? It was bliss. To sit down and write the outline. To discover how one scene transitioned to the next. How each interaction rested on what happened before while laying the ground work for what came next. How everything, every page, every moment, was somehow all interconnected. All those sly breadcrumbs you could scatter, giving hints to what waited ahead. How the characters' journeys unfolded through action and inaction, dialogue and silence. How everything was plotted and planned and carefully thought out before ever putting fingers to keyboard.

It felt amazing to hear those keys clicking again and to see that black pixel spill across that white. And to *know* I could still write? Thank god!

But that unfinished opus haunted me. Like my immortal Martuk, it felt alone and abandoned. In my

VOLUME 2

mind and my heart, what that book could be and what the concept could accomplish refused to die.

Fast forward to Spring 2010. Lunch in Greenwich Village with a friend of mine, a film producer. Between bites of delicious—albeit overpriced—burger and sips of sugary soda she asks how the book is coming along. You know, the one I started almost two years ago?

"It's not," I said before going on to bellyache about the unrelenting torture of having to face that unblemished page.

"Well, what's the story?" she said.

And I told her about Martuk. His youth one thousand years before Christ. His mortal death on an altar in Uruk at the hands of those priests in red and gold. The ancient evil draped in darkness finding him, infesting him. The despair of the no longer mortal Martuk discovering himself trapped in Life Everlasting.

His anger, his bloodlust, his revenge driving him to do the unspeakable. His immortality in 1st century Jerusalem. His loneliness and despair. His shocking brief brush with an unforgettable, unexpected love. How he turns to a false messiah in his desperation for healing. Or for death. His tortured modern life in Paris, plagued by an endless past that follows him like shadow and ghosts that, like him, cannot die.

"Great concept," she said. "But what's your story? You just spelled out a great idea—which would make a great film, by the way, so we should talk later—but what's linking one thing to the next? How does this 'what' happen?"

I don't remember what I said in response. I might have shrugged. I do know I took a bite of a french fry

WRITERS ON WRITING

and chewed it very slowly. As if this predictable strip of fried potato was some never-before-seen discovery bequeathed to me by the culinary gods. Some unexpected experience I needed to savor and relish.

In fact, not wanting to talk with my mouth full, I might have chewed that damn thing thirty, forty times.

One thing I'll never forget is that thumping thud in my gut when the pillars of my life as a budding fiction writer collapsed with a simple question.

But she was right.

I had no idea what Martuk's story was.

But that wasn't the stake in the heart.

"So, what does your outline say?" she said before taking a bite of her burger.

That, right there, those were the five words that sliced through my skin, stabbed through my middle, and pinned my precious pretensions to the bottom of my crumbling coffin.

So, um, yeah, my outline?

I didn't have one.

Oy to the vey.

I'll never forget her sigh. The deep disappointment in that drawn out exhalation as she shook her head. The shame in knowing that my monumental, perhaps even historically atrocious screw-up was out in the open for all to see.

Or at least that's what it felt like.

My friend was right, though. The same tactics I used time and again to tackle writing a screenplay should be, nay, needed to be, used when writing a book.

So, buoyed by that glimmer of light at the end of the I Guess I Can't Write a Book tunnel, I sat down and outlined the What of what *Martuk . . . the Holy* was

VOLUME 2

about. Plotted the Who and the How. Found that, even with the first half of *Martuk* written—not perfectly or even prettily, mind you, but still written—I wasn't in as bad a shape as I'd thought I was. Through this outline I discovered that, unbeknownst to me, a much more interesting, perhaps better, story was waiting in those hidden spaces tucked beneath the words I'd already put on the page.

This orderly arranging of what *Martuk* could be reignited my excitement. I once again found myself driven by inspiration, rushing to the computer to methodically plot the plot and set the scenes. Not that they'd be followed to the letter, of course.

Because outlines are guides. Roadmaps, if you will. They're not intended to imprison your creativity or stifle your voice. They're there to help keep you on-track when you wander and point you back in the right direction if you get lost.

But that lunch was *Martuk's* saving grace. The embarrassment, the humiliation, the realization of how greatly I'd messed up, all of that saved not only my first book, but my career as a fiction writer. From there followed not only the finished *Martuk . . . the Holy* and *The Wounded King, The Elder* and *Red and Gold*—part of *The Martuk Series,* an ongoing collection of short fiction inspired by *Martuk*—but also the full-length sequel, *Martuk . . . the Holy: Proseuche*. From there followed award-winning short stories, a book deal and a treasured relationship with one of the best presses in the business.

You could even say that thumping thud in the gut during that disastrous lunch in Greenwich Village unlocked my writing career.

WRITERS ON WRITING

Talk about turning a frown upside down.

But let me back up for a moment to share with you what an outline is. Or at least what it is to me.

It's nothing fancy and you're not going to find an example of it in a How-To book. For me, like everything I do, it's casual and conversational, eschewing rules and regulations in favor of inspiration and creativity.

It's an email, basically. And then a Word Doc. But first it's an email. Written and sent to yours truly. It's a list, usually bullet pointed, broken down by Act—Act One, Act Two, Act Three (shades of the screenwriter in me)—of where I think the story's going to go. But, more importantly, it's a guide. And it's what works for me. Casual. Conversational. Easily amended and changed.

Try it. If it works, great. If not, play around and find what works for you. And then write those words.

Even if they're crap.

And we're back to that again.

You see, I'm a huge proponent of bad writing. Not the *publishing* of bad writing, of course. Not the all-out frontal assault we see these days of hack writers burdening their readers with their worst just 'cause they can or they don't know better.

But writing crap? For yourself? To get the gears moving?

Yeah, do it.

Because—say it with me, kids—they're words on the page! And you should never underestimate how great it feels to get those words out and see them grow up big and strong into paragraphs and stories and books. Even if most of it will be deleted during edits.

VOLUME 2

And they should be deleted. They're supposed to be. Although their lives are brief, their jobs are clear. Crap's sole purpose is to get you writing again. To shake off the dust. To get you going. To build up your confidence. And to get rid of the pristine perfection of that damn white page.

Of course, there will be those who disagree with me.

"What? Write horribly? No! Never! There's enough shyte out there to begin with! We don't need more! You should do your best. Be your best. Always!"

Hey, welcome back, Writer's Block.

The above is a clear example of what I believe is the root of writer's block, at least for me: the fear of being imperfect. Of doing it wrong. Of somehow writing the wrong way or of being bad or not being absolutely brilliant right out of the gate.

I suspect the *fear of doing it wrong* stops most people from doing anything at all. Stops our stories, stops our voices, kills our careers. Even stops countless first sentences from ever clickity-clacking their way onto the page. Because, god forbid, what if that first sentence really, really sucks?

Good! Let it suck. Ignore it. Fix it later. Allow yourself to do your worst. Let it be okay. Just keep writing because your fifteenth sentence might be accidentally great. And the thirty-fifth sentence might be awesome. And that fiftieth? That five thousandth? Brilliant.

This is why I urge people to write crap. This is why I insist it's a good thing to do. In some cases, why it might be the *only* thing to do. Because when you write crap, you see that not only is doing your worst

WRITERS ON WRITING

survivable, it can also be fun. Want to know how to loosen up? Have a ball writing bad.

And then shock yourself by stumbling into something so golden you never would have been able to create it had you *not been writing.*

See how that works?

Remember, your worst doesn't need to ever see the light of day. It never needs to be read by anyone but you and it should never be the thing you present to the world as an example of your work. Its sole purpose is to put words on the page and pole vault the writer in you out of mute and over the fear of being bad.

But you'll never get to your best if you're afraid of your worst. So, when you find yourself stuck, begin a dialogue with yourself and refocus your attention. Sit down and write out your thoughts, your musings, your ramblings.

Hell, work on your outline.

And then, once again calm and armed with the What and How of your story, the map for where you and your readers (they're out there, trust me) are going, settle in and, if need be, write your worst. Because that's the only way you're going to win the Battle of Blank Page and discover your best.

Talk about sweet irony.

WRITERS ON WRITING VOL.3

CREATING EFFECTIVE CHARACTERS

HAL BODNER

When it comes to creating effective, realistic characters, much of the advice given to new authors winds up being completely useless to them. Whether the technique is one espoused by a New York Times best-selling novelist or by a college professor during a Creative Writing course, the challenges inherent in the advice are often identical. The eager freshman novelist or struggling short story writer is given nothing more than a metaphoric painting of a house which then purports to guide him in constructing the building in real life

There's no actual blueprint, no primer course in electrical wiring or on how to install the plumbing. Worse, the puzzled author has no clue what the final house is supposed to look like. No one stands by to tell him it might not be a good idea to hang the toilets from the ceiling, or to caution him against building the stair cases upside down.

It's no wonder that new authors are frequently puzzled and frustrated. "Listen to your characters,"

WRITERS ON WRITING

they're told. "They'll speak to you and tell you about themselves." How on Earth is anyone supposed to work with *that*? It's not an example of good literary advice; it's an invitation to psychosis. Trust me, if you ever hear any of your characters murmuring at you from your keyboard, my suggestion is to increase your dosage immediately.

Joking aside, there actually *is* something valuable to be learned from this advice, but it doesn't help at all with the *creation* of characters; instead, it is a technique for more fully fleshing them out. There's more to be said about that, and we'll get to it later. For now, I'll say merely that my sympathies are with those poor new authors to whom these kinds of non-specific comments must evoke a sort of mysticism that hinders, rather than helps, the creative process.

They don't provide the writer with the kind of blueprint for creating a character that many inexperienced authors long to have. And, of course, there's a reason for this. There is no step-by-step method; creating fictional characters is not like baking a cake where so much sugar and so much flour, if mixed in the right proportions, yields a specific result. Traditional "How To" instruction is rarely helpful. Instead, the teacher needs to provide examples and hope that one or more of them resonates with the student. In the best relationships between literary mentors and hopeful authors, the more experienced writer has the opportunity to use the student's own work as a foundation for teaching, much in the same way that a master sculptor might physically guide the hands of an apprentice while teaching him how to sculpt clay.

VOLUME 3

That doesn't mean that there's no hope of learning other than by sitting at the feet of a modern day Shakespeare. There are tons of specific techniques and tricks that can help. But creating characters—as I will undoubtedly repeat many times before the end of this essay—is as much of a craft as it is an art. But, we'll get back to that distinction in a little while.

In the meantime, I'd like to share with you a little anecdote about how I was asked to write the article that you are currently reading. If I may be permitted to digress, I promise it'll be worthwhile time in the end.

I was initially shanghaied into writing this essay because of an old friend I'll call "Sally."

Sally is a brilliant, multiple award winning author of thrillers. Not too long ago, it seems that someone from the Los Angeles Chapter of the Horror Writers Association (whom I will call "Jason" in order to protect him from Sally's wrath—which is a volatile and terrible thing!) was volunteering as the Guest Coordinator at a literary convention. As most readers probably know already, this is a thankless job as it mostly involves wrangling all of the invited guests and making sure they get to where they're supposed to be on time. Sally was one of the guests of honor and due to speak at a panel. Forty-five minutes before the panel was scheduled to begin, Jason went to her hotel room to collect her. But Sally was nowhere to be found.

If any of you have ever been to one of these things, you'll recall that the most interesting events usually take place in the hotel bar. Fortunately, Jason is a pretty smart cookie, and Sally's reputation had preceded her. So, with the panel about to shortly

WRITERS ON WRITING

convene, he headed immediately to where the spirits were being served and . . . viola! There was Sally, regaling a handsome young bartender with stories of how she won her first two Edgars, the Bram Stoker and, more recently, the Shirley Jackson Award.

Jason had little problem prying Sally off the bartender. After all, there was a wooden bar separating them . . . or rather, there was a wooden bar *protecting* him. From what I hear, he was blond and rather beefy, and Sal sometimes finds it difficult to restrain herself when she meets an attractive young man who is her "type" . . . um . . . I meant to say . . . when she meets an attractive young man who is *one* of her "types" as our Sal is very liberal where her preferred "types" of men are concerned.

Sal had, of course, been drinking. She's a New Yorker, and though it was only ten in the morning where the convention was being held on the West Coast, the sun was already over the yardarm in New York. In Sally's mind, that meant it was perfectly fine to have a cocktail or three with lunch. The fact that it was far too early for lunch to be served in California was certainly not Sal's fault, was it? She'd just have to make do with the cocktails alone.

While my old friend is capable of speaking at great length—and even appearing intelligent about what she's saying—after downing up to a third of a bottle of vodka, on this particular occasion, she appeared to have been drinking scotch. In fact, she'd been drinking a fair amount of scotch, perhaps enough to suffice for a round at a Glasgow pub. Even so, the speaking part wouldn't have been a problem. Once Jason had convinced the bartender not to file sexual harassment

VOLUME 3

charges, all he had to do was drag Sally to the panel on time.

Navigating out of the bar and up the stairs to the conference room was, however, beyond Sally's physical abilities. Worse, the esteemed author had reached a point where her vocal chords were sodden enough such that the volume control seemed not to be working. An argument with a potted plant ensued. The dispute escalated into mild fisticuffs between Sally and the plant and ended only when the flailing of fists and branches was strenuous enough to cause Sal to evacuate some of the scotch.

There is a lesson to be learned from this. Just as your mother cautioned you against swimming immediately after eating a heavy meal, it is equally as unwise to physically over-exert yourself by trying to murder a ficus so shortly after consuming large quantities of over-priced spirits. Fortunately, Jason reports that he was able to maneuver the remains of the plant's pot into position in time and avoid the convention promoters being hit with a hefty cleaning bill for the carpets.

The rest of the story is, I'm happy to say, far too boring to relate here except to say that Sally was, as always, brilliant and witty on the panel. By the end of the weekend, she'd decided that Jason was her new Best Friend Forever. Sal's infatuation with Jason had not worn off when she called me at roughly four in the morning the other day and insisted I write this essay. The conversation was short and sweet and basically consisted of a short monologue on Sally's part. "Hal, you've *got* to do something for Jason. You simply *must*! He's just *fabulous,* and *he's doing wonders with*

WRITERS ON WRITING

the Los Angeles HWA Chapter and he's got this nonfiction thing due for Joe Mynhardt, and he's got absolutely no time to do it. It's for Crystal Lite . . . no, Crystal Lake . . . down in Australia or South Africa somewhere. I forget which, but it's that place where they have lions and kangaroos walking the streets. Darling, you *must* do it! On Jason's behalf, I'd consider it a personal favor if you would . . . oh damn. The cat just threw up on the rug. Gotta run. Kissy kissy."

I was baffled, but not by the substance of the conversation. Sal is not only a marvelous promoter who very freely hands out tips to all of her good friends, but she's also one of those people who seems to know absolutely everyone who's anyone and delights in matching them up to help each other out. Rather, it was the timing of the thing that troubled me. Usually Sally wakes up around noon—my time, which meant that when she called it was only seven in the morning in Manhattan. Morning makes Sally break out in hives. Of course, she might have still been awake from the night before, but I think that's unlikely as none of her words were slurred.

Then, the reason came to me like a veritable bolt from the blue, to work an already overworked cliché . . .

Sally does not exist!

I just made her up. Yes, mes amis. Sally is naught but a fictional *character*.

But you feel you know her, right? Just a little? At the very least, you probably know someone *like* her. Granted that I was unable to do full justice to the character of Sally in less than a page, but nonetheless, I hope I had you fooled. You may certainly have convinced yourselves that the *events* I described were

VOLUME 3

blown out of proportion for comic effect. But I'm betting you did not realize from the start that "Sally" was entirely fictional.

That's called creating character. And I will blushingly admit that there is, indeed, a certain amount of art involved. But it requires an equal amount of craft, as well. Moreover, to do it effectively, it usually takes a little more than a page or two, though in truth, I've known authors (myself included) who can do it in a matter of a few lines if necessary. If we look more closely at "Sally"—which we'll do in a moment—we'll discover some very specific tricks I used to help create her as a character.

But before that, let's get back to those platitudes and bits of helpful advice that may have been doled out to you in college. Very probably, everything you've ever learned in a creative writing class, or by participating in a writers' group, or on a weekend authors' retreat is probably absolutely valid—as far as it goes. The litany of instructions usually goes something like this: observe people around you to discover interesting things about them; base characters on real life; give them interesting "quirks"; tell your audience how your characters feel because character is more than mere description.

In the right hands, I'm sure that all works just fine. But, for many authors wishing to master the techniques, creating a character that way is a lot like struggling to read an instruction manual in Swedish. It's far better and far more of a learning opportunity if someone shows you how to put together that IKEA bookcase you just bought, the one that's still in pieces spread out all over your living room carpet.

WRITERS ON WRITING

So let's get down to the nitty gritty, shall we?

There are some obvious fundamentals you can use in order to create believable characters. The most fundamental way is to describe them physically. This is what I call creating a character "directly." But there is a danger to not taking this technique far enough that, not to mince words, can easily lead to flat and boring characters who lack all semblance of a distinct personality. There's a technical word for that, by the way. It's called bad writing.

On the other hand, many authors successfully use the technique of direct character creation. Often, to one degree or another, the elements of a particular character may indeed be physically based; it's how those elements are *used* that make the difference. Cyrano de Bergerac's deformed nose is only the tip of the iceberg; in itself, it is merely a contrivance. But his *character* comes from how he *relates* to the deformity, how he reacts to other people's comments about it, how his perceived ugliness has created a huge insecurity and a hair-trigger temper among other traits. That is the genius of the author, Edmond Rostand, and even more impressively, he did it in French!

But too many less talented or experienced writers may assume that describing the physicality is enough. They either forget about the emotional impact the physicality must have in order to seem real, or they ignore the possibility that different people may react very differently to possessing identical physical traits.

Alternatively, a writer may introduce a character with vast paragraphs of background exposition which detail their entire lives to date. Unless you're an

VOLUME 3

extremely skilled writer, this practice should probably be avoided as, in most cases, it is the quintessential example of what your college professor meant when he told you, "Show. Don't tell."

We may read pages and pages about how little Amelia was cruelly ripped from her mother's breast and sold into white slavery, spending her tenderest years as a scullery maid before being forced into a life of prostitution. Often, the author's intent is to provide a rough sketch for the reader to latch on to so that the plot can move forward. The writer may believe that he must make the reader familiar with Amelia's motivations in order to understand why she is about to do whatever it is she does.

For several reasons, this is a flawed way of thinking and, in most cases, an example of inferior craft. First, it usually bores the reader with information that he does not really need; very often, there's too much exposition for the reader to fully digest anyway. It's far more interesting and effective to *show* your audience how Amelia responds to the obstacles and plot twists that you throw in her way. If you're not able to create believable situations to which your character can react truthfully, if you're not able to use words to sculpt a character that leaps off the page with vitality, then no amount of background explanation is going to help you.

How many times have you read a book with cardboard characters who are fundamentally interchangeable except for some minor physical difference? How often does an author distinguish his creations only by the "roles" they play in the plot? How many times have you been forced to constantly flip

WRITERS ON WRITING

back and forth through a novel until you find the page where various characters were introduced, simply because the author has provided you with nothing distinctive that allows you to remember who is who?

We've all found ourselves wondering, "Sam . . . Sam . . . which one is Sam? Is he the surfer with the club foot? Or is he the one who was injured in the accident? No, that's not right. Sam is the guy having the affair with the other guy's wife! No, wait. The guy having the affair is Bill. Who the hell is Sam?" In cases of truly bad characterization, we may even find ourselves trying to recall whether Sam is the "blond one," "the fat one," or "the dentist!"

In short, merely *telling* the reader who a character is directly—either by physical description or via a lengthy mini-biography of the past events which have supposedly influenced the character into becoming who they are—requires a mastery of language and storytelling that most writers don't have. Those of us who *can* do it may also find that we can't *always* do it well; a lot depends on the specifics of what we're writing. In short, though this kind of "short hand" character development can be made to work, it's very difficult, and it's usually done badly.

Ironically, the easier method is also the more effective method. I usually refer to it as creating characters "indirectly," and the technique has many wrinkles to it.

Instead of showing your readers solely by means of a physical description, you must dig deeper. Show your readers also what the character does, how the character reacts, how they feel about things. Dialogue can often be the most effective way to do this. Even

VOLUME 3

better, if you're good at what you do, you can sometimes write pages and pages of nothing but dialogue without a single "he said" or other dialogue tag and your readers will still know exactly who is speaking, how they feel about things and, in some cases, what they are doing while they speak.

The dialogue trap to be wary of is this: Don't use it as a substitute way of burying your reader in all the extraneous information that you were originally tempted to put into the background exposition. That's sometimes referred to as an Information Dump, and it's almost impossible to do well. There's nothing worse than expository dialogue that goes on for pages and adds nothing to the plot or characterizations. It exists only because the author mistakenly thinks the reader needs to know it. However, the truth is that it is the *author* who needs to know the information, not the reader. Putting it onto the page serves no function; it is tantamount to a cordon bleu chef presenting his guests with a sheaf of written recipes instead of the feast they were expecting.

Now, let's revisit "Sally" again, the character who spaketh not a word until the very end. Nor was there a single adjective used to describe her physically. Nevertheless, I'm hoping most of you conjured up some mental image of her slumped over the bar and flirting with a bartender half her age. Or maybe it was the suggestion of her wrestling with the doomed ficus before throwing up on it that triggered a picture in your mind. My point is that, as an author, I was entirely comfortable leaving Sally's physicality to your imagination. What she looked like was not important for my purpose, which was to make you believe she

WRITERS ON WRITING

was a real person. And I used some tricks to do it, tricks which serve as examples of indirectly creating character.

First, I blended reality with my fictional creation. Novelists do this all the time when they set a story in a real place. We use the realities to which the reader can relate as a springboard for the fantasies we wish to weave. Ira Levine's *Rosemary's Baby* provides what is possibly the quintessential example of that technique. We see how Rosemary reacts to extraordinary events taking place in the most ordinary environment and, by seeing how she copes as things spin out of her control, we learn a hell of a lot about *her*. Had the reader been unable to witness the strength she summons as the creepiness intensified (and when weaker folks would run screaming into the night!), her actions at the end of the book when she finally sees her baby would make no sense.

To better ground "Sally" in reality, I mentioned Jason because I thought it likely that if you were reading this piece, you would know that the HWA Los Angeles Chapter is a real group. You would have no reason to doubt that "Jason" was not a real member (Yes, "Jason" is also a construct of my imagination, I'm afraid). I also gave Jason virtually no character of his own. I made him unimportant, giving you no reason to doubt his existence. He was merely a mechanism, a red herring if you like, who was invented so that you would accept him at face value; thus, he gives further credence to the more colorful character of "Sally." It's a kind of literary magician's trick involving misdirection. The theory is that, if I can get a reader to accept that *one* fictional character as real, the reader

VOLUME 3

is less likely to doubt the existence of a second fictional character.

Second, I set my little scenario at a convention, knowing many of the people reading this would have attended one. Then, in order to set y'all up for my pulling the wool over your eyes with the fictional "Sally" . . . *I cheated!* (I know, I know. I'm hanging my head in shame.)

The way I did it was by drawing you in and inviting you to share an "inside" joke. I alluded to how the bars at conventions are often more popular than the actual event. By directing your memory to your own experiences at the bar at that wretched romance/horror/sci-fi convention that you once attended, I performed another small feat of literary misdirection. Perhaps you even recalled that there was drunken guest of honor at the bar? After all, these things have been known to happen!

I got you to buy into the scene as a whole, and if I did it well enough, you never once stopped to consider that I had an ulterior purpose for doing so. I grounded the whole thing in reality and never once gave you enough time nor any reason to wonder if "Sally" might be a fictional construct.

Finally, just in case you were a particularly clever reader, I exaggerated for humorous effect. Did I truly try to convince you that an award-winning author beat up a plant and vomited on it after practically raping a bartender? Of course not! On the contrary, I expected you to reject my hyperbole while retaining a belief that the underlying character of "Sally" was either real or, perhaps, a thinly disguised version of a real person. You might even have wondered who "Sally" was in real

WRITERS ON WRITING

life. It's the old *Victor/Victoria* ruse. Toddy creates the "Count" as an obvious fraud. Everyone is so busy trying to find out who the Count *really* is (because no one believes he's an actual count) that no one stops to think that *he* might actually be a *she*.

In a few more pages, who knows what else we might have learned about Sally after witnessing her antics on the panel. Would her drunken state render her boorish and insulting? Or would she be completely charming until, without warning, she simply passed out face down on the podium in front of hundreds of adoring fans? How about Jason? What's his stake in all this? Is he the long-suffering volunteer, somehow managing to overcome obstacles while chewing antiacids the whole time? Or is he a male Eve Harrington who is set on ruining the great, but tragically alcoholic, writer's fame for nefarious purposes? What happens if one of Sally's multiple boyfriends waltzes in and it turns out he's also Jason's ex-boyfriend, a bisexual with whom Jason is still in love?

If you know your characters, if you have them firmly in your mind, the answers to the questions I just asked will start that mystical process that some authors refer to as "listening to" your characters. This is the psychosis I humorously referred to at the beginning of this essay, and now, we see that it isn't psychotic at all! I've also heard writers speak of it as letting the characters "take us places." It's another little trick—and a lovely one it is, too! If you've set them up properly, your characters will begin to react to the elements you provide and the things you throw at them in their own unique ways. Often, I find my people taking me in directions I had no intention of

VOLUME 3

going. One NY Times Best-selling author who I know—and I promise you that she's a real person this time—calls it "learning from my peeps."

When this happens, I've found it's almost always best to go with the flow so that I can find out where it leads. Sometimes, it opens entire vistas of plot and character interaction that I hadn't considered. Other times my characters will "take" me to a place where I emphatically do *not* want them to go—usually because it mucks with the plot I've already got in mind. Then, I have a choice. I can alter the plot accordingly or, as I more often do, I can go back to the specific event that started the character down the "wrong" path and simply rewrite the event to evoke a different reaction from the character. Usually, that will put things firmly back onto the path I prefer.

Nor is it necessary to use only one method to create a character. Mixing and matching is encouraged! Here's an example from one of my own novels, *Mummy Dearest*, where I've woven a bunch of techniques together.

In another darkened bedchamber, the only sound was light breathing from the naked body, fast asleep, tangled in white satin sheets. Suddenly, there was an audible click from the night stand and the room's peacefulness was shattered by a raucous voice singing, "I had a dream! A dream about you, June!"

The sleeper came groggily awake, his blond curls tousled, his blue eyes bleary. "Thank you, Ethel, dear," Troy Raleigh murmured as he stretched out one lithely-muscled arm, grabbed the Ethel Merman

WRITERS ON WRITING

alarm clock, and tapped her gently on the head to shut her up before she could tell him how swell things were.

Troy stretched languorously, yawning and emitting tiny squeaky noises of pleasure as his muscles and joints popped. He tossed aside the sheets, flipped over onto his tummy, his perky little rear end bared for all the world to see, and shoved his head under the pillows. Five minutes later, just as he was drifting back to sleep, the silence was once again shattered as Ethel belted out "There's NO business like SHOW business!" with musical abandon, and if possible, even louder than before.

Troy shot bolt upright and grabbed the clock. "That will be quite enough from you!" he said irritably and shut it off. Then, as if to make amends for his terseness of a moment before, Troy kissed the plastic Mama Rose on her nose before replacing her carefully.

Ten sentences. Two hundred thirty-five words. Four short paragraphs. Yet, if I've handled things properly, my readers should already have a handle on the essence of this character. Moreover, I've not had to really *tell* very much by way of description other than that the character is blond, has blue eyes, and is in good shape. Frankly, out of everything else in this excerpt, I find those physical characteristics to be the *least* effective elements that define this character.

Now, let's examine the excerpt in greater detail. Let's dig a little deeper and see what we find out.

We open on a naked man sleeping on white satin

VOLUME 3

sheets, and he has . . . what? An Ethel Merman alarm clock! It's the clock that does it; everything else leads up to the clock. It's quirky, campy. and makes the reader ask, "What kind of a guy has an Ethel Mer . . . ? Oh. I get it now."

Further, look at some of the word choices: "tiny squeaky noises," "flipped onto his tummy," "perky little rear end." There's a juvenile quality to this verbiage mingled with a kind of cheery optimism. Even the alliteration furthers the theme. Go ahead, say the words out loud: perky, squeaky, tummy. The very sound of them creates a certain mood, an ambiance if you will, that creates an aura around this character. If you believe, as I do, that many readers' brains will allow them to internally "hear" the words they are reading, so much the better.

Now combine these facets with the blond/blue thing and the "lithely-muscled arm," and a picture starts emerging. I could just as easily have described Troy *directly* as, "an overly effeminate young man with curly blond hair, an innocent yet mischievously elfin expression and a gym-toned body." But the waking up scene does the same thing. It's much more fun to read. And, if the image of that odd little clock strikes a chord in my reader, it's a more memorable experience.

It's true the readers do not know everything about Troy Raleigh. But this is the first time he shows up in the book; the audience doesn't need to know his entire life story. At this point in the novel, as an author, I need to give my readers only enough detail to create the most basic image of who Troy is in their minds. They need only to grasp what I call the "essence" of the character; I can supply the fill-in stuff later. Also, I

WRITERS ON WRITING

want to confess that since Troy appears in two earlier books, this passage is tailored more towards refreshing familiarity than towards the initial introduction of a character, but the techniques are the same.

On the other hand, *I* need to know vastly more than my readers about Troy, even at this early stage. All that stuff that would otherwise constitute an Information Dump needs to be at *my* fingertips. Why? Because I can use all those lovely little details in a myriad of ways.

I can dole them out slowly, dangling tidbits of information to keep my readers wanting to know even more about this character. Or I can reveal something major, a big hidden secret or tragedy, at a later time in order to create an emotional effect. I can move the plot along, or perhaps complicate it, depending on the nature of those hitherto unrevealed details of a specific character. If I'm J.K. Rowling, I may even be able to use all that unrevealed information to create a cultural icon while, at the same time, dragging people back into the bookstores and movie theaters because they want to know more ... More ... MORE!

I *love* indirect ways of establishing character. I recall a friend who was working on a book about an assassin. His protagonist enters a restaurant, sits with his *back against the wall*, orders food, and when the waitress drops something, he reaches out and snags it out of midair *without taking his eyes off the door*. We immediately know this guy, as well, don't we? Moreover, we may even know a little something—without any specifics—about the plot and possibly why he's in the restaurant. Our assumptions about the character may turn out to be completely wrong, but the

VOLUME 3

author has given us that bit about the man watching the door and has infected our imaginations with some tantalizing clues to consider.

So, since I'm running out of space unless I want that guy who lives where the zebras and lions are roaming the streets to beat me to death with a red editor's pencil, I'll wrap up with the following advice:

Always try to find external and indirect ways to reveal your characters through what they do, how they react, what they say or by the way other characters respond or relate to them. Certainly, you should know what they look like and how they dress. By the same token, you'll need to know their backgrounds—extensively. But, save the direct character development techniques as fall-backs for the much more effective indirect method. Your job is to create vibrant characters in interesting ways and, hopefully, to leave lingering fond memories of your peeps in your readers' minds long after they've read those two little words I'm about to type . . . The End.

FICTIONAL EMOTIONS; EMOTIONAL FICTIONS

JAMES EVERINGTON

So, you're a writer. You've written a story. And that story has done its thing, and found itself a goddamn reader. Someone is *reading your work* (and no matter how successful you become, you should never let that fact cease to delight and thrill you). So what do you hope for, as they turn the pages?

Maybe you hope they empathise with your characters.

Maybe you hope they laugh or cry.

Maybe you hope they feel angry or scared or comforted by what you've written.

Empathy; laughter; comfort—whatever you hope for, we're talking the language of emotion here. Of *feeling*.

But what exactly do we mean when we say that a book made us *feel*? And more importantly, what techniques can we use to choreograph and orchestrate the emotional responses of our readers?

I'm not talking about whether you want to make your readers feel happy or afraid or angry or guilty.

VOLUME 3

Those are the basic units of human experience that I don't need to explain to you. Think of those emotions as different colours; what I want to talk about is the different *brushes* you can use to paint in any of those hues.

The best way to understand the potential emotional reactions of your readers is to analyse your own as you read. So in this piece I've tried to categorise my own responses as a reader. Be warned: These categories are no doubt very loose, blurry, and biased towards my own reading and writing preferences.

Seeing Characters as You: The Reader is the Character

One of the most obvious ways to emotionally manipul . . . sorry, emotionally engage your readers, is to give them a character with whom they are immediately invited to share headspace with. A central character through whose eyes they can view your fictional world, whether those eyes be behind rose-tinted spectacles or black designer shades.

Many contemporary children's and YA books use this technique; a protagonist is introduced in Chapter 1 and becomes in effect the reader's surrogate as they move through the story. Readers share this character's triumphs and feel the sting of their setbacks and reversals. It's a particularly useful way of approaching fiction set in a fantasy world, for it allows you to introduce the setting through the subjective viewpoint of a specific character, rather than dry recitals of imaginary dates and events. Fictional worlds live when readers experience them emotionally.

WRITERS ON WRITING

In terms of technique you've probably already thought this one through: introduce the main character as soon as you can, make them sympathetic with a few adorable flaws, make them roughly the same age as the demographic you're writing for, use a first-person or close third-person point of view and voila! Emotional connection, right?

Beware, though. The smallest slip, the slightest action by your main character which isn't in keeping with the reader's view of them can break this emotional bond. When readers complain they didn't find a character's actions believable, what they are often saying is that the character acted in a way *that they wouldn't* (or don't think they would anyway, which amounts to the same thing). And sometimes the author's desire to create a character that is sympathetic leads to creations that are bland and insipid. No one wants to share headspace with someone who's *dull*.

Much of so-called literary fiction's claim to be more "sophisticated" than commercial fiction derives merely from the fact that the character readers are invited to emotionally identify with is unattractive or abnormal in some way: a murderer (*The Outsider*), a dropout (*The Catcher in the Rye*), a child-molester (*Lolita*). And one of the reasons reading is a valuable activity is precisely because it allows you to *emotionally* experience the world from someone else's perspective, which may be radically different to your own. But it's a rare book that invites readers to wholeheartedly identify with an irredeemably vile character; most will mix in other techniques to give a more nuanced view. Such as:

VOLUME 3

Seeing Characters as Other People

Another approach to your characters is to present them not as surrogate selves but as other people—characters on a stage in front of your readers. Rather than invite your readers to empathise with a character, you can invite them to sympathise or condemn them, to *judge* their actions. Much as we do with people in real life.

Obviously, if you are using the first technique we spoke about for one character, this is how you'll be presenting all the other characters emotionally. In your climactic scene where your viewpoint-heroine bests the story's villain, if you cut away briefly to describe the Big Bad's rage at being foiled, you're only doing so in order to heighten the reader's vicarious feeling of the heroine's triumph.

More interesting is when your readers' emotional response doesn't correspond with those of *any* of the characters; look at how writers like Jane Austin create scenes where the characters appear to themselves to be acting civilly and rationally, but the reader can perceive the more human reasons for their behaviour underneath, such as pride and, uh, prejudice. This approach doesn't mean we can't *like* the characters; Emma and Elizabeth Bennet are some of the most loved characters in fiction, in part because of their flaws.

A different approach is used by Stephen King in *Carrie*, in which the story is told from multiple perspectives. We experience the novel both from inside Carrie White's head and from the perspective of those around her. As such, we alternatively feel her

WRITERS ON WRITING

actions to be both perfectly understandable and utterly monstrous. The different points of view King utilises during the story dramatise this paradox. They dramatise it *emotionally*.

Atmosphere

Of course, emotions don't have to have anything to do with characters at all. It's an odd fact about writing that you can describe almost anything, no matter how unfeeling, in ways designed to emotionally engage the reader.

This is especially important in horror writing, where a sense of dread is frequently achieved by describing everyday locations in such de-familiarising ways that they seem full of portent and threat. In the brilliant opening to Shirley Jackson's *The Haunting of Hill House*, the sense that something is very wrong about the building being described is palpable, but there is no viewpoint character to be experiencing this; it's all in *our* heads. Of course, this kind of effect is not just limited to unease. Different writers might evoke atmospheres of resignation, bucolic peace, or comedic goodwill.

Think of atmosphere as the background music of your narrative; it should be persistent but not without variation. It should start off in the background but may or may not build to a crescendo.

Atmosphere is generally built up by how you select and write about small details, not grand gestures or events. There's no reason for the atmosphere to correspond to the gravity or otherwise of what's happening in the story, and some of the best effects occur when the two are opposed. If you have

VOLUME 3

characters blissfully unaware of the mounting tension the *reader* is feeling, then they will feel it all the more.

Game-playing, Plotting, and Climaxes

The plot of a book drives the character's emotional responses, but as readers we also respond to it on an entirely different level—because we *know* it is a plot.

When you successfully spring a twist at the end of your story, or reveal the identity of the murderer in a whodunit, the reader will respond emotionally. In a sense, you have been playing a game with them: They have been trying to guess the ending whilst you've tried to stop them doing so (whilst still playing fair and leaving enough clues). There's something pleasurable about being tricked by Agatha Christie in *The Murder of Roger Ackroyd* and then looking back and seeing how that trick should have been obvious to us all along. And that "Aha!" moment of realisation is an emotional response that comes only from stories, not from life, which doesn't play games.

More broadly, just knowing a story is nearing its end shapes the reader's emotional responses to what occurs. We don't have to think about what the events of *Romeo & Juliet* mean to the poor sods who are left to pick up the pieces in the months and years afterwards, because *we're* already back outside of the theatre, blinking in the light.

So think carefully about the ending of your story, not just in terms of events but in terms of an emotional crescendo or epiphany. Where and how you choose to *stop* will colour your readers' emotional understanding of all they've just read.

WRITERS ON WRITING

The Sound Of Music

Being able to actual *write well* is of course key to evoking any emotional responses in the reader. But separate and beyond that is the way a well-crafted sentence can evoke an emotional response in the same way a piece of music can—by the way it *sounds*:

> *"Dying is an art.*
> *Like everything else,*
> *I do it exceptionally well.*
> *I do it so it feels like hell.*
> *I do it so it feels real."*
> ("Lady Lazarus," Sylvia Plath)

Or if poetry is too much for you on a blurry Saturday morning, how about this from Douglas Adams:
"He turned slowly like a fridge door opening." (*Dirk Gently's Holistic Detective Agency.*)
I'm not sure there's much point in trying to explain that—you either get it or you don't. Either feel the *rightness* of those words in that order, or you don't. Subjective, sure. But as much a part of the emotional experience of reading as anything else.
Of course, we don't just appreciate words as pure sound; meaning, contradiction and context all contribute to the tune. But pay attention to the music of your words.

Intellectual Emotions

I read somewhere that we all belong to one of two

VOLUME 3

camps with regard to facts: those people who think it's only worth knowing something if it's of practical *use* and those who value knowledge for its own sake regardless of its utility.

The fact that I've remembered this, when it's never been of the slightest use in my life, probably tells you what type of person *I* am.

I think for those of us who value knowledge for its own sake, the use of intellectual ideas in a piece of fiction can trigger a peculiar kind of emotional response, one which is hard to describe (we really need a specific word for it). *Flatland* by Edwin A. Abbot is about a society of two-dimensional beings (in the mathematical sense) who one day encounter a three-dimensional person. It's a satire about how limited our own perspective might be, and it works almost entirely because of the play of intellectual ideas—and that's the best way I can describe it, as "play."

Intellectual play doesn't have to be this overt for it to emotionally engage readers; figurative uses of language often work by contrasting two disparate ideas. Dickens's *Bleak House* opens with the image of a Megalosaurus waddling along the streets of Victorian London, and the enjoyment we feel from this is at least in part due to the intellectual dissonance at the notion not just that dinosaurs might still live, but that they might live in Holborn.

Fill in the Blanks

Of course, we all know that at least some of what the reader feels when they read our stories will be due to their own lives and experiences. And there might seem

WRITERS ON WRITING

little we can do about that. After all, no writing technique can allow us to influence what emotional baggage readers are carrying when they open the pages, can it?

Well, no. But as a writer you can decide how much space you allow for readers' own feelings. Many of the techniques we've been talking about are *controlling*—they attempt to dictate what the reader should be feeling at any given point in the narrative. But some books go the other way: they present events in such a flat, neutral way that the reader is tempted to fill in the void. *Less Than Zero* by Brett Easton Ellis uses this approach—it presents to us scenes so flat it's like an itch we can't quite scratch. We ascribe motivation, beliefs, and emotions to characters based on their actions without any textual justification for doing so. Rather than trying to control what we feel, Easton Ellis simply gives us enough empty space to feel what we will.

To return to the analogy that atmosphere is like background music: Imagine a film with no incidental music at all, and you have something like *Less Than Zero*. And certain readers will hate that silence. It's not just a subjective matter of taste, it's that some readers will turn away from the blankness rather than attempt to fill it.

When the reader has to do much of the emotional heavy lifting for the duration of an entire novel, it can be wearying. But this technique can be used on a much smaller scale, presenting an event in plain terms with zero emotional window dressing. Consider:

"Gerald died that afternoon." (*The Longest Journey,* E.M. Forster)

VOLUME 3

In the spirit of blankness, I'll leave you to decide what you think about that sentence yourself.

And Finally, One Specifically for Authors:

Of course, there's one other type of emotional response you've probably felt in response to a piece of fiction. That crippling sense of bitter envy and self-doubt when you read something so bloody good it makes any talent of your own seem insignificant and counterfeit in comparison. *That.*

But remember that feeling. Make it your aim, whatever other emotional responses you conjure in your readers, to make other writers suffer by writing something *stupendous*.

HOME, SWEET HOME

BEN EADS

You've finished your first book. Congratulations! It's time to find a *good* home for what you poured your time, sweat, blood, and tears into. Certainly, there are plenty of dark fiction markets looking for your hard work. Sadly, the majority of them are "for-the-love" markets that don't pay you. Or worse: insidious presses that prey on a new author's work. Some are headed by someone who *thinks* he/she can edit and only publishes his/her friends. So, before you cast fate to the wind, let's find out how to find a *good* home for your work. We'll be covering "small" presses in the beginning of this article. The "Big New York 4" and self-publishing will be covered toward the end.

You may already have a good home in mind for your dark fiction. Shoot for the stars! Why give your work to a "for-the-love" press? You deserve compensation for your work, right? And why go for a mediocre press? I would say go for *Cemetery Dance*, but as of this writing, March 7, 2016, they are closed to unsolicited submissions. No worries. As the saying

VOLUME 3

goes: There's plenty of fish in the sea. Once you've found a press that you're interested in, the first step is to see whether or not it's reputable. A simple Google search of the press is a good place to start.

Who is the editor of the press? Editors do more than correct grammar—they are the lifeblood of the press. How long have they edited work professionally and for how many award-winning authors? Also, who are these editors publishing today? Are they publishing well-known authors? Award-winning authors? You need to ensure the editor is accepting and helping publish amazing work. If the press you're interested in passes the above tests, then it's time to contact a few of those authors they've published.

This is quite common. Be professional and polite. Let them know your intentions, and ask them the following: What was your overall experience working with them? What was it like working with the editor in final edits? Did the press help you market your book, or did they just publish it and walk away? How many professional interviews did they arrange? Was there anything that you felt could have been done better? Anything I should be concerned about?

Folks, this is a very small world we live in, especially the world of dark fiction. Word gets around. In fact, my novella, *Cracked Sky* did . . . in a bad way. I didn't do the above, and this is what happened: I received no email stating whether or not a certain publisher would accept or reject my novella. I didn't expect them to. Per their submission guidelines—always, always follow those—they stated the editor would not reply back to submissions. The only exception being an acceptance email. This should have

WRITERS ON WRITING

stopped me dead in my tracks, but it didn't. Time passed, I didn't hear back from them, and the time frame—I think it was two months—passed.

A few days later, I received a private Facebook message from an author saying the following: "I really enjoyed reading your novella! So-and-so from the press sent me a copy." Yes, ladies and gentleman, the egg was on my face. The editor of this press—a well-known Grade A asshole—gave my novella away for fun. Why did this occur? Again, folks, there are plenty of insidious presses out there. Please let my example be a warning. I cannot stress the negative impact going with a less than reputable press can have on your career. It's all in the suit you wear. Thankfully, after asking some award-winning authors for advice, I found a very good home for *Cracked Sky*.

Before we dig deeper, I want to let you in on a little secret those award-winning authors shared with me: No matter how many drafts you put your book through, always have it beta-read by professionals in the field. It took me years to find the beta-readers I have now, and I am eternally grateful for them. But there's something better than a beta-reader: an actual professional editor. Yes, my dear friends, amazing editors like Richard Thomas of *Gamut Magazine*, and Kate Jonez of Omnium Gatherum—the latter is my publisher, and I have nothing but amazing things to say about them—do editing on the side. More on how to find great editors will be covered later in this article.

Whatever they charge, it's worth every cent. These editors will test your love of writing. Trust that. They will pore over your manuscript with a red pen and catch anything and everything that will get you

VOLUME 3

rejected by most presses. Even better, both help you find a good home for your work. How can you beat that? Not only have you grown as a writer, now you have someone going up to bat for you. I cannot stress how important it is to have your manuscript as good as it can possibly be *before* submitting.

When working with professional editors, let me caution you: It's not for the faint of heart, nor is it for authors whose egos are as big as the Goodyear blimp. You must love writing. It will probably be the biggest challenge you've faced as an author yet. Good! And welcome to the club! If you're having trouble understanding some of the notes they've made in your manuscript, then please contact them for clarification. This is normal, and they'll appreciate you communicating with them.

Any professional editor will know exactly where you're at, and what help you need. That said, they're not psychics. And yes, they can be wrong. My advice? To write is human. To edit is divine. We have Stephen King to thank for that, and he too uses beta-readers and editors. I'm reminded of a coffee table book that was published about fifteen years ago. I'm having a very hard time tracking that gem down, but if you can find it, buy it! It takes Stephen King's first few novels and shows you the first chapter of each that Stephen sent to the press. Then, it shows you what the editor did to the opening chapter. This will show you that even the best of us need editors.

I also remember finding myself stuck between a rock and a hard place in final edits. *Cracked Sky* had two problems, and I thought I had a fix that would kill two birds with one stone. I wrote Kate Jonez and asked

WRITERS ON WRITING

her if my solution would work, and she gave her approval within a day. Working with an editor is akin to collaboration. The more open you are to possibilities, the better the final edit will be. Should you find yourself not able to fix something, then contact the editor and phrase your question like this: "I'm trying to . . . " you can insert whatever you're trying to accomplish here, and be clear and direct that you're having trouble understanding. Again, this is quite normal.

Despite all your hard work and research in finding a good home, I cannot guarantee you the press will be around forever. Nor can I promise you that you'll sell millions of copies of your book. But if you follow these simple steps I've outlined above, you'll be delivering high quality work to top-quality presses.

Now, on to "The Big New York 4." So, you'd like to submit your book to one of them. Awesome! If this is your first book or you've only had short fiction published, you're at an extreme disadvantage. But don't let my words stop you. It's perfectly safe to submit to them, but you'll need to hire an attorney should you actually get an acceptance. You'll also need the help of an agent. Most of them require that an agent deal with them directly. I've heard horror stories from authors who signed a contract without having an attorney read it first, and they had their book returned to them with a bill enclosed. Yes, those authors are blamed for the book not selling well—the publisher did no promotions whatsoever—and they had to pay the press back. The same aforementioned rules apply to "The Big New York 4."

For the most part, authors start—and even stay—

VOLUME 3

in the small presses. Small presses are where the best talent is, and fans of dark fiction know this. If you have a good book, small press or large press, it's going to sell well as long as they have a great marketing plan. If your book is selling well with a small press and a "Big New York 4" press contacts you with a $50,000 offer on your next release, take it! But make sure you have an attorney read the contract first.

Should you choose to self-publish, awesome! Simply skip googling a press, writing their authors, checking out the resume of their editor, and go straight for a professional editor. Whether you self-publish or not, we're all subjective to our own work. In your case, working with a professional editor is vital. Let me repeat that: Working with a professional editor is vital. The only problems? Most review sites and professional podcasters won't interview you or review your work. Worse, you'll also have to market it yourself. I'm not saying don't self-publish; I'm just making you aware of the extra work you'll need to do.

I cannot recommend joining the Horror Writers Association strongly enough. You'll find resources such as lists of HWA approved editors and agents listed in their member's only section. Should your publisher fail to pay you, close up shop, etc . . . The HWA's grievance committee is there to help you. The benefits are vast!

Should you have any questions or concerns, reach out to well-known authors and ask away! That's what we're here for, and our philosophy is: We're all in this together, and we wish you the best of luck, my dear friends. Feel free to hit me up at beneadsfiction@gmail.com.

YOU

KEALAN PATRICK BURKE

BACK IN 2008, divorce and economic necessity saw me rejoining the workforce as a fraud investigator. It was a good job. The pay was respectable, and there was plenty of room for advancement. And I was good at it, possessing as I do (according to my employers) the type of analytical mind such posts require. I did the job for two years. What I didn't do during that time was write. And every day that passed without putting pen to paper, a little piece of me died. That's because writing has never been a hobby for me, but a vocation. As far back as my memory goes, I have always written stories, and when the opportunity presented itself to come to America and try my hand at doing it professionally, I jumped at it. And it worked. Over the course of eight years I wrote four novels, two collections, edited four anthologies, and placed over seventy stories in professional magazines. My novella *The Turtle Boy* won the Bram Stoker Award in 2004.

I had, at least by my own humble standards and aspirations, arrived.

VOLUME 3

When real life intervened, as it frequently does, and I found myself working a job that required me to leave home at 6 a.m. to catch a series of buses so that I could be at work at 8 for a twelve-hour shift, and then endure another two-hour gap between work and home on the return journey, I was left with no energy to write. But the ideas never stopped coming. If anything, they came faster and harder than ever before. But worked trumped everything else. I have known writers who can work long, arduous days at what my friend Norman Partridge (himself a day-jobber) calls "the joe job" and somehow manage to come home and crank out a couple of thousand words before bed. But I've never been one of them. I'm not a multitasker. I commit to one thing and do it to the best of my ability. Everything else suffers as a result.

But I'm a writer. I need to write. *Have* to write. I am nothing without it, and when I'm not doing it, I'm not me, not being true to myself. That may sound like hyperbole. I assure you, it isn't.

By 2010, the digital explosion was in full swing, and I found myself coming home to stories about authors making a decent living (and in some cases much more than decent) selling their backlist via Amazon, Smashwords, Apple, and the like. So, while my energy level was not ample enough to permit excursions into fantasy land, it was sufficient enough for self-education.

So, this brings us (*finally*, I hear you say) to the point of this essay. In those few scant hours after work and before bed every night, I taught myself everything I could about digital publishing from formatting to upload, covers to promotion. Of course, many of the

WRITERS ON WRITING

aspects were already familiar to me from my years in the print publishing business, but in many ways, digital was like hitting the restart button. It was alien territory, intimidating and strange. But, I told myself, if it worked, if it even made bill money, my life would be a whole lot better.

I started small, using the four books in the Timmy Quinn series as my test subjects. I had a little experience with Photoshop, so I knew how to make pictures that would serve as semi-decent covers, thereby helping me avoid the expense of hiring someone to do four of them for me. I uploaded the books and went to work. Sales were slow at first, but I was heartened to see them selling at all. In my first month, I made enough to pay the water bill ($42.26).

I put what I'd learned into practice, and there was no reason it should have worked, no guarantee that anything would come of it but disappointment.

It took almost four months.

I made *The Turtle Boy* free. And sales of the three other books exploded.

Buoyed by this result, I added more of my backlist. They sold, too. My figures rose, my income rose. A few months later, I was able to quit my job and return to writing. I wrote daily, continued to learn (the very definition of writing), and finally wrote the final book in the Timmy Quinn series, which readers, to their credit, had never given up hoping would come. I wrote more and I wrote better.

I was home, right where I belong, and the writing, which I'd feared would have atrophied over time, was right where I left it.

That was six years ago, and I have been writing

VOLUME 3

since. And when not writing, I design book covers through my company Elderlemon Design to subsidize the writing.

And all because I was dissatisfied with denying myself the one thing I truly wanted: to write.

Because if you're a true writer at heart, nothing will keep you from doing it. In the intervening years, I've kept on writing even when the sales ebbed (as they will, no matter your level of success) and it looked like the economic bottom was once again going to drop out from under me (and that has happened a lot more than once), but I persevered, because you have to. And whenever an obstacle arose that stood between me and what I do best, I found a way around it, learned the nature of that obstacle, and defeated it.

People can, and often do, help you on the path to where you belong. Whether it's a parent, spouse, friend, teacher, another writer, we seldom do this alone. I've lost count of the number of people who have helped me on my way, but I've never forgotten them. I would not be here without them, getting to do what I do. But when we write, we're alone. Even if you write in public, the size of the crowd around you is redundant. You are not there. You're inside your head where nobody else can reach you. You are alone in a world of your own creation. And as magical as we all know this to be, it can also be exhausting, taxing, draining. Writing is hard. It's fraught with self-doubt and intimidation. Adapting to the ever-changing world of publishing can seem daunting. But it shouldn't. Not if you focus on the thing that matters most: the writing. Only the story matters, not the medium of delivery.

WRITERS ON WRITING

Because that's what we do. We're storytellers.

It would have been so much easier to keep working as a fraud investigator. By all accounts, it was a safe, secure, reliable job with medical and dental and paid holidays. But I did it only because I had to, while suffocating the other more predominant compulsion I have carried within me my whole life. To an outsider, my decision to quit was a foolish one, and I deserved every shitty thing that happened as a result.

And what happened was success, because I needed to take one more chance to see if I could be true to myself, and there was nothing I wouldn't do to make that happen.

True writers exist to tell stories because when we don't, we're mere shadows of ourselves. If writing is something you can take or leave, that's good for you: You're a hobbyist, a casual writer, and there's absolutely nothing wrong with that either. Some friends of mine are casual writers, and to be fair, they generally seem happier than the rest of us.

Because for the rest of us, it's write or die.

We write because we must.

If there's a point here, it's that the writer, when faced with opposing forces, must do everything in his/her power to circumvent or overcome them. The need to write is not an arbitrary thing—it's ingrained, and unlike less benign compulsions, it should never be repressed. Deny yourself the luxury of writing, and you deny the world your words.

Find a way to write them or you'll never truly be you.

And you're what we need.

HOW ABOUT THEM FREE BOOKS, EH?
(OR, RATHER, THE ART OF BECOMING A BOOK REVIEWER)

NERINE DORMAN

IF YOU'RE A complete bookworm, it means you probably go through about three or four books a month. Even if you've gotten with the times, buying those books as electronic editions, which tend cost less than physical books, it still adds up. And if you're like me, you'll also keep an eye open for any story bundles, specials, discount codes, and giveaways. We don't always have time to go to the library, and sometimes they either don't have what we're looking for in any case. Or the book is out or, worse, stolen.

Yet... piracy. The temptation to download and the ease with which we can track down that book we're desperate to read is always whispering. Just type in the right keywords in the search engine, and voila! A bunch of options pop up. I mean, surely this practice doesn't actually hurt authors, right?

Think again. It costs money to produce a good book. Not only has the author spent months, if not years, working on the book folks are itching to read, but chances are good that even if the book has been self-published, an editor, illustrator, and designer have all been involved in the process of taking an idea and giving it form. All these people would have needed to be paid, either by the author or by the publisher.

If a book doesn't move physical units, we have a problem.

I've heard people argue that, gee, golly gosh, exposure is wonderful. The more people read the book, the more chance an author has being discovered, right?

In an interview with the Open Rights Group, author Neil Gaiman had this much to say about piracy: "That's really all this is. It's people lending books. And you can't look on that as a lost sale . . . What you're actually doing is advertising. You're reaching more people. You're raising awareness. And understanding that gave me a whole new idea of the shape of copyright and what the web was doing. Because the biggest thing the web was doing is allowing people to hear things, allowing people to read things, allowing people to see things they might never have otherwise seen. And I think, basically, that's an incredibly good thing."

While Gaiman is certainly not hurting financially from any lost sales, he speaks of piracy from a position of security, as an author who is able to support himself financially doing what he loves and does best. Not all authors have that grounding.

If you want free books to read, go visit your library. Or make use of vast online resources like Open Library or Project Gutenberg, where thousands of public

VOLUME 3

domain works are available for free—and *legal*—download. What's even better is that as each year passes, more and more works are creeping into the public domain. There aren't enough hours in the day for you to read all those books. If you haven't already acquainted yourself with reading books on electronic devices such as your smartphone or tablet, do consider this as an option. Even if you claim to be hung up on the tactile sensations of holding a physical book in your hands, there is something to be said for the ease of lying back on a couch with a phone or tablet or reading in the dark without having to worry about turning on the light that may bother your partner.

But let's get back to authors and reviews. Every year, authors spend many, many hours promoting their writing. This might be as simple as sharing excerpts or interviews via social media or as elaborate as arranging a book launch or preparing a stall at a convention. It's all fine and dandy to be an author, but if you're not putting out word that you have books available, then you're never going to reach your target market. So many books are released daily on digital platforms such as Amazon, Kobo, iTunes, and Smashwords, to name a few, that new authors often find themselves lost in a veritable avalanche of new titles.

Yet if an author spends too much time promoting and making noise, eventually the eyes of folks in their media streams will glaze over.

"Oh, look, Polly's talking about her book again." [yawn]

However, there's one sort of promotion that's pure gold, and that's word of mouth. When a trusted friend

WRITERS ON WRITING

turns around to tell me, "Hey, that's a great book," then I usually sit up and take note. Why? Because generally my friend won't have a financial stake in whether a book sells. If someone I know genuinely likes a book and thinks I would, too, I'll have a closer look at it. And then I'll note the reviews and decide where to take it from there.

Repeat after me: *Word of mouth is gold.*

Which brings me to the thankless task of book reviewing. Book reviews are among the best word of mouth an author can get (apart from a friend shoving their dog-eared copy of *Twilight* in your face while frothing about Edward's sparkly skin). Here's another little secret—if you set yourself up as a book reviewer, you need never wonder whether you can afford to buy yourself books. Authors and publishers will approach you to request that you read and review their books. In fact, they'll shower you in books.

Reviews and ratings on sites such as Amazon and Goodreads help authors' books get noticed. Just as good is if their books are reviewed for newspapers and magazines or mentioned on radio shows and podcasts. It doesn't really matter where books are discussed, but the more potential readers get to hear about books, the better the chance that an author will have someone pick up their book.

A steady reviewer never lacks books to read. Granted, they might not always be the books that the reviewer would pick up off their own bat, but they'll be exposed to a good cross-section of titles and build up a solid knowledge about the tropes prevalent in their chosen genre—which in turn informs how they evaluate titles.

VOLUME 3

If you want to set yourself up as a book reviewer who has their pick of books to read, there are dozens of places where you can post your review. The most obvious is to set up a personal blog. Another is to join groups on social media where people share book reviews (hint: there are plenty on Facebook). Many vendors, such as Amazon, Kobo, and Smashwords also allow reviews to be posted on their sites, which help visitors decide whether they will make a purchase. You can also start reviewing for print media by contacting the books editor of a local magazine or newspaper. With regard to the latter, don't be shy. Just send that email. Most books editors welcome reviewers and may even be able to help you out with review copies. Though I feel that there's a perceived prestige attached to having one's reviews appear in print, remember also that unless the publication uploads the content to their website later, the review you've written is ephemeral. More lasting are the reviews on actual vendor sites such as Amazon, where people who're already looking to buy books will be scanning through reviews to decide whether the book they're interested in is something they'd like to commit to purchasing.

The most important fact remains that you need to identify which platforms you want to use, then start using them. Obviously, the more cross-posting of your reviews you do, the more attractive you'll make yourself as a potential reviewer to authors and publishers.

As an example, once one of my reviews appears in the newspaper for which I write, I post it to my blog, post it to review groups on Facebook, then also paste it to the book's profile on Goodreads, Amazon, and

WRITERS ON WRITING

Kobo. I then follow up by sharing my blog post via social media such as Facebook, Tumblr, Twitter, and sites such as G+, using appropriate hashtags like #fantasy #reviews #shortfiction #horror or anything else that I feel is appropriate to help draw readers looking for particular subjects to follow. If my review is positive, I usually tag the author in question if I'm following them on the particular platform. The reason for this is that unless I actively draw attention to my blog post, it's generally going to sink without a trace in all the noise (authors tend to share/reblog/retweet positive reviews—which helps your visibility in return and may lead to further requests). Amusingly enough, reviews for material that are used in set reading for educational institutions often are more popular than others, and I attribute this to good tagging and thank my friend Google.

With a plethora of social media platforms available at present (and by the time you're reading this article, my advice is probably already going to sound quaint), all I can advise is that even if you start out with few people actually following your updates, it's vital that you not give up before you've given the platform a chance (hint: tag your posts so people can find if they're doing searches for particular content).

For those of you who're not in the know (or who're feeling a little at a loss for where to start), I'll quickly run through the basics of getting set up. Chances are good that you're already on Facebook. Perfect. Twitter? Yes . . . No?

If you're going to be serious about spreading a good buzz with regard to reviewing books, Facebook and Twitter are both important, because this is where

VOLUME 3

you're going to post reviews to your stories (and this is where a load of potential readers hang out). If you're on Facebook, you might want to see if you can search the groups to find any book clubs or groups that encourage members to share reviews. There are numerous book clubs on Facebook—some even tailored to specific genres. Pick three or four that you like and that you'd feel comfortable posting in. Make sure to understand what their rules are for posting (for instance, many don't allow links to external sites due to spam), and get an idea of the general tone of the group. On Twitter, you can follow your favourite authors and publishers (in fact, I suggest doing so as this is an excellent way to keep up to speed with new developments in the industry). Get to know how to navigate on the platform and which hashtags (#) are relevant. For instance, if you're reviewing a lot of young adult (YA) fiction, you'd tweet using a hashtag such as #ya or #yalit.

If the book you're reading is fantasy, you might post your link with the hashtag #darkfantasy and #review.

Twitter will often shorten links on your behalf, so even though you might Tweet:

I enjoyed KINGDOM by Robin Young
http://nerinedorman.blogspot.co.za/2015/09 /kingdom-by-robyn-young-reviews.html #review #historical

Your Tweet's actual link may appear something more like this:

WRITERS ON WRITING

nerinedorman.blogspot.co.za/2015/09/kingdom-by-robyn-young-reviews.html . . .
#reviews #historical

I always advise folks who post on Twitter and Facebook to use images in their posts, as often people will scroll through their timelines and, to be honest, text-only posts tend to get lost. An eye-catching visual, such as a book's cover, may hook viewers to click through to the actual link of your review.

Now, let's get onto blogging platforms. There are loads of sites that are great for blogging, but the two that appear (at time of writing) to be the most popular are WordPress and Blogger. Both have their pros and cons, so do a little research and decide which platform appeals to you the most and you are comfortable using. What I like about posting my reviews to my blog is that I retain full control over my site, whereas posting to sites such as Goodreads, Amazon, and elsewhere means that I'm at the mercy of their admin. Not that I make a habit of posting the sort of content that would be controlled by admins, but I do believe it's important to have at least one venue where I can fully curate all my writing.

So, get comfortable setting up your blog. The rule of thumb is to keep it simple but attractive. See what works on other book bloggers' sites, and decide what you'd like. If you feel a bit overwhelmed, don't go overboard. Just set up the very basics, and don't clutter with lots of extras. Get into the habit of posting regularly, maybe once or twice a week, and remember to share the links with a picture to your blog via your micro-blogging platforms such as Twitter and

VOLUME 3

Facebook. The great thing about blogging is you can generally discover some interesting things by looking at your statistics, and discover which posts are the most popular or which search functions may have led people through to your site.

The great thing about using Blogger is that it's part of the Google tribe, which means you can set up your blog so that each update automatically posts to another (largely underrated) social media site: G+ (which is linked to your Google profile if you use Gmail). While using G+ is not essential, in my experience I've found that despite it being a bit of a damp squib in social media circles, it's not quite dead in the water. Yet. (Though this may change in the future.)

I also like cross-posting my reviews to my Tumblr blog and, once again, remember the all-important #hashtag that will help your post show up in searches. Even if you don't have a lot of people following or commenting on your blog, keep at it. Keep posting. Follow people whose blogs interest you, comment and reblog, and you'll gradually see that others begin to follow you.

Twitter itself is a useful micro-blogging platform, and in my experience, it plays nicely with your other social media if you take the time to set it up. For instance, I've made it so that all my Goodreads updates automatically go out as Tweets—which is useful. That being said, don't completely automate your social media. If you become what is essentially just a spambot, you'll find yourself bleeding followers. Ditto for setting up a schedule of automated Tweets. Be personable, be nice, and be human.

WRITERS ON WRITING

A word of advice: If I see you posting the same Tweet round about the same time every day, I unfollow. It's a fine line between sharing links and having that all-important human touch. Use Twitter to share a little of the interesting things that you do: for instance, a visit to the library or perhaps your experiences browsing a second-hand bookstore. Keep things light, informative, and real, and you'll be well on your way to building up a respectable following. A little bit of humour goes a long way. Trust me.

The same goes for Facebook. Generally, I've found groups to be a better bet than pages, as Facebook has set it up so that you need to pay to boost posts from your pages. A neat trick I've learnt with Facebook when posting book reviews is to attach the photo first before adding the link to an external site like my blog. That way, the image that shows up is the actual picture you've attached and not some random graphic Facebook draws from the website (which could be a banner or a logo or simply nothing at all). With social media being so visually driven, you really do need some graphic element to draw potential readers' eyes and entice them to click.

While there are piles of review sites out there, and it certainly will make you incredibly popular with publishers and reviewers if you cross-post your reviews to sites such as Amazon and Kobo, where people make their purchases, one site that plays incredibly well with your other social media (like Facebook and Twitter) is Goodreads.

Although Goodreads is owned by Amazon, the content it provides is largely driven by passionate readers who post their reviews and interact on the site.

VOLUME 3

A host of features is available on Goodreads, including groups and lists, with functions such as newsletters and giveaways that are incredibly useful to authors and publishers. If you take the time to build up your profile on Goodreads, you may find authors contacting you here to review their books. At any rate, Goodreads also provides a fantastic way to keep track of all the books you've read and when, as well as marking books for your ever-increasing to-be-read pile.

Don't expect miracles overnight with regard to popularity ratings on your social media, but be patient, play around with how you can link the accounts, and post regularly—cross-post and share links across the media—and you'll gradually see an increase. Most importantly, find a method that works with you. There is no one way to build a reputation as a reviewer.

A word on creating a profile: It always helps to put up your review policy on your assorted sites, space allowing. Here you tell authors and publishers how they can contact you, and what sorts of genres you welcome. Often, authors will trawl Goodreads and Amazon and query you based on your previous reviews, but it definitely helps to have your preferences posted clearly either on your blog or website, or on your Goodreads and Amazon profiles. What do you like reading? What do you not want to see? How can authors contact you? Do you do interviews with authors? Is your blog available for guest posts or blog tours? Are you currently accepting review requests? This is all important information.

So, you've read a book, and it was horrible. What do you say? Remember, a review is written for other readers in mind, and not to stroke the ego of an author.

WRITERS ON WRITING

However, sometimes a book can be so awful that you really have nothing good to say about it. In those cases, it's perfectly acceptable to decline to review it. Simply tell the author that you're not the right reader for the novel. Or, if you can, find some aspects of the novel that were good, and sandwich the bad between the good to give a balanced review. It's not so much *what* you say but *how* you say it that counts.

Some reviewers tag authors when they post the reviews online—and this is absolutely fabulous with a great review. You may want to refrain from doing so if it's not a stellar review. Authors are not faceless entities who churn out words. They are thinking, feeling people who've poured hours of their lives into their words, no matter whether they've written utter dreck (in your opinion) or created a literary masterpiece (also your opinion).

If an author (or any other person) ever gets abusive with you about what you've written about a book, the golden rule is DON'T FEED THE TROLLS. Don't engage with them. Don't reply; don't respond in any way. The internet is ephemeral, and the storms in teacups pass. If need be, block individuals who are horrible, and get on with your life.

When you craft your words, your chief goal is to share with your readers what you thought was great (and also not so great) about a novel. Try to avoid simply retelling the entire plot (thereby giving spoilers), but it's perfectly all right to introduce a story by giving a bare-bones account of what readers can expect, for instance:

Frodo, a hobbit who lives in the country, is tasked by the wizard Gandalf to carry his uncle Bilbo's ring

VOLUME 3

to the elves in Rivendell, only that first step into adventure leads into an epic quest not even the wizard could have foreseen.

See what I've done there to paint in the very basics for a well-loved fantasy classic? You do not have to give a blow-by-blow account of the entire plot. You do not need to tell readers what happens in the end. But what you *should* be doing with your review is whetting readers' appetite to make them *want* to read the rest of the story. When writing reviews, I like to touch on the aspects of the writing that I enjoyed, and yes, if there are things that didn't blow my hair back, I make mention of them but try to sandwich them with praise so that my review is balanced. A good review says more about the book that's being reviewed than about the author (or indeed the person writing the review, for that matter). So, while your personal likes and dislikes are important, do try to realise that just because you don't like something doesn't mean that everyone else should agree with you. While it's probably not possible to write a completely objective review (you are, obviously, being asked for your opinion), it's equally vital that you don't allow your personal tastes to completely overshadow what you're trying to say about a book.

I like to keep things fairly chatty and informal when I write, and my reviews are anywhere from between 250 words to 600, depending on where my review is being published. Reviews destined for print media tend to have a stricter adherence to word count (for obvious reasons—ask the book's editor what they want), but if I'm writing purely for my blog and associated online destinations, I can write longer—

WRITERS ON WRITING

bearing in mind that the average reader's span usually wafts off into the nether realms after 600 words.

[What? You're still reading this article; well done!]

Now, you may ask, where are your free books?

Well, apart from trawling your local library or visiting wonderful sites such as Open Library or Project Gutenberg, you can also sign up at NetGalley, where hundreds of publishers put up the advanced reader copies (or ARCs as they're more commonly known). That's right. You can have your pick of novels—often well before they're released into the wilds—for free. All you need to do is write a few hundred words worth of review that goes out either to a publication, blog, or onto sites like Amazon or Goodreads. Easy peasy.

Remember that reading is fun—share the love. We read because we often want to temporarily escape the madness of real life.

References:

https://www.techdirt.com/articles/20110211/003844
    13053/how-neil-gaiman-went-fearing-piracy-to-
    believing-its-incredibly-good-thing.shtml

TREATING FICTION LIKE A RELATIONSHIP
THE IMPORTANCE OF VULNERABILITY

JAMES EVERINGTON

WE ALL PUT up walls.

You do it; I do it. Many claim not to do it, but when was the last time they shared their darkest secrets with you? Cried in your presence? Let loose a torrent of raw emotion, be it positive, negative, or otherwise in front of you?

That's what I thought.

Of course, everyone's different, and there are exceptions to every rule, and blah blah blah, but let's be real here, okay?

No one likes to get hurt.

No one likes to feel foolish.

Nobody wants to be the one who cries.

I've been married for nearly twelve years to an amazing woman. Counting our overlong courtship (my fault), we've been together closer to sixteen years. I know her better than anyone, and she knows me like no one else. We've been through three pregnancies and childbirths together, we've counseled each other when

WRITERS ON WRITING

loved ones have died or gotten sick, we've been as intimate as two people can be.

Yet we still put up walls.

When life gets busy and we have twenty-nine events scheduled in a three-day span and we're both tired and one of us says something callous or even something innocuous that the other one misconstrues, we withdraw a little. Because we hate being hurt. We hate feeling foolish.

We don't like being vulnerable.

In time, my wife and I hammer away at those walls and eventually return to normal, and thankfully, "normal" for us means being good to each other. Being vulnerable.

What does all this have to do with your writing?

Everything, my friends. Everything.

No matter what anyone tells you, writing is a tough gig. People can talk all they want about muses and beauty and the ethereal blaze of discovery, but when you get down to it, there are more important things than a poet's soul:

Toughness.

Endurance.

Work ethic.

Determination.

The fact is, there are a billion aspects to this business—not the least of which the fact that it is indeed a *business*—that can drag down a writer's spirit. Bad reviews. No reviews. Poor sales. No sales. Competition. Insincerity from peers. Disappointment. Worry. Frustration. Self-doubt (insert more troubles here).

Don't get me wrong, friends. I love being a writer.

VOLUME 3

I wouldn't trade this profession for any other, and every day I'm allowed to write and interact with readers is a blessing.

But I won't lie. Sometimes it's hard.

When you consider all the difficulties writers experience, it's perfectly understandable that the vast majority quit at some point. At times, the negativity can be crushing.

It's enough to make a person put up walls.

But you can't.

When you begin to withdraw into a protective shell—on the page or in life—you effectively blunt the pain you feel on the page or in life. This is appealing, of course, because it diminishes the risk inherent in investing in relationships (in real life or on the page), and at heart, most of us are risk-averse. We fear the unknown. We'd rather know what's going to happen tomorrow rather than worrying about it. We like assurances that we won't be hurt or made to look foolish.

There's only one problem with this isolationist approach.

We don't feel joy either.

We don't feel truly thrilled when life dazzles us with unexpected surprises.

We don't truly love.

I'm very proud of every book I've written so far. Oh sure, when I reread my work from four years ago, I find things I'd do differently now, word choices I wish I could fix.

But aside from these technical areas, the biggest difference between the Early Writing Me and the Current Writing Me is this:

The Current Writing Me is more courageous.

WRITERS ON WRITING

No, I'm not talking about following the plot where it goes—I've always done that. I'm not talking about my heroes risking their lives and leaping off of burning buildings to save babies (though that does happen in one of my novels).

What I'm talking about is the willingness to let readers see my heart.

You see, there's genuine vulnerability inherent in the reader-writer covenant. Or at least there should be. How much a writer decides to reveal is up to him/her, but I can tell you, the more emotionally raw the writer is when crafting a tale, the more powerfully the story will resonate with readers.

And I'm not necessarily talking about flattering or endearing raw emotion either. You know, the kind of writing where you can pretend you're being emotionally raw with your readers when what you're actually doing is portraying yourself as a sensitive, good-natured human being while keeping the reader at an emotional arm's length.

Take the following passage from my novel *The Nightmare Girl*. The protagonist, Joe Crawford, is a good man, but he's not perfect. In the scene from which this passage is taken, Joe finds out to his disgust and fury that his good friend (Police Chief Copeland) has discovered one of Joe's workers (an idiot named Gentry) spying on Joe's wife in only her bra and underwear (and engaging in auto-erotic behavior whilst peeping on her):

> *Joe stood mulling it over, not wanting to ask the question but knowing he needed to anyway. "Was Michelle . . ."*

VOLUME 3

"She was near the window," Copeland said. *"A little ways in. She was sitting there in her bra, looking at something."*

Joe's voice was barely a croak. *"That's where the computer is."*

"Well, I didn't take the time to figure out what websites she was on. It was embarrassing enough seeing her there wearing hardly any clothes."

"You don't think she knew Gentry was there?"

Copeland took a step back from him, his expression aghast and more than a little irate. *"Man, don't you have any faith in your wife? Of course she didn't know she was being gawked at. The hell kind of question is that?"*

Joe blew out disgusted breath, took a couple steps into the road. *"Man, I'm an idiot. I don't know what the hell's wrong with me."*

What's the big deal with this passage? you might ask. The big *deal* (says the author incredulously) is that my protagonist isn't behaving like a protagonist.

He's behaving like a person.

I'd like to say that men are one hundred percent trusting of their wives, that they never harbor petty thoughts or irrational worries. And let's be totally honest here—jealousy is not an attractive or admirable emotion. But aren't we sometimes petty? Aren't we sometimes insecure? Don't we sometimes doubt people whom we know to be trustworthy because our baser natures bully our thoughts into uncharitable realms?

WRITERS ON WRITING

No? Then you're a better person than I am. Actually, you're a better person than anyone I know.

They say that fiction is the truth inside the lie. Even better, someone once said that fiction is telling lies about people who never existed in order to tell us the truth about ourselves. Which means it's our job as writers to tell the truth even when it's unpleasant.

Especially when it's unpleasant.

What you see in that exchange with the police chief is that for all Joe's good qualities—and there are many—he has his faults. And I'm not talking about the manufactured fictional flaws, the kind of flaws-that-aren't-flaws that allow the characters to remain pretty much perfect. Giving a character a limp or a scar isn't giving the character a serious flaw because limps and scars aren't imperfections. Not really. They're backstory markers or physical mysteries, but they sure as hell aren't flaws. And they come with zero risk.

Having a character question his faithful wife's virtue, even if it's only momentarily? That's risky.

I wouldn't have written an exchange like that when I started out because I would have been too afraid of breaking the arbitrary rules I learned from my stacks of fiction-writing books and the million or so strident "Don't Do This!" blog entries I devoured while cutting my authorial teeth.

You know why? Because I didn't want to be perceived as foolish. I didn't want people to hurt me with their judgmental words.

Sound familiar?

Without realizing it, I used to attempt to remain *in*vulnerable. Strength was my mantra. If I learned enough rules and toed the lines drawn by those who

VOLUME 3

knew more than I did, I figured I'd disarm my future critics and reside in a criticism-free zone. By erecting a wall of knowledge, I could remain safely within my literary castle, and no one would call me a hack, no one would reject me.

Not that this thought process was a conscious one, of course, and like I said, I really love my early work. And it's not what I said in those books that illustrates the point of this essay, but rather what I didn't say.

I didn't get naked.

See, it's the author's job to describe the gleam of the vehicle's new paint job, the glimmer of polished chrome. But he also has to pop the hood and dismantle the carburetor; he has to flay open the upholstery and take a Sawzall to that oil pan.

He has to show the audience his crankshaft.

Ahem. *Clears throat.* Sorry.

The point is, our job as authors is to constantly dig deeper. It's not enough to delve below the surface of a character's psyche. The human mind is an infinitely complex network of neuroses and convolutions, self-deceptions and desires. And by writing characters as though we're building Lego helicopters—*white brick here, red block there*—we're shortchanging ourselves and our audiences.

Lest you think that being vulnerable is exclusively limited to negative moments in our stories, allow me to offer the following passage as proof that being vulnerable in our writing can be an edifying, love-affirming practice, as well. This scene is near the end of the book, after Joe, his wife Michelle, and his daughter Lily have been put through hell. And despite all that's happened, Joe still isn't sure that the nightmare is over. He's leaning over the railing of his sleeping daughter's crib and grasping her shoulder. He begins to tremble, then to weep, and finally to sob. After a time, Joe and his daughter have the following exchange:

> "Daddy?" a voice asked.
> Joe stared down at his daughter, became instantly aware of how hard he was gripping her shoulder.
> "Sorry," he said, though his voice was so husky the word was indecipherable. But it didn't matter. He'd relaxed his grip, and Lily had shown no sign of discomfort, was showing nothing at all but concern for him. Her lucent brown eyes picked up some of the starlight slanting through the sides of the curtains, and in them he saw the same look Michelle often wore when he was beating himself up for something.
> He cleared his throat and whispered, "Sorry, honey. I didn't mean to wake you."
> His voice broke on the last word, the sobs still refusing to completely abate, and all of a sudden Lily was rising from her nest of pillows and toys and reaching for him. He stooped over to meet her, thinking she wanted to be held, but rather than simply resting her forearms on his shoulders as she ordinarily did, this time her slender arms enfolded his neck, hauled him down into her embrace with astonishing strength. Joe scrambled for some comforting word or phrase, but his chest was

VOLUME 3

still quaking, the wet heat in his throat scalding him, robbing him of speech.

But his daughter, he now realized, was speaking, was repeating something over and over, her voice a soft, soothing whisper.

"You're safe," she said. "You're safe, Daddy."

Joe clenched his arms about her, a violent sob racking his body. But though he'd leaned into her, she somehow supported him, somehow helped him remain upright. Worried he'd collapse the whole crib and send her to the ER, he made to pull back, but she only tightened her hold on him, said, "Shhhh. Shhhh, Daddy."

"Lily," he tried to say.

"You're safe," she repeated. "You're safe."

Tears streamed over his cheeks, and though he fought it, the silent, quaking sobs took him then, rendered him powerless. He leaned against his daughter and wept, wept as he hadn't since the miscarriage. The heat in his chest became a boiling inferno. It spread through his shoulders, his arms, down his abdominal muscles all the way to his toes, and now he let it flood through him, gust out of him, his daughter whispering to him all the while. She had turned three earlier in the month, but in her voice, in her unwavering, loving embrace there was something maternal, something ageless. She whispered to him and nuzzled her lamb-soft cheek into his neck, and told him he was safe, and when he'd

WRITERS ON WRITING

finally regained control of his emotions, when he was at last able to draw back slightly and gaze into her liquid brown eyes, she was making a face at him, a face she often made when he'd fallen silent and she wanted to make him laugh. They called it her surprise face.

Joe looked at his daughter's wide eyes and open mouth and began to smile, despite how messy he was with tears and mucus.

Okay, we all react differently to different things, and maybe that doesn't hit you at all, particularly out of context. But I can tell you I'm extremely proud of it, not only because it fits these characters and this story, but because it's raw. It's charged. It's emotional.

It's vulnerable.

And I'm not just talking about my character being vulnerable, though he certainly is that. I'm talking about me, as a man, being vulnerable.

There are all sorts of silly stereotypes, but one of the most pernicious is that men can't be nurturers. As a father, I can tell you that I get emotional about my kids every day. I cry at least three times a week. I shower them with love. I play with them every chance I get.

But I'm far from perfect.

I sometimes get frustrated. I can be irritable, particularly when I've just written my three thousand words for the day, and my brain is in a fog. When I do a bad job, I ask their forgiveness, but that rarely feels like enough. At times, I feel like they're supporting me as much as I'm supporting them.

That weakness, that need for help is echoed in the

VOLUME 3

above passage. I wish I could be strong all the time, but there are times when I need my kids to tell me they love me. It shouldn't be the case, but it is.

Do you see? Admitting this to you was difficult for me. I opened myself up for your judgment. I took a risk.

And if you want your fiction to resonate with readers, you have to take risks, too. You can't just toss your characters out there as fictional human shields while you remain safely hidden behind your keyboard.

You have to reveal *your* heart, too, with all its flaws and worries.

And when you do, your characters will resonate with readers in a way they couldn't have otherwise. As a result, your readers will open themselves to your characters.

In relationships it is vital that we strive for vulnerability. It's how we tear down walls between our loved ones and ourselves.

On the page, we have to do the same thing.

WRITERS ON WRITING
VOL. 4

BLUNT-FORCE TRAUMA
HOW TO WRITE KILLER POETRY

STEPHANIE M. WYTOVICH

BLUNT-FORCE TRAUMA is defined as a serious, sometimes fatal, injury caused by a blunt object or surface. It's a physical act. A beating. A bludgeoning. It doesn't always have to be thought out. It can be an accident, a spontaneous act fueled by rage, by sorrow, by passion. Or it could be the result of something methodical, well-planned. Maybe the inflictor had been contemplating the idea of murder, getting the feel and taste and scent of homicide all over and inside his or her body. Blunt-force trauma is visceral, raw, and either way, it's the resulting aftermath of one's instincts and morality at war. It's an assault on the body, but the trauma also leaves a lasting impression on the mind and the spirit, as well.

And that's what poetry is all about.

It's the meditation on and exploration of the wound and how it came to be.

I started writing poetry—probably like most of you—in my teens. I wrote in journals for years, but I never let anyone read my work because I had a hard

WRITERS ON WRITING

time talking about a lot of issues and concerns that I was having at that point in my life. My then-therapist mentioned that if I was having problems exposing, accepting, and expressing my pain, that I should try poetry as a way to dissect the images and emotions that I was stuck on or having trouble moving past. She told me poetry would step in and be my medication, my catharsis. If I wrote every day, I would feel better.

And so I did.

At first, my pages were filled with line after line of purple prose—a style of flowery, overdramatized language—and it was dark, and sad, and borderline gothic in a way that gave emo a run for its money. But having said that, my bad poetry did something that was a necessary and important part of learning the craft: It taught me to be honest, to put exactly what I was feeling, and how I was feeling it, right on the page. It gave me permission not to hold back, to be frank with myself, and to do and say what I needed to in order to tell my story.

The blank page let me yell. I could scream and curse and draw blood and it accepted it without complaint or fight. It let me get angry, and it was there for me when I needed to cry. I wrote without revision like that for years, just filled journal after journal, notebook after notebook, and when I went to college, I used Duct Tape to bind them all shut so no one would ever read them (at least not without a struggle). I spent a year or two reading nothing but poetry, and it was at that point I realized that while I liked what I was doing, I didn't have a style, a niche. I was writing memoir, but I wasn't exactly writing prose. I was incorporating elements of speculative fiction, but I wasn't quite

VOLUME 4

writing horror. I got really frustrated and realized that when it came to writing poetry, that I was more or less a verbal loose cannon and that I had no idea what I was doing at all, other than being honest about my fears.

So I went home one weekend, ripped open all of my journals, and flipped through them one by one as I took notes in a separate diary. I collected images, phrases, connected themes and motifs. I analyzed the demons that had been following me for years, and I accepted the darkness that was still lurking inside of me and causing conflict.

I made a collage of my injuries, my lesions, and my bruises. I watched myself grow up, listened to my heart break, and I revisited the places in my mind that I went to when I needed protection. Then when I had what I needed—my style, my niche, my memories—I threw those journals into a fire pit and said goodbye to weakness, to suffering, and to vulnerability as I watched my past burn while I paved a new path for my future.

That was the day I remember becoming a poet. It was in that moment when I accepted my scars not as something that made me weak, but rather as something that made me strong, that I found my voice. Not just my poetic voice, but my voice as a woman, as a feminist, and as a soon-to-be writer with a flair for confessional poetry and a dark, speculative edge.

I independently studied poetry for years after that. Outside of my classes in college, I read voraciously and I took note of my reactions to certain poems and artists. I read poets from different countries, from different religious affiliations, genres, and gender/sexual preferences. I took notes on how I felt after reading their work, and I studied their structure, their habits, their tells. I went to readings, I listened to lectures, but when I would sit down to write, I always felt as if I were knocking on a door that was never going to open.

How was I supposed to get into the asylum of my mind?

What was my poetry lacking? Where was the intensity? The blunt-force trauma?

I asked myself these questions and thought long and hard about them. I had spent four years studying literature and art history, but that was only a part of me and a fraction of what I wanted to do with my writing. That's when I made the decision to go to graduate school, where for another two and a half years I did nothing but study horror and learn about gore and murder, monsters and madmen.

At that point, my muse developed a face.

And a motive.

And a weapon of choice.

Meshing literary and speculative fiction together was something that I felt—and feel—strongly about. I think there is something hauntingly beautiful to be said about confessional poets tapping into the vein of horror and dark fantasy to expel demons and exorcise angels. It brings together the classics and the contemporaries, and it allows one to experiment with form, structure, and line. I started out with free-verse and then moved on to prose poetry. I wrote murder poems, killer prose, and blood ballads, and to me, that was the edge that I wanted and needed, and horror gave me the formula to make it happen.

VOLUME 4

STEP ONE: FIND YOUR MOTIVE

Every killer, just like every poet, has a motive, even if that motive is not having one. Think about what you're writing, and why you want to write it. Are you angry? Are you upset? Are you healing? Are you inflicting a wound? This is the moment when you grab hold of your emotion(s) and dissect them to perform a psychological autopsy and discover your intent.

Something that has worked well for me in the past is making a word collage. I'll write down words that I associate with the emotion I'm feeling and then connect them to images and phrases that come to mind as a result. Sometimes these phrases work themselves into the poem and other times they help form the backstory or the setting of the piece.

Another brainstorming activity that I've used is to write a dialogue with or between characters to better shape them and understand why they feel and act the way that they do. In many ways, you're playing therapist in this stage and trying to better understand where the aggressions/regression is coming from.

STEP TWO: CHOOSE YOUR WEAPON

This is both a literal and a figurative step in writing your poem. When writing killer poetry, there needs to be a destructive force in some manner whether it's the threat of something physical like a knife, or something figurative like loneliness or madness. Keep in mind that the choice of weapon will have a say in character building and also affect the style of the poem based on the sounds and motions that are associated with it

WRITERS ON WRITING

while it's being used. The weapon will go hand-in-hand with the motive and ultimately lash out at the protagonist.

This leads us into the next weapon that you need to be aware of which is your structure. Are you writing in the form of a prose poem so it feels more like a story? Is it free-verse? Is it experimental or composed through a stream of consciousness? Think about how you're *telling* your story. Is it through images? Is it through emotions? Are you comparing and contrasting? Are you making an analogy? The structure helps to build character and voice as you put flesh on your murderer and victim.

STEP THREE: PLOT MURDER

This is the nuts and bolts stage where you think about the importance of line, syllable count, breaks, and stanzas. Do you want short lines with lots of bite? Would you rather use long, flowing lines that wrap around the page creating a cat and mouse game? Will you be direct or speak metaphorically? Will you use poetic devices such as alliteration and personification?

Aside from these being important questions that should be asked before writing any poem, it's especially important with horror poetry because you want the structure and manner of the poem to mimic the ideologies and style of your killer or victim. For instance, if the killer is a hit-and-run kind of guy or gal, you'll probably want to use something short and to the point. However, if your antagonist has more of a torture-porn appetite, he or she is going to want to play with their toy(s) and drag matters out to better enjoy

VOLUME 4

them. Long, sweeping lines with lots of detail and focus on the human body might work better here.

Point of view is also up for discussion at this point as poetry doesn't always have to be written in first person point-of-view. You are permitted to be a bystander rather than a lead, and you can still write in the vein of confessional poetry through another character's eyes and actions.

STEP FOUR: EXECUTE

The execution stage is the climax of your poem as motive, weapon, and action all come together to inflict pain. At this point in the writing process, I usually refer back to my word collage to tap into the emotional attachment/detachment that I felt when I first started working on the piece.

Remember that the action of the scene will reflect the characterization that you've chosen in regards to structure, style, and word choice. Every killer has their hang-ups and preferences, just like every final girl has something that she has to overcome in order to realize she can survive. Make sure the action suits the character and the killer fits the crime. Tension and pacing will be crucial here and should be considered heavily when choosing where to break your lines and shape your stanzas.

STEP FIVE: EXPOSE THE WOUND

The denouement and its subsequent conclusion should expose the wound and the vulnerability of the poem. This should be honest and raw, and regardless of your

WRITERS ON WRITING

style of writing, provoke a reaction from your reader. Think of this stage as the part where the coroner writes "blunt-force trauma" on his or her report. Don't hold anything back. Show your readers what your characters are seeing, feeling, hearing, smelling, and tasting—even, and maybe especially, if they are dead/dying. Let us feel the blood on our hands and experience the cold sweat running down our neck. Your characters are living the repercussions of the threat, but you want your readers to have a visceral reaction to the danger and feel that at any given moment, they could have easily been the victim.

These five steps will help to visualize your poem by means of structure, character, and voice. While you're meditating on murder and motive, you're also performing an assault on the five senses by using your words as weapons. Each syllable becomes a quick stab, each caesura a right hook. By being honest with yourself and using real life experiences and fears to help shape your writing, confessional poetry can meet speculative prose by incorporating fact and fiction, memory and nightmare.

So expose the wound, examine the fear, and close the case.

Dead or alive, the poem will stand as a testament of life.

HAPPY LITTLE TREES

MICHAEL KNOST

"When you write a book, you spend day after day scanning and identifying the trees. When you're done, you have to step back and look at the forest."
—Stephen King, *On Writing: A Memoir of the Craft*

WHEN IT COMES to developing characters and set pieces, I can't help but think of the late Bob Ross on his PBS television program, *The Joy of Painting*, as he painted what he called "happy little trees." With a soft voice and relaxed pace, he offered viewers insights into execution and theory as he effortlessly produced breathtaking scenery. The more I learn about the craft of writing, the more I think I know why Ross's little trees were so happy.

Ross used the wet-on-wet oil-painting technique. He would add fresh paint on top of still-wet paint rather than wait for each layer to dry, which allowed him to paint trees, bodies of water, cloud formations, and mountains in a matter of minutes. And he didn't simply paint each element in a single layer. Each began with simple strokes, little more than colorful smudges. Adding layer after layer, Ross transformed blotches of

WRITERS ON WRITING

paint into intricate, lifelike formations; bit by bit, stroke by stroke, layer by layer, smudges of paint became trees, mountains, entire landscapes.

With the same patience, you must focus on every little detail for each individual tree (think, *character* or *set piece*) when writing your story, but your character is a collective entity—made up of hundreds (possibly thousands) of details. He or she is like an onion—shaped entirely from multiple layers. Individually, these layers are so thin you could literally read a newspaper through one. But with an adequate number of them, you have something powerful enough to not only spice up the mundane, but also bring tears to the eyes.

Let me introduce you to Billy Bob (layer). He lives in Harlan, Kentucky (layer). His favorite pastime is hunting and fishing (layer). He chews tobacco (layer) and loves flannel shirts with the sleeves ripped off (layer). Think you have this guy sized up? What if I told you Billy Bob is a neurosurgeon? The character you just had in your mind has changed completely. Adding a fresh layer of paint to another layer of fresh paint is important because the two elements mingle, adding realistic dimensions and depths. This is one type of what I call *relational influence*, which can be as simple as adding that one detail that turns a stereotype into a unique individual. Remember, *every* detail should contribute to the whole.

But even with complex, layered characters or set pieces, you can't just focus on a single tree without considering its regional copse—just as you can't focus solely on a single branch without imagining the entire tree. That doesn't mean you can't see the tree because

VOLUME 4

you are focused on the forest, but that you need to notice, as you write, how each specific element blends with all the others.

Once each individual is fleshed out with appropriate layering, it is time to examine the forest. That's when all your trees, clouds, and rivers work together to become the fascinating scenes you intended from the beginning. *Relational influence* also describes two (or more) individual entities sharing multiple layers.

Think of each scene as a single canvas in a series of paintings that, when placed next to one another, create a complete panoramic experience. It's a good way to examine how the continuity of the forest depends on the intricate layering of the individual trees: wet paint on wet, in Bob Ross's scenes; word on word and paragraph on paragraph in your writing. If you fail to properly flesh out characters and small details, you will more than likely fail to properly flesh out the story and its themes.

The last thing you want is a character standing out from the background like she'd obviously been Photoshopped into the scene. Good Photoshopping (as well as painting and writing) requires elements to reflect or affect one another.

When Bob Ross painted a mountain range behind a lake, you could be sure the mountain was mirrored in the water. And just as placement of the sun will affect shadows on everything else in the scene, each character (or story element) in your tale will affect all other characters and set pieces in some way.

Let's take another look at Billy Bob. What if we learn his father took him hunting and fishing when he was younger? Gave him his first chaw of tobacco? And then we learn this was the only time he really connected with his dad. Billy Bob didn't just develop a love for these things on his own; it is a direct result of specific influence from a relationship in his life.

What if we learn the death of his father (who passed away from complications of a neurological disorder) was the impetus for him going into the medical field? It's easy to see that the shadow of his father's death (and life) still influences him. We may not always recognize it, but the people in our lives can have great influence on us . . . why would we not show this in the characters and set pieces in our fiction?

This means relational influence ensures the writer is *showing* rather than just *telling*. To be honest, I think Bob Ross nailed it when he said, "If I paint something, I don't want to have to explain what it is."

Relational influence allows the reader to size up the characters and set pieces for herself, evaluate the clues (layers), and then form calculated perceptions. In other words, it allows her to appreciate the depth of the forest while examining every individual tree.

IN LIEU OF PATIENCE BRING DIVERSITY

KENNETH W. CAIN

BEING RATHER NEW to this writing gig, I'm still finding my sea legs. My focus, however, remains the same, always striving to improve as a writer. There's much to learn, and around every corner comes a new lesson. There's a vast ocean of information out there to absorb, the sort of knowledge they don't always teach in a classroom. It's accrued over time, coming out of experience more than anything. That's why, when first asked what I thought was the most important quality to possess in writing, I responded with my best intentions and claimed patience preceded all else.

Being successful at most anything requires a great deal of patience, especially in a career where everything you put out there becomes so permanent. And patience has always been something I've struggled with myself. You learn it soon enough, though. Sit on any shortlist for a year and you can't help but find the ability. Jump that to two years or more and you'll have mastered it, right? Not necessarily, as patience comes

WRITERS ON WRITING

on a sliding scale, requiring little one day and more than you can muster the next.

Patience is required at most every step of publishing, too. I spoke in Crystal Lake Publishing's *Horror 101* of its importance in getting your work out there. To reiterate, make sure you are always putting out the very best work you can at any given time. You'll also need patience to accrue sales, to gain readership, to make acquaintances, to have people "like" you on social media. All of it takes a great deal of perseverance, and before long you'll find you are inundated with requests to "like" or visit or join or support, requiring even more patience. Many of those requests, but not all, demonstrate a lack of patience to one degree or another. Therefore my initial response did not come without forethought.

I've altered my opinion on this topic as of late. I've come to believe that avoiding the generalization of characters is what's most important. It's an easy trap to fall into, more so than one would think. Many of us have grown up with generalizations. We see them on a daily basis and after all, aren't we initially taught to write what we know?

I'll admit my first realization came as a hard slap to my face. Well, at least that's what it felt like. The editor for my first book didn't do anything to me in a physical sense, but instead asked what should have been an easy question to answer. She wanted to know why every woman in my book came off as being so frail. Her saying this stung my pride, too, because it hadn't been my intention to portray that sort of narrow-mindedness. I appreciated her bringing this to my attention so early on in my career.

VOLUME 4

My gut reaction was to disagree, of course, because I don't think all women are frail. Not one bit. After stewing over the question for some time I reread my manuscript and understood what she'd meant. It wasn't that I'd attributed the word "frail" to each and every female character description, but I'd depicted these women as needing men. That had been a generalization I'd wanted to avoid, too, because I wanted to paint at least two of those female characters in the exact opposite light.

So what happened to me while writing this book that led to my oversight? Did I somehow get my lines crossed and confuse the characters? Or had I simply drawn from the many ways in which women are often portrayed to us in books, movies, and television shows? I've come to find it's more than that. It's not only about female characters. It's about all of them, every color, every race, every size, every sex. Yes, there are generalizations to explore in writing, ones that many people will say are off limits or in poor taste, but they exist nonetheless. Not every character needs to find themselves carved from the same cloth.

People are much like snowflakes. No two are alike. While some of us may share an endless list of similarities, we are all different to some degree. Therein lies the truth to characterization, the secret ingredient to creating a successful story.

We writers want our characters to feel real. Therefore it would be an injustice not to allow them to make the same choices we have from the time we took our first breaths into this world up until the day we breathe our last. We need to allow them to choose their beliefs, their preferences, what they look like, whether

WRITERS ON WRITING

they are fat or skinny or somewhere in-between. Only they know what sex they will be, or the color of their skin, what clothes they'll wear. If you listen well enough they'll divulge their every secret down to the last detail. They'll let you know what makes them real. It's up to you then to give clarity to their persona to the best of your ability.

One of the first ways writers often fail in this is to divulge these details like a grocery list. They'll paint a picture of a character somewhat to this effect:

Red hair framed her pale, white face. She was both tall and slender. Kept her nails painted red and wore lipstick to match. When she spoke, she did so with a soft yet seductive tone.

Listing details in this manner often loses the reader. So we must find better ways to seed these qualities of our characters throughout the entire story. We must also determine which traits matter.

Stephen King cited an excellent example of this in his book *On Writing*. In his example, he spoke of a room with two windows and flowing drapes. In the center of the room sat a couch and in front of the couch a table. On the table sat a cage and inside of the cage was a white rabbit with the number 8 painted on it. What drew your attention? The rabbit, of course. King's serves as a great example of how little you need to reveal, so if you haven't read the book yet, you should do so soon. I'm obviously paraphrasing, but King went on to discuss how the reader then draws the picture of that scene in their minds, and how several different readers might perceive the same scene in different ways. Some might see a black number and others a red one. Some might picture a Victorian end

VOLUME 4

table and others a ratty old wooden table. The point is to engage your readers and allow them to fill in the blanks.

So, the next question becomes: What is necessary? Do you have to mention hair color or race or even sex? Well, much of that depends on your story and what you're trying to achieve. We don't always want to paint the same tired old picture. Can you imagine Monet painting the same few water lilies over and over? Instead he chose to show them from different angles, utilizing different colors and scenes to the best of his ability. The variety of ways in which he portrayed them is what added to his legacy. So you must ask yourself: How do you want your writing to be perceived?

If you want to paint a visual landscape for the reader, you might mention the red hair against a dreadful background. There are certain generalizations that come to mind when we consider red hair. That picture surely depicts passion standing out from the surrounding trepidation. Or it could display the focus of a love interest. Or fury among the meek. We don't want to create any character that appears to have been formed using a cookie cutter, so we must be careful when and where we apply these details. In truth, the mention of red hair must do something to move the story forward because if we achieve nothing by mentioning the color of the hair, then what's the point? Leave it to your reader. Let them become invested in your character of their own tastes. You can paint that same picture without mentioning hair color, but only you can decide whether the impact will be as strong. Regardless of how you paint the scene, many readers will not see the

WRITERS ON WRITING

same picture you had in mind. That is part of the beauty in a well-told story.

You can work what details are necessary into your story through exposition. For instance, if you want to talk about skin color, you can write about sunburn or a birthmark or some other skin blemish. You don't ever have to come right out and mention what color your character is if you're clever enough. A simple mention allows the reader to see things about the character we aren't always privy to. For instance, a character with rough calluses could be a hard worker or a killer or poor. We don't have to come right out and say any of this. Let the reader speculate and divulge what you need to as the story progresses. Perhaps you might mention the calluses early on, then later reveal the *how* in which the character earned these calluses by having him or her visit their parents at a dilapidated farmhouse. This way the reader can put these things together for themselves and build those connections that keep them interested in your characters.

After we breathe life into a character we then need to break that mold. Throw it away each and every time we apply pen to paper. We don't need to create token characters to make our stories real. We need to allow our existing characters to become what they will, what they wish to be. Let the world create itself and don't be afraid to put yourself in unfamiliar shoes. It's only by this reasoning we are able to experience what they experience. And that is the only time we need to explore those generalizations, so that we can better understand what made these characters who they are today. How did their struggle define them?

As of late, I've been striving to do just that, writing

VOLUME 4

not only what I know, but what I do not. Writing from different and unfamiliar perspectives. It's been a breathtaking experience at times. Whether I'm successful or not, this is what I wish to create. I want to depict real people in the best way I can. Not the same old people, but ones who truly matter. I want to tell the real story, and I've come to learn that creating real characters leads to a successful story.

So the next time someone asks you what you think is the most important quality of writing fiction, consider characterization in lieu of patience. Consider diversity and enlighten your craft. Treat your readers to a real experience. Allowing your characters to breathe and come to life on their own transcends generalizations. Most importantly, the reader creates the most important aspects of the characters themselves. This is the recipe for a story with impact, one that leaves a lasting impression with the reader.

NETWORKING IS SCARY, BUT ESSENTIAL

DOUG MURANO

WRITER. WHAT POPPED into your head when you read that word? Did you think of an awkward loner slugging it out word by word in a darkened, cluttered room? I'm betting there's a good chance, that this oh-so-clichéd character invaded your mind, even if you didn't invite it in.

To be fair, there's a reason why this archetype persists in pop culture: There's a kernel of truth to it. Yeah, a lot of us are a little strange; eccentricity is what fuels these engines of creation. What's more, as a species—and I'm talking specifically about writers, here—we're often introverted and fiercely independent by nature. We require a measure of solitude to get our heads around an image or to refine an idea to its essence.

But making a career as a writer (or an editor, which is how I'm attacking the business more often than not these days) means more than sitting alone in a room of your own and putting words down on a page. It means positioning your work within the business,

VOLUME 4

building support within the community of your peers, getting your work out in front of readers and enticing them into dropping their hard-earned dough on something you made.

Most of the time—and it doesn't matter whether you're working with a big publisher or a micro-press—accomplishing these things means you have to do some networking.

I know I'm probably losing some of you after offering up that word, but I hope you'll hear me out on this. If you cringed just now, it's probably because you're picturing exchanging business cards and lame small-talk in carefully orchestrated social situations. Or, if you're anything like I used to be, you might have an extreme negative reaction to the idea of networking because your stomach turns at the thought of joining any type of "good ol' boys' club." Yet others might recoil at the word because of an overwhelming sense of helplessness at the thought of finding where to begin this effort.

Let me address these concerns, briefly, in order. First, however unlikely it is, I can't guarantee you're never going to have to choke down a cocktail at an awkward networking mixer, so it's best if you just get your business cards ready, pick your poison, prepare for the worst, and hope for the best. Second, there's a difference between the type of networking I'm talking about and joining a "good ol' boys' club" in that it's more about supporting your community and finding your niche than it is about trading favors. I'll take much of the remainder of this essay describing what this means in practical terms, as well as addressing the third concern: How to get started. I can't and won't

WRITERS ON WRITING

supply step-by-step instructions on how to build your network because I don't have all the answers, and because your journey will likely be different than mine has been thus far.

Here's what I'll do, though: I'll give you two anecdotes from my career that, I hope, will illustrate what I'm getting at. Then, I'll break down those two stories into a few easily digestible nuggets that you can take with you out into the world. Sound good? Good.

Story 1: Finding my fit

By the fall of 2013, I'd been knocking around the small horror press scene for about five years. During that time, I'd placed a number of stories with various indie horror presses, including a handful of professional sales, and had served at a small publisher as an assistant editor. Even so, I could feel my momentum flagging and found myself at something of a crossroads. Sales came slowly and the press I'd been working with as an editor had gone on indefinite hiatus. All in all, it seemed like the right time to shake things up and try something new. It seemed that it might benefit me to take a more deliberate approach toward professionalism.

I'd joined up with the Horror Writers Association a year or so before then, but hadn't put much more into my membership than my annual dues. I decided that I should change that, and, as luck would have it, around that time, I received a mass email from the organization, soliciting volunteers for two positions: One was a membership verifier, who would review applicants' credentials; the other was the

VOLUME 4

organization's communications and public relations director. Although I'd spent several years as a public relations professional, I applied for the membership verifier position. My reasoning was that it'd be a way to dip my toes further into the organization without overcommitting myself. In other words, the PR director spot sounded like a lot of work. So, I sent a quick note to the contact email, along with my résumé, and expressed my interest in the position.

The response I received, less than an hour after clicking SEND, changed the trajectory of my career. It came from then-president of the Horror Writers Association, Rocky Wood. Rocky thanked me for my interest in volunteering with the HWA, and, having reviewed my qualifications and experience, wondered why I hadn't instead applied for the communications and public relations position.

Two things occurred to me. First, when the president of the organization you're trying to crack into personally invites you to take a position of great responsibility within said organization, it's a good idea to go ahead and take him up on the offer. Second, I wondered if, by sending my résumé along with my original query, whether this was the result I had subconsciously hoped for. I wrote back immediately and said I'd take the job.

I was right. It was a lot of work, and I spent dozens and dozens of hours working on behalf of the HWA and its interests. But it was also a treasure of an experience. For the next year, I immersed myself in all things HWA and remained in almost daily contact with Rocky regarding happenings within the organization, plans he had made for the future, promotional

WRITERS ON WRITING

opportunities and general questions about the genre. Rocky proved to be a wealth of information, advice, perspective and guidance, but he also allowed me to grow into my role within the organization and pursue my own ideas.

The most consequential example of this took shape in the lead-up to the 2014 Bram Stoker Awards. I requested permission from Rocky to send a short list of interview questions to all of our nominees for the purposes of posting the responses at the HWA's official site. I proposed that the series would serve as a way to promote the HWA, the Bram Stoker Awards and our nominees' work. To Rocky's great credit, he saw potential in the idea, agreed, and made sure I had everything I needed to pursue the initiative. I didn't think any of the authors would respond to my questions, but to my surprise, dozens of them did. The interview series became Know a Nominee, and soon I found myself in personal contact with many of the top practitioners of modern dark fiction. I didn't realize it at the time, but this list of contacts would prove invaluable, which leads me to . . .

Story #2: *Shadows Over Main Street*

Shortly after agreeing to serve as the HWA's communications and PR director, I received another career-altering electronic message. This one came from a gentleman by the name of D. Alexander Ward. I honestly don't recall whether he reached out to me via email or through social media, but I'll never forget that he had this crazy idea that we should put together an anthology that would mash up the mythos of H.P.

VOLUME 4

Lovecraft and the fictional town of Mayberry, made famous on *The Andy Griffith Show*.

Before I go any further, you need to understand I'd never met D. Alexander Ward in person or over the internet. Although we'd shared a few tables of contents in genre anthologies, I'd never spoken to him before in my life, and yet here he was, pitching this idea my way, even though neither of us had any experience assembling anthologies.

My first gut reaction—and I've told him this, so I'm not making any news here—was to tell him I wasn't interested. I knew almost nothing about Ward at the time and I thought his strange idea represented an endless array of intellectual property nightmares.

But my wife urged me to see where the opportunity would lead, and I'd be lying if I told you Ward's enthusiasm for the project didn't infect me. It didn't take many conversations with him before it seemed as though doing the book wasn't just possible, but inevitable. I agreed to team up with him, but suggested that we remove the Mayberry link altogether and broaden the theme to include anyplace in small-town America. He agreed to the approach.

The problem was we didn't have a publisher or a reputation for successful execution of such a project, and it seemed our prospects for contacting authors were somewhat limited. The way forward looked bleak, but then it occurred to me that not only did I have a number of contacts on file, but they were among the most talented members of the horror community: Bram Stoker Award nominees. We ran our idea by a number of the authors who had participated in my

WRITERS ON WRITING

Know a Nominee interview series, and before long, the project picked up momentum.

The project eventually became *Shadows Over Main Street*, one of 2015's bestselling and most critically acclaimed horror anthologies. On the strength of what I consider to be a stellar table of contents, the book spent months as a top 10 horror anthology on Amazon (and even briefly occupied the number-one spot), and set the stage for everything that has come since, including our follow-up projects, *Gutted: Beautiful Horror Stories* and *Shadows Over Main Street, Volume 2*. Because Ward took a chance on me, and I took a chance on him and his project, we've had the opportunity to collaborate with some of the most talented horror writers of our time—or any time.

So, What Does This Mean?

As I mentioned in this essay's introduction, it's unlikely your journey as a writer or editor will take the same route as mine did, but I think we can extrapolate some lessons—I'll highlight five for brevity's sake—from my experiences that you can apply to your life. Here we go . . .

Find a mentor. Your first step in building a network should involve finding a person, or persons, who know more about what you hope to achieve than you do. I was lucky. My mentor found me and put me in touch with dozens of other mentors who have helped me along the way.

VOLUME 4

Make yourself useful. It's not enough to join a professional organization like the Horror Writers Association. You have to get involved in the life of the organization. I see it all the time on social media: Some horror writers gripe that they don't get anything out of their yearly HWA dues. Well, I didn't get a whole lot out of my membership either until I got involved. It's easy to heckle from the sidelines. It's not so easy—but it's oh, so gratifying—to use your skills and talents in service of something that's bigger than you are. Just like anything else in life, you get out of it what you put in.

You're networking all the time whether you know it or not. A few months into working on the project that became *Shadows Over Main Street*, I asked D. Alexander Ward what in the world compelled him to reach out to me, a complete stranger, and pitch his project. He said he liked my writing style and, based on some comments that I'd made on social media, he thought I'd be the type of person who would appreciate his idea.

The opportunity that sounds crazy or scary is the opportunity you should pursue. Your date with destiny is probably going to look an awful lot like work. Don't shy away from it. Keep an open mind and go where the energy is, even if it's not what you had in mind. Sometimes it only takes a little finesse to take a good idea into great territory.

None of this replaces working at your craft and delivering a solid product. No matter how much

WRITERS ON WRITING

networking you do, and no matter how successfully you navigate through the publishing community, you still have to put the time and effort in that it takes to make something people want to read. Networking might help you cut through the noise, but once you've done that, you need to make sure you've done the work.

Thanks for taking the time to read this. Now, get out there and hustle!

ARE YOU IN THE MOOD?

SHELDON HIGDON

As WRITERS WE have lots of cool things to make the story, or novel, cooler. Kick-Butt things like theme, symbolism, foreshadowing, atmosphere, tone, and mood. You'll see I didn't include plot, setting, well-rounded characters, dialogue, description, and action. If I missed one, my apologies. Nonetheless, these are very important. Without them you only have a blank page. Without them you can't have the aforementioned kick-butt things like mood and atmosphere. I look at it like this. Plot, setting, well-rounded characters, dialogue, description, and action are the primary colors while theme, symbolism, foreshadowing, atmosphere, tone, and mood are the secondary colors. These secondary add to the primary. Sometimes they add without your knowing, such as theme.

Now before I get going, let me explain what I consider mood to be. Some consider mood and atmosphere to be the same. Some consider mood and tone to be the same. And there is nothing wrong with that. Not at all. I'm only adding my two cents on why I consider mood and atmosphere to be two different

WRITERS ON WRITING

things. Mood and tone as two different things. These items are related, but instead of being brother and sister, they're more like cousins.

Mood and Tone

Mood is how the reader feels about the story. Not plot per se but the connection to it through feelings. Tone is the writer's attitude toward the story and/or reader. Basically, how she or he feels about the story. Tone stays constant throughout the entire novel. However, mood changes throughout the entire novel. By the way, key word here is *feels*.

If you picked up a book and the first page was tense, serious, dark, then the rest of the book will follow suit. The tone is set. It sets the stage. Plot aside, it tells the reader what kind of story they're about to read. However, if its tone is dark and serious, can humor appear in it? Yes, of course. But these humorous bits don't change the overall tone. They're simply moments of mood. A brief moment of laughing, happiness. Action aside, mood helps create a peak and valley effect, up and down, like the hills of a roller coaster. But not the only effect. Sometimes the hill can go way up and then plateau. Or it could go way up and then go right back down. It can vary.

Let's take a paragraph from Stephen King's *The Shining*. A scene where Danny is in room 217. *shudders* Remember that room, right?

> "Time passed. And he was just beginning to relax, just beginning to realize that the door must be unlocked and he could go, when the

VOLUME 4

years-damp, bloated, fish-smelling hands closed softly around his throat and he was turned implacably around to stare into that dead and purple face" (218, King).

So how is the above paragraph related to mood?

The first part of the sentence, "Time passed. And he was just beginning to relax, just beginning to realize that the door must be unlocked and he could go . . . ", creates a mood of relief not only in the character, which it shows since it's the character's point of view, but in the reader, as well. Danny, and the reader, feels that the scary moment he lived through before this paragraph is now over. After all, time has passed, so that means nothing has happened for a bit, right? He's also beginning to relax. He can catch his breath. He's also realizing that the door to room 217 is unlocked and that he can go. Freedom! No more monsters. Yay! But wait, is it really over? " . . . when the years-damp, bloated, fish-smelling hands closed softly around his throat and he was turned implacably around to stare into that dead and purple face." Not by a long shot! Now Danny's mood and the reader's have changed to terror, fear. Mood, or feelings, rose and fell in the same paragraph. A roller coaster effect. Up and down.

The mood is caused by the plot in this scene, but Danny's mood adds to the plot, which is a realistic reaction. Secondary adding to the primary. Imagine if Danny's mood was nonchalant. This scene wouldn't work the same. And the reader wouldn't have much investment in this scene or Danny, as well.

Remember the old Mood Rings? It was a cheap costume ring with a fake gem on top that would change

WRITERS ON WRITING

colors according to the mood you were in at the time you wore it. So green could have been envy or something. I don't recall what the colors meant but you get my meaning. Moods change. You ever wonder what kind of mood a coworker is in while heading to work? You hope they're in a good mood so your work day will be good. If not then your day will be . . .

If your work day is in an office and it's mundane every day then that's the tone of your office. Same thing every day. Same dress code. Same cubicles. Boring, right? Type, answer calls, type, answer calls, check for the latest TPS Report, answer calls, type . . . . That's the tone. As a worker you can change your mood *within* the office about your work or job. How you feel about it.

Or what if it's your honeymoon and you're at the airport with your new husband waiting to board a plane to Cancun. You're happy. Excited. Elated. The future is wide open. Then your cell rings and it's the police. Your father has been in an accident. Sorry, but he didn't make it. Happiness gone. Excitement deflated. Your mood has changed in a single moment. Single scene. But what about the people around you? The businessmen and women scurrying about? Pilots rushing by with suitcases pulled behind them. Passengers wait, sitting at computer stations, charging their phones and laptops before they fly off. The tone of the airport is the same. It hasn't changed because of the new bride's phone call from the police. It still goes on. Again, the new bride's mood changed within the airport. Within the tone.

Now let's say a terrorist attack happens at either the workplace or the airport—and we know that these

VOLUME 4

horrible things happen unfortunately—would the tone change? Assuming these two examples are part of a book where the tone is thrilling, suspenseful, action-packed, then no. Because the tone of the two imaginary books would carry on as planned. The tone wouldn't change to humorous unless that was the tone from the get go. If the tone was humorous, or funny from the start, then these two examples would be brief moments of mood in the novel.

Mood and Atmosphere

I consider atmosphere to be associated with setting not mood. You've seen when someone in a movie lights candles in a bedroom and turns off the lights and throws on some Marvin Gaye or Barry White? Well, what are they doing? They're creating atmosphere. It's the character(s) who'll reflect the mood in this setting. And that mood would probably be love or lust, depending.

If I ask you to give me a spooky setting at night, for a horror novel, what will your answer be? Probably a haunted house or graveyard. Now if I ask you to describe them you'll probably tell me that the house is old, dilapidated. Has a lean to it. Paint is chipped, peeled, and faded. Roof sags. Doors creak. A flight of wooden steps moan beneath footfalls. Cobwebs adorn nearly every corner. Torn, yellowed wallpaper cover weak walls. The air is musty. Stale. And what of the graveyard? Some headstones are broken, cracked. Covered in moss. Others lie in the dead grass as ankle high fog rolls over them. Inscriptions worn away from weather. Wilted flowers sit before them. The air is cool,

WRITERS ON WRITING

damp. The graveyard is silent. The bare trees' arthritic fingers spread out creating shards of broken shadows across it all. The wrought iron fence is rusted but still keeps in the dead. For now.

What you gave me isn't mood but atmosphere. Atmosphere describes a place, setting. Mood describes a person's feelings about someone or something. Could be a loved one, a car, or a place like a graveyard or haunted house.

So if you were put into either the haunted house or graveyard at night your mood would probably be fearful or anxious. Once you left, your mood would change to relief, happiness. But the haunted house and graveyard would remain the same.

Speaking of haunted houses let's use a snippet of another example, but this time from Shirley Jackson's *The Haunting of Hill House*.

> "Sitting up in the two beds beside each other, Eleanor and Theodora reached out between and held hands tight; the room was brutally cold and thickly dark. From the room next door, the room which until that morning had been Theodora's, came the steady low sound of a voice babbling, too low for words to be understood, too steady for disbelief. Holding hands so hard that each of them could feel the other's bones, Eleanor and Theodora listened, and the low, steady sound went on and on, and the voice lifting sometimes to a breath, going on and on. Then, without warning, there was a little laugh, and the small gurgling laugh broke through the babbling, and rose as it laughed, on

VOLUME 4

up and up the scale, and then broke off suddenly in a little painful gasp, and the voice went on.

Theodora's grasp loosened, and tightened, and Eleanor, lulled for a minute by the sounds, started and looked across to where Theodora ought to be in the darkness, and then thought, screamingly, Why is it dark? *Why is it dark?*" (119-120, Jackson)

There are a few things happening in this example. In the beginning we are set up for the ending, with Eleanor and Theodora reaching out and holding hands. We're also given a tad bit of atmosphere with the room being "brutally cold and thickly dark." And the mood? It's nerve-wracking, not only because we, and the characters, are in the dark but because of the unknown babbling voice, at first low and steady then increasingly becoming louder, coming from the room next door. Shirley Jackson has created mood with repetition.

"The low, steady sound went on and on, and the voice lifting sometimes to a breath, going on and on."

She continues in the second paragraph, but this time reminding us, with repetition, that we're in the dark. " . . . looked across to where Theodora ought to be in the darkness, and then thought, screamingly, Why is it dark? *Why is it dark?*"

What I've given you here is only a piece of a fairly long scene. The strange voice continues babbling, then rising and falling, on and on throughout the remaining scene building to the point where Eleanor can't stand it anymore. Our hearts are racing. For Eleanor bravery

WRITERS ON WRITING

comes out of character, possibly necessity, and in the end she's had enough. With the lights back on the way they had been left, she comes face to face with a shocking revelation. I'm not going to ruin the surprise for you, so if you haven't read this novel, or know of this scene, you should search it out, and not only see how the mood escalates, but experience Eleanor's terrifying discovery with her.

Earlier I spoke about the roller coaster effect, the up and down feeling that mood can create, but here it didn't do that, instead it kept rising (and continues to do so in the rest of the scene.) The coaster took us up that first high hill. The clickity clack clickity clack of the chains pulling us and the characters along. It's a tall hill. So tall that Eleanor can't take it anymore. We can't take it anymore either. Eventually we get to the hill's crest. That's when Eleanor's discovery hits her, us. From here the mood could speed downward or flatten out. But it'll change again. We and the characters just don't know when or how.

No matter what genre you write, mood is necessary when it comes to not only the character but to your story, as well. Above I've shown how it's used in characters. How mood can change within a scene like at the airport. Or how it can change because of a person like a coworker, or how a place can affect your mood like a haunted house. A place can cause mood to change or a person can change mood. Or a person can willingly change their mood depending on that other person or place. Like working in the cubicle and typing all day, forgetting the cover to the TPS Report. How often have you been around people who have a negative mood and so you keep a positive mood to

VOLUME 4

keep their infection away? And since my opinion is that mood is tied to the character, it can affect the story.

If you have a character that is prone to mood swings (changing moods) then imagine the scenarios she or he may find themselves in. It would create many tense or humorous scenes that could change the story and affect other characters involved. Talk about ups and downs.

In the beginning of this I mentioned that the key word was feel, or feeling(s), and when it comes down to it, if the character reveals their mood throughout the novel accordingly, then the reader will feel with them. Remember, mood is how the reader feels about the story, and how they feel about the story depends on the character(s) and her or his mood.

"But isn't mood just another way of saying how the reader cares about the character? And because they care they'll read on?"

In order to care about the character there's more to it than just mood, or how the reader feels about the story because of the character's own mood within it. In order to care the character has to be fully fleshed out. Realistic. Have flaws. Strengths. Internal and external scars. Not perfect but perfect. Y'know? Someone who saves a cat from a tree but isn't a cat person because of her or his allergies. And added to this would be mood. Is she or he worried, nervous about the cat stuck in the tree? Maybe this person is afraid of heights. How does this character feel? I want to know this person who saves a cat even though they aren't a cat person or are afraid of high places. Like I said previously, secondary color added to the primary color.

WHAT IF EVERY NOVEL IS A HORROR NOVEL?

STEVE DIAMOND

LET ME ASK you a simple question:
What do you think "Horror" is?
I ask this question a lot. In fact, it's become a habit of mine whenever I'm on panels or when people are asking me what I write. You see, I write Horror. Generally, when people hear this, and I ask them what they *think* that means, they go straight to blood and scream-soaked slasher films and torture flicks. In fact, I'd say a good chunk of the time these same people have a look of disgust on their faces when they answer me. For the longest time, this sort of response actually got me down. How could people only think Horror was that one thing? How could people not see how excellent and varied Horror actually is?

So, then, what *is* Horror? If it isn't just the genre that only deals in the spray of blood and the accompanying screams, then what exactly is it?

Therein rests part of the problem. The word, "genre." You see, when I began thinking of Horror less as a genre, and more of an element, it all began to click in my head.

VOLUME 4

One of the standard definitions of Horror is the strong feeling of fear, dread, and shock. Now, is there anything in that definition that excludes it from any other genre? Or limits it to one special area? Nowhere does the definition state Horror can *only* be used in certain situations. If anything, that definition of Horror should be *liberating*. All the tethers that bind your impressions of Horror should be severed by that definition. Horror belongs everywhere, in every story you read and write. Hitchcock, Laurel K Hamilton, Jim Butcher, Douglas Adams, Tolkien, Agatha Christie . . . Horror is in all of their works.

Several years ago, when I was struggling with the blanket perceptions that come with being labeled "only a Horror writer," I began looking at all the novels I'd read and asking myself a simple question: Is there Horror in this novel? Look closely there. I didn't ask if the novels *were* Horror novels, but if Horror was *in* those novels.

Let's start with a novel by the guy who got me reading Fantasy, Terry Brooks. I read *The Elfstones of Shannara* back in 1992 for the first time. *Elfstones* is Epic Fantasy that contains all the classic tropes of that genre. An epic quest with a magic sword. A Dark One that needs to be slain to protect the world. Budding romance. It *also* has legions of demons that want to break into the world and kill everything. In fact, most of the novel is about demons stalking our protagonists, killing them one-by-one as they flee in terror.

Yeah. There is definitely some Horror in there.

One of my favorite authors is Joe Lansdale, who has been known to write a Horror story or two. But one of my favorite novels of his is *The Thicket*. It's a

WRITERS ON WRITING

Western (and, in my opinion, one of the best Westerns ever written). It's about a boy who hires two bounty hunters to track down his kidnapped sister. And yet, the horrors that are perpetuated by the "villains" and described in the novel often stretch the story into definite Horror realms.

Think of Horror as an element that you can add to any story you write. Think of it as an element in any story you are reading. George RR Martin? Yep, he has Horror (and I don't just mean in his pure Horror stories). Michael Connelly? Totally. James SA Corey? Come on, now you're making it easy on me. Tom Clancy? Have you read *Without Remorse*?

Movies and literature have had a long-standing, secret series of affairs with Horror, and I think this is because of what Horror adds to, or accentuates within established genres. When I write anything, conflict is key. There MUST be conflict in the story. There MUST be love and fear for the main characters. What I feel Horror does better than anything is make you fear for the lives and sanity of the main characters.

When you are in book nine of a series, how much do you actually fear for the main characters? It's a bit like watching your favorite TV show and knowing your favorite character is perfectly safe because they appear in the preview for the next episode. A fair bit of the tension is robbed, isn't it? The tone of the entire show or novel is changed, and often times the author is forced to manufacture other sources of conflict and fear to keep the reader invested.

Let's compare this to pure Horror novels, which in large-part are stand-alone stories. This, by itself, takes away your comfort in knowing that your favorite

VOLUME 4

characters will survive until the next book in the series. Guys like King and McCammon do this extremely well. Most of the time, as readers, we simply *don't know* if the characters are going to make it. And if, by some miracle, they *do* survive . . . will that be a fate worse than death?

Think about that for a minute. Think about how you can add those strong feelings of fear, dread, and shock into your own stories. What does it do to them? When you add Horror to your Fantasy novel, what happens to your story, and to your readers? How about your Sci-Fi story? Your Western? Even your Romance novel? My, my. How the stakes change when you do that.

You may ask, "But, will people accept that? Have authors really been doing this all the while?"

For decades (centuries, even), Fantasy authors have been taking monsters and adding them to their stories. Not just to give the heroes something to fight. Monsters exist to hold up an imperfect mirror to ourselves to remind us how far we can fall, and how much worse humans can be than monsters. Yeah, these are Horror elements in your Fantasy stories.

Westerns are all about fear of the unknown, and living on the frontier in isolation. These same themes are what make Horror so amazing. I've just described most Westerns . . . and Lovecraft. And maybe you are even thinking, "Hey, that sounds like Sci-Fi, too." You'd be right. I mean . . . we've all seen *Alien*, right?

My point is this: anything you write, you can add Horror to. It's simply another tool in your toolbox for creating stories. It will change the tone of your story, but maybe that's what your novel needs to separate it

WRITERS ON WRITING

from all the other ones just like it. When I'm selling my novel, *Residue*, it is very simple for me to say, "Oh it's a YA Horror novel." Or, if they say they don't like Horror (weirdos) I can say, "This is a YA Paranormal Thriller." It's easy and it's true, because *Residue* is all of those things.

Horror isn't a limited factor. It's the element in fiction that raises the stakes in everything you write. Whether we are talking about the supernatural, or the psychological, the hack 'n' slash, or the monsters (both unnatural and the human variety), we can and should include them in any story we write. Adding Horror elements to other genres keeps your writing fresh, the conflict real, and the readers legitimately invested.

Remember, just like people aren't made up of one single thing, neither is Horror. That variety is what makes things interesting. So, try putting some Horror in your stories . . .

. . . I promise you'll love it. Cross my heart and . . . well, you know.

DESCRIPTION
YOU CAN'T WIN, SO DON'T PLAY

PATRICK FREIVALD

THERE ARE AS many ways to write as there are writers. Writing as an art is inherently subjective, and that's why a lot of writing advice is crap. What works for you might not work for someone else, and vice-versa. That said, if you're writing with the intent to be published, there are often a lot of conventions beyond the grammatical and syntactic rules of English that you shouldn't break without intent and purpose. These range from little petty things like "never use adverbs" and "don't use similar names for your characters"—both of which exist for good reason and can be violated for good reason—to even pettier things like "don't use towards, forwards, and backwards when you can use toward, forward, and backward." But they also encompass Big, Important Things like not overwriting.

Instead of delving into a detailed discussion of what overwriting may or may not be, especially since there's more than one kind and a lot of disagreement on the subject, let's do an experiment.

WRITERS ON WRITING

Read this description once through:

"Brian stood 6'2" at full height, and looming over the ornate wooden table he still towered next to Sarah in her seat. His button-down tweed jacket took up half her chair-back and forced her to lean too far forward, the preposterous Victorian throwback at odds with his bright red Nikes and knee-length gym shorts. The big man's green and white striped shirt batted against the side of her face, an assault of rough polyester weave every time the wind blew through the open, stained-glass window. His arm hair tickled her shoulder, warm and unwelcomed. Steady, even breaths blasted her with the fetid stench of that morning's chimichanga, cumin, sour meat and sour cream mingling with the faint, rich smell of furniture polish and the sweeter notes of her floral perfume. Her stomach turned."

Okay, now cover it up and don't look at it, then answer these five questions about the scene conjured in your mind by the paragraph. Don't worry about being right, just being truthful to the picture in your head.

1. Is Brian muscular, or fat?
2. What color are the stripes on his shirt, and are they vertical or horizontal?
3. Was it a beef or pork chimichanga?
4. Where are they?
5. What time of day is it?

Of course this wasn't a fair test. The only question you can actually answer is the first half of number two. And yet, in attempting to answer them you'll find that you've pictured the scene in your mind in such a manner that there are a gazillion details you didn't read but that your

VOLUME 4

brain supplied anyway. The color of the table and whatever makes it ornate, some vague notion of what Sarah looks like, the shape and size of the room (based on some assumption of where you think they might be), what sort of flowers her perfume smelled like.

The ratio of details you actually read to details that your brain supplied is probably somewhere far south of one to a thousand, and some of the details your brain conjured almost definitely directly contradicts something I'd described.

And this is why a lot of writers overwrite.

I could bog down the description with a lot more detail—it's a T-shirt and it's way too big on him, the table was an oval five feet across and ten feet long with a swirling pattern cut along its edge like molding in an old house and four legs cut like lion's feet with six claws apiece, and it was definitely a steak chimichanga, and he's flabby and soft and pale, and blah blah blah. And none of those things would actually make the scene more vivid to the vast majority of readers, who are probably going to skim them and make up their own picture anyway. Even the reader who faithfully reads every word will end up with a picture in their head quite different from the one I intended, no matter how much detail I pour into the scene.

Overwriting is about control. Like a movie director, writers want to conjure very specific images in the reader's mind, paint in all the little details to get what's in the author's head through the page and into the readers unadulterated. It's not a game you can win, so it isn't one you should play—given enough detail to be unambiguous, and you'll have bogged down your plot and bored your reader to tears.

WRITERS ON WRITING

The truth is that nobody reads your book and gets out of it precisely what you want them to. Books aren't movies, and you have zero control over what images appear in the reader's mind when they read a particular sentence or turn of phrase. "Jim chewed on the pencil a while before taking it out of his mouth and scrawling his name on the paper." There's not a lot there, but your brain probably made it a plain, wooden pencil rather than a mechanical one, Jim right-handed instead of left and white-toothed instead of a hard yellow-gray, and the paper white and blank except for his messy signature.

. . . and unless any of those missing details are important to the plot or characterization, it's perfectly acceptable to let the reader assume them however they want to and keep on trucking with the narrative. The important information here is that Jim is apparently nervous or at least hesitant, and after you borrow his pencil you should probably wash your hands. The rest is just filler, and including it will both slow down your story with irrelevant details and do nothing whatsoever to improve the accuracy of what the reader is picturing vis-à-vis what you wanted them to picture.

Any given person, object, or scene can be explained with somewhere around three details—too few is fine if the details aren't important so it doesn't matter if the reader gets it totally wrong, but you want to have enough to anchor the mood and the emotional impact because, after all, emotional impact is why you're describing whatever it is in the first place (you might protest at this point that you're describing the table as ornate because the library it's in has ornate tables and not because of some sort of emotional hook; but that's

VOLUME 4

not true, because you set the scene in the library—that library—for a reason, and that reason probably has nothing whatsoever to do with the exact size, shape, and color of the tables. If it does, because the secret compartment in one of them becomes important later, then of course you need to include enough detail to give the reader the impression that they could have picked up on that were they just a little more perceptive. But if it doesn't, cut it or gloss over it).

Describing characters follows the same rules. Exact heights, weights, hair shade, and so forth generally get in the way of narrative flow. Depending on the book and the mood you're trying to evoke, "a hulking, square-faced mofo with a bad rug and a Burt Reynolds mustache" could be more than enough detail, even without any indication of hair color, eye color, what clothes or jewelry this person is wearing, and so forth. Maybe you want to add that he smells like onions and baby powder; make that determination when you need to.

It's not that all the detail doesn't add flavor and character, it's that you can pluck all the right strings without it and end up with a stronger, more vibrant story for its absence. The same story with fewer words means that your reader is more heavily immersed, more effectively swept along, and I'll point out again that every rule can be broken. In *American Gods* (or maybe *Anansi Boys*) Neil Gaiman spends a couple of pages describing a tree, and it's one of the most kickass descriptions of a tree in the history of descriptions of trees. He could have lived without it, and the story would have been fine, but damn was it a cool moment. I'm glad he left it in.

WRITERS ON WRITING

So for all my talk about what not to include, there are things that you should include that a lot of writers don't do well enough. A scene becomes vivid when the reader engages at least two and preferably three senses, so pick which three senses best evoke the scene and hammer them good.

Sight is the easy one, the most predominant, and rightly so—humans are primarily visual creatures and that's how we take in most of our information. Stick to a few pertinent details and let the reader fill in the rest and you can't go too far wrong here. If you're anchored in a POV you don't need to say that the character saw something, you can just describe it happening—and the same is true of other sensory verbs most of the time.

Smell is a funny one because we often say what things smell like (onions and baby powder, for example) without describing what those smells smell like. Onions can smell great, sweet and caramelized in soup or on a fancy hamburger, or they can smell pungent and acrid and sour. Baby powder smells chalky by default, so maybe that doesn't need an additional descriptor. But there's a noted and important difference between "he gave off a light bouquet like caramelized onions and baby powder" and "his armpits reeked like rotting onions inadequately masked with baby powder."

We often shortchange sound except in dialogue, and when we don't our descriptions tend to be matter-of-fact. "Frank couldn't get back to sleep because of the birds chirping outside his window" is probably fine in most cases, though "Frank couldn't get back to sleep through the piercing trills and whistles of the birds

VOLUME 4

outside his window" follows the same general rule that smell does—geese sound a whole lot different than chickadees or cockatoos, and while it might not be important it's more vivid if you not only make them too loud but are specific in the manner in which they're annoying Frank. The annoyance is the important detail, the rest just helps you get there.

If you want a crash course on how to incorporate touch as a sense in your writing, you can't go too far wrong by reading a couple of romance novels. Obviously the types of sensations in a thriller or horror novel or romance novel might be very different, and how much the sense of touch is emphasized will vary a great deal between genres, but it doesn't hurt to start with authors notorious for overdoing it and then paring back what you learn to a suitable level for what you're trying to do.

Of the five major senses, that leaves us with taste, which (technique-wise) isn't much different from smell, except that for some reason it's a whole lot trickier. It's easy to overdo taste because everybody has a pretty good idea of what things taste like, unless you're trying to describe something exotic, in which case you're almost forced to use analogies to more familiar things. The vast majority of readers will know what a cherry tomato tastes like, so unless for some reason this cherry tomato tastes different than a standard cherry tomato, you can probably get away with skipping taste altogether in favor of the other senses as it pops in the chewer's mouth and squirts sweetly acidic liquid against his teeth. Or whatever. We often use incorrect but somehow appropriate words to describe taste, like the thick, cottony taste of just-

WRITERS ON WRITING

woke-up-with-a-hangover mouth (which of course doesn't taste anything like cotton).

In describing any of these senses, it's important to keep in mind the exercise we started with: your reader isn't going to get out of it what you want them to. Let's take the oniony guy above. The first description is weird but not unpleasant, while the second is recoil-worthy and gross, and the precise smell is not nearly as important as the reaction you want the reader and the character to have to that smell. The details don't matter; they *can't* matter, because the reader is going to get most of them wrong anyway.

What color was that guy's shirt in the first example, again? His shoes? What was his name? What three things did his chimichanga-breath smell like? How tall was he? It wouldn't surprise me if you couldn't reliably answer most of these without double-checking, but I'd be shocked if you couldn't tell me how his looming over Sarah made her feel.

It's at once aggravating and freeing to realize how little control an author has over what the reader is going to experience. We put all these words on the page with care and precision only to have the imagery, meaning, and details trampled by every single person who reads them. We're not movie directors; we can't control what the reader sees and hears the way they can control what goes on the screen and out the speakers. Every reader's experience is going to be different both from what we experience and what other readers experience, and there's not a damn thing we can do about it.

But by recognizing and embracing that powerlessness we can turn our attention and our craft

VOLUME 4

to what we can control, which fortunately for us is what truly matters: the emotional impact. Focus on that, and make every word on the page serve it.

LONG NIGHT'S JOURNEY INTO ... THIS?
A FIRST-TIME NOVELIST'S ODYSSEY

WILLIAM GORMAN

WRITERS TAKE STRANGE journeys. Some of us plot these journeys out carefully, others just fly along by the seat of their pants. We find ourselves navigating from point A to point B, from B to C, then from C on to D and E and to F and even beyond. Then we find out the journey *still* isn't over.

First off, let me say that I think writing is a form of art. It can be done almost anywhere. But it can be messy. There's a business side to it also. It takes time, and practice. You have to love to read—a lot. With novel-length fiction there might be plenty of research to do in the beginning, and some of us often live with characters in our head for weeks or months before actually jotting anything down. At some point you have to come up with a good title that sparks the imagination. Then there's the rough, first draft . . . working every day and coaxing it out of you, stutter stepping at times, second-guessing yourself. Breaking the paralysis of self-doubt and following through and

VOLUME 4

at last pulling it all together into a finished manuscript, only to have to revise and repeat and revise again. Even then, is it ever truly finished? I mean, what sane person does these types of things?

No comment.

In my own case, I started out when I was young, writing short stories for various small press magazines during the big horror boom of the 1980s and early '90s, created in the wake of Stephen King's wild popularity. After collecting countless rejections, I sold most of those scary stories and saw them published, too—all except for one (the yarn in question was called *Widow's Walk*, about a Victorian-era bride with a particularly nasty curse on her lovely, undying head. It was accepted and slated for publication when the woman who ran the 'zine passed away rather suddenly at a young age. Next, after a proper period of mourning for her *and* for my story, it was again picked up and ready to go when this latest publisher up and disappeared with funding for the project, including money some of the authors had given in advance for extra copies, which included fifteen bucks of my own. After that fiasco, a second woman died upon agreeing to publish *Widow's Walk*, a much older lady this time, leaving her magazine's fate in limbo and leading rumors to swirl throughout the small press hidey-holes that perhaps my horror tale was *itself* cursed. But that's another story altogether). For better or worse, I decided here to try my hand at my first novel. As it happened I was corresponding with Clive Barker around then, getting autographs and exchanging letters with him through a California P.O. Box, sending him some of my published stuff, and in one of his notes

WRITERS ON WRITING

to me he typed the words: *Now it's time for your novel.* So I set about it . . . because when Clive Barker says to do it, you do it. And a grand tome it would be, one about grief and aching darkness, about pulling oneself up from that darkness, and ultimately making a stand against supernatural evil.

I wrote fifty pages or so and hit a wall, stopped dead in the water, began sinking like a stone, like that tourist's body in Aickman's *The Wine-Dark Sea*. I left the pages in a stack and let it sit awhile, allowed the words to gel for a few days, then I read it all back.

It wasn't there, what I had written—what I *needed* to have written. Not there. I didn't have it. Didn't have my own authentic voice yet. I had the characters, sure, had their backgrounds and dialogue, motivations, their loves and hatreds and their fears. I knew them intimately, had been living with them in my head for weeks and months, but I didn't understand what I was writing about. Didn't know enough about aching grief and darkness, I guess, or finding the courage to make that ultimate stand. Not yet.

Short stories were a lot different than a full-length novel, I realized.

So I put it aside and worked on something else. I gathered a bunch of spooky local legends and strange myths from my Illinois hometown and compiled them into a little collection, *Ghost Whispers*, the first of its kind for my neck of the woods. The kind that hopefully gives off an unholy chill just having the volume close by on the nightstand. Anyway, while it was in progress I would send fragments of stories to a ghostlore scholar I knew, a professor of folk heritage and oral storytelling at Southern Illinois University, to see what

VOLUME 4

he thought of them. He kept writing back and telling me, *No no no, you're forcing it. Not being yourself. Do over.* So I'd rewrite it and send it again, until finally (quite by accident, once I had stopped overthinking things) he wrote back and told me, *That's it, right there. The last story you sent. You've found it. That is your voice. It's a true and natural voice, one the reader will always trust. Write everything in that voice from now on.* So I did, because he was right. After the ghost story collection was completed, I pulled the stack of novel pages out of a desk drawer.

I was ready, it seemed. A bit older. I'd spent several months delving into the grief and aching darkness of my own hometown, writing about tragic death, forgotten souls left behind in shadow-haunted cemeteries, and about unquiet spirits which lingered still, hungering after all these years. I had even lost people close to *me* during that time. This was it.

The odyssey recommenced.

I went through my manuscript and kept the good stuff, jettisoned all the rest, and then began anew. Because that's what writing is: sifting through the garbage and tossing it, getting it to be less and less garbage, getting it to where it isn't bad. Working every day at it. *Coaxing.* I had sketched a very rough outline for the book, mere bones over which my story would be draped, and now I let the thing meander where it wanted. It was hard going—writing always is for me—but after a while the novel started to come alive, growing, morphing, refusing to stand still.

Its skeletal outline was always there, though, to draw me back in if I found myself wandering too far out.

WRITERS ON WRITING

This was well after the horrors of 9/11, but I set the novel's time period at just before 9/11 for my own nostalgic purposes. I let the narrative lead me as I created it, trusting the process, looking forward to the culmination. Doing it all in my newly discovered voice. I changed the title to *Blackwater Val* and it just felt right. The original title, *Malignant Regions*, became the name of my main character's fictitious first novel in the book. I wrote mostly at night, because I'm a creature of habit and that's what I've always done. Write at night. But I suffer from migraines, so the computer screen was sometimes unbearable. Frequent breaks became necessary. Mass quantities of Dr Pepper were consumed.

One method I used to keep pushing forward was to visualize an actual physical copy of my book, the published product, to imagine the weight of it in my hands, the feel of it between its own two covers.

Later in the game I developed a bad habit of revising things as I went along, going back and changing words, second-guessing myself. Distractions, distractions. More stutter stepping. Don't do this if you can help it . . . unless it works better for you, of course.

When I finally finished *Val* and put the last period in place, the real revisions began. I went through and trimmed it, nipping here and tucking there. Started over at the beginning and did it again, going over it with a fine-tooth comb. My eyes tired from the tedious experience, my mind wearied of it. I grew to hate the manuscript, and my own ineptitude as a writer, but at long last it was done. I could do no more with it, or so I thought.

I started sending it out, once I'd broken that

VOLUME 4

paralysis of self-doubt yet again, and quickly learned of a terrible, dreaded thing called "the synopsis." It seems most publishers and agents want to look at a condensed summary of the entire submission, and not just the blurb-sized kind either—some want a one-page synopsis, or a three-pager, or the full ten-pager. The pits of the underworld bubbled up around me, calling my name; I could hear the howls and infernal laughter, and ignored it as best I could. In time, I found my publisher. Or they found me, one or the other. Excitement flowed, contracts were discussed and signed, and good wishes were shared all around. I breathed a sigh. All of the hard work was about to pay off.

Then I was paired with an editor who informed me that new rounds of rewriting would soon begin.

What fresh hell is this? I remember thinking. Had I come all this way, toiled and agonized and struggled through my seemingly endless journey, just to arrive at *this*?

The answer was yes. I worked on it over that winter. There were disagreements on some of the cuts, because we didn't see eye to eye on everything, but I made most of the changes suggested. Not all. An extra four to five thousand words fell away, and the novel ended up being tighter, leaner than before. Now it was truly ready. A publication date was set for the following spring. More waiting began.

My book cover for *Blackwater Val* was ultimately revealed, and a gem of a cover it was indeed. I loved it then and I love it now. Love the feel of it in my hands.

From the initial outset of this odyssey to its long-awaited climax, almost five years had gone by. Good

WRITERS ON WRITING

grief. In hindsight, I must say that I lucked out and landed with a great publisher (you know who you are, JM). The book was well-received, and some readers have told me how they were moved to tears by my story.

Since then, I have come to several conclusions. They are thus:

Writers take strange journeys. Messy ones. Writing is about not overthinking things. It's about sifting through the garbage, getting it to be less and less garbage. It's about being yourself, finding your own authentic voice. Once you do that, I believe you'll never have to wait for inspiration again. Fear of rejection? Get over it now, because you're going to be rejected. We all are. A friend of mine, mystery writer C. Hope Clark, was rejected seventy-one times by agents and then another dozen or so times total before selling her first novel. Never give up. Just seclude yourself and make the time to write; it doesn't matter in what genre, or on what subject. Coax that first draft out of yourself, then revise, craft it and polish it. Be prepared to revise it again. And yet again. Don't get too distracted or discouraged. Tap your deepest emotions until you have an extraordinary story down. You will need at least one good person to use as a sounding board, to let them read the work and give feedback on it. A different perspective. Remember, wonderful things happen by accident sometimes. Your novel will be continually in a state of change while you write it, growing, borrowing from other things and morphing, refusing to stand still. Real writers stick with it and keep chipping away until it's done, until that last period is in place. Persistence is the key, or so I've been

VOLUME 4

told. And if you find yourself getting bogged down with it all, just visualize the finished book, imagine the weight of it in your hands, the feel of it between its own two covers. It helps.

When you finally hold that completed novel in your grasp, when someone tells you they were moved to tears by the story within, or by your heart-stopping ending, you'll realize as I did that all the *fresh hell* you went through was worth it. Well, that's about all I can say.

Oh yes, one more thing. Watch out for bad advice.

There's plenty of it out there, a veritable reliquary of bad advice. A romance author on social media once told me to never write anything more than fifty thousand words, *ever*, in any genre, because most poor readers couldn't cope with something that big. Not in this day and age.

Wow. Right? Sorry, lady, but some of my favorite books—the ones I love and that have stuck with me for years and years—have been books of a hundred thousand words or greater.

Avoid bad advice at all costs. Once you are ready, once you've learned the basics, the mechanics of writing, and you've found your voice, do what you want. Don't worry about word length until you have to, but don't go wild with it either. Don't worry about what's trending, or about "kill your darlings" or any of the other worn-out metaphors and clichéd catch-phrases making the rounds. The odyssey belongs to you, to tackle and conquer however you may.

In the end, the best advice I can give is this: don't take anyone's advice, including mine. Just write with passion. Write what you're passionate about and make

WRITERS ON WRITING

that passion spill off the pages and into the reader. Make them want more. Try to write every day (or night—Dr Pepper helps) if you can, to keep the forward momentum going. Other than that, do whatever the hell you want to do. Plot your own course, or simply wing it as you go along. You are the master of your own journey, after all . . .

And who am I to give advice?

I AM SETTING

J.S. BREUKELAAR

SHIRLEY JACKSON'S *The Haunting of Hill House* is one of my favorite haunted house novels of all time. Those familiar with the novel will know that the whole world of Hill House is made, as John Gardner says, in a "single coherent gesture, as a potter makes a pot, or as Coleridge puts it, copied from the creators' infinite mind, in the process of the infinite, I AM."

What this I AM means in terms of setting is that the world of your novel, whether it is set in a haunted house or on a distant planet, needs to be continuous and in conflict with character and plot. The effect is that the world not only feels believable and true, but is a world—no matter how strange or foreign—containing characters and experiences that break our hearts and sear our souls. Characters require our absolute belief in them and setting is the crucible of that trust, that connection. As Herman Melville wrote in *The Confidence Man,* set on a nominally haunted steam boat on the Mississippi River, our first and last job as writers is to "present another world, but one to which we feel the tie."

WRITERS ON WRITING

Fiction at its most complex, and we writers of dark fiction inhabit that realm, is an art of becoming, of transformation—horrifying or rapturous—and the locus of this transformative power of fiction is place. When we write place well, we immerse readers in settings that feel so real that they become us. Both reader and author internalize them at some level, and become better or different, in the certain knowledge that Westeros, or London Below, or The Sprawl, or that Galaxy Far Far Away is a There, a There that existed before us and will exist after we are gone. When setting works, it should speak that simple truth. When setting doesn't work, it's often because it seems to be imposed from the outside, from a utilitarian vantage point that reduces the characters to chess pieces or action figures and the author to a set-designer.

Full disclosure: I was dragged across countries and hemispheres as a child, so setting, or place, is a subject dear to my writer's heart. I learned very early on not to take any place for granted. It is this estrangement that impacts the fictional worlds I create. But feeling out of place comes with the territory of being a writer, so even if your fiction is set, like Shirley Jackson's, right in your back yard, maybe there are ways that you, too, can make it strange.

1: Setting is action.

Setting is where the action takes place, yes, but the separation between the inner world of the character and the outer world of the story is always contested ground. Every scene in your chapter or story should in

VOLUME 4

some way place the characters in an uneasy relationship with the setting that is a projection of the psychic, emotional, and inter-personal obstacles the story throw at them. Beginning writers have a tendency to look at setting as static—the sun glistening on the lake, the snowflakes whirling, and so on. That's all very well and good, but every 'act' of glistening, every moment of whirling, should have consequences. In other words, the setting has, no less than the characters, a job to do over and above creating atmosphere, and that is to escalate the action. If the sun glistens on the lake then the consequence of that should be that the character must visor their hands over their eyes to peer more closely into the shadows. The whirling snowflakes should sting the cheeks of your character, or mingle with her tears, or with the ash from the cabin in the woods she just set on fire. Setting, as the inimitable Dorothy Alison says, is your door into the story, inasmuch as it is your character's desire out of it, and your job is to find that opening.

I set my novel *Aletheia* in a remote lake town, struggling to forget its dark past. When a hard-scrabble clan of trouble-makers, led by Thettie Harpur, returns to the town in their flotilla of dirty boats, the major story conflict is immediately obvious: 'there goes the neighborhood.' But I tried to make all aspects of setting consequential to that conflict, to create a world in terms that escalate the action in the opening scenes:

> *By the time Thettie neared the camp grounds, her vision was jumpy from lack of sleep, black flakes at the edge of her eye. She*

WRITERS ON WRITING

shivered in Archy's cast-off sweater. Between the lake shore and the woods was a row of new solar-paneled log cabins, behind which ran a scraggly line of budget-priced trailers for retirees and fishermen, itinerants and the terminally ill who came back year after year or who never left. A face suddenly appeared from the window of an old double-wide, and Thettie's flesh rippled. A scarf or veil obscured the face as it followed Thettie's progress, and she heard the strumming of a distorted guitar. Thettie quickly turned away and just as quickly looked back—she didn't want to—but the face was gone, and the music, too.

Word of the Harpurs' return had started to spread and a small posse gathered in the parking lot. Thettie fluffed out her hair and unbuttoned the top button of the sweater. She felt their eyes on her. The ridge behind the village blocked the rising sun and blurred the outlines of the waking world. Disembodied headlights moved slowly down Main Street. New smells in the air. The unfamiliar grind of an espresso machine from where the drug store used to be, rosemary in the fresh-baked bread from a new bakery at the end of the block.

'I'll be damned.'

Ten years since they'd left and it had transformed from a forgotten lake town into something from the future.

We all know that every scene in fiction is advanced

VOLUME 4

through conflict and moves through a rough event-crisis-resolution pattern. What many of us forget, especially when we're starting out, is that setting is our first tool for etching that pattern into the reader's consciousness. In the scene above, I used setting to reveal as much about Thettie, my protagonist, as I conceal. The face at the window, the sun-starved morning—these will all play a role in the micro-world of the novel. But these elements also serve to amplify the Big Story question: can anyone ever really go home again?

So the first rule of setting is that at every point in your world-making, it should express both the minor and major conflicts of the story you are trying to tell. And connected to that, setting should force the characters to interact with it no less than they do with other characters, or within themselves. It's never just a static background and it will fail as setting if that's your approach, much as a character will fail if you make them flat. Setting, like character, is depth. Place is action. It ripples across flesh. It lies.

2: The devil's in the detail.

There are details in your fictional world, just as there are details in the real world that set off a psychic crisis, or that moment of unresolved emotional conflict in your writer that sets the plot in motion. In Shirley Jackson's novel, as you may remember, one of those details, in a memorable scene, is the cup of stars. On her way to Hill House, the protagonist, Eleanor, watches a little girl at a roadside café refuse to drink her milk unless it's from her favorite "cup of stars."

WRITERS ON WRITING

This detail comes to symbolize the gap between (female) desire and its gratification—a gap only crossed in fairy tales, and in nightmares.

In my novel an early detail is a covered-up crack in the pavement. This opens an unhealable wound in Thettie, one that will force her to make a series of decisions that will impact the rest of the story:

> *Her body remembered, before her mind could argue, to avoid a wedge-shaped crack that was no longer in the sidewalk. As she stepped over where she was sure the gap had been, Thettie noticed fine lines webbing the new mica. She froze. At her feet, a small fissure seemed to widen as she watched, like something shifting deep below the surface. Beneath the spot—she was sure this was the spot—was a deep vertical slit that had once split the old sidewalk. Cassie and Frankie always said it looked like a giant mouth, and it had just been here, she was sure of it. It had cut all the way down to the soil and was tufted with weeds and crowded with chunks of asphalt like broken teeth—and it always tripped one of them up, either by accident or on purpose. Could turn a spectacular wheelie into a dramatic lose, cross-bar slammed into pubic bone, that old cement mouth with its broken teeth laughing at their pain. Thettie held her breath, as if she were on thin ice, instead of six inches of brand new mica. Don't make any sudden moves, she told herself. When she no longer could feel or see the cracks*

VOLUME 4

in the sidewalk getting any bigger, she carefully stepped away from the treacherous grin that lay, she guessed, much too close to the surface.

Catherynne M. Valente has written that "Most stories, at their core, involve someone finding out that What Everyone Knows, is or is not true, and what they do with that information." This moment of revelation—often deceptive—is often triggered by an anomalous detail in the setting. That is plot. It's that simple.

So you want to think about a detail or two that comes from setting and which is the key to the door of unresolvable emotion. The door can be seen as an uncrossable fissure between what the character sees and what everyone else knows. Whether cups of stars or asphalt grins, detail must seem both to come organically from setting and from within your character's own conflicted soul. Effective setting is always both continuous with and in conflict with character, and this duality of setting is as much a part of the rising action as any other. Set the clock ticking and think about how every detail in your scene presents your character with a choice. A trinket on the road: Will she pick it up or drive over it? A window: Will he jump through it or close it? A lover's laptop: Will he open it, or toss that out the window, too? The devil is in the detail.

3: Where's the door?

In Dorothy Allison's famous essay, *Place*, she describes setting as no less than the "search for a door." The very

WRITERS ON WRITING

notion of a search carries with it a trunkload of unresolved desire. Of looking for something that we want, or think we want, that cannot be found, or which turns out not to be what it seems: love, home, family, victory. What are your characters' unresolved desires? What are yours, and how does the setting both lead *to* them, and away? That should be the question you ask of setting at every point. Let's takes another look at *The Haunting of Hill House*:

> *At one spot she stopped altogether beside the road to stare in disbelief and wonder. Along the road for perhaps a quarter of a mile she had been passing and admiring a row of splendid tended oleanders, blooming pink and white in a steady row. Now she had come to the gateway they protected, and past the gateway the trees continued. The gateway was no more than a pair of ruined stone pillars, with a road leading away between them into empty fields. She could see that the oleander trees cut away from the road and ran up each side of a great square, and she could see all the way to the farther side of the square, which was a line of oleander trees seemingly going along a little river. Inside the oleander square there was nothing, no house, no building, nothing but the straight road going across and ending at the stream. Now what was here, she wondered, what was here and is gone, or what was going to be here and never came? Was it going to be a house or a garden or an orchard; were they driven away*

VOLUME 4

forever or are they coming back? Oleanders are poisonous, she remembered; could they be guarding something? Will I, she thought, will I get out of my car and go between the ruined gates and then, once I am in the magic oleander square, find that I have wondered into a fairy land, protected poisonously from the eyes of people passing? Once I have stepped between the magic gateposts, will I find myself through the protective barrier, the spell broken? I will go into a sweet garden . . . . She laughed and turned to smile good-by at the magic oleanders. Another day, she told them, another day I'll come back and break your spell.

Eleanor's initial journey to Hill House, her heart's deepest desire, is broken by gates and gaps, hard descents, and winding climbs. It conceals as much as it reveals and makes us want to stay on the page as urgently as we need to turn it. In your stories, look for an event, suggested by setting, by a literal wrong turn, or maybe two, that triggers an emotional crisis. This is your way into the story

In *Aletheia*, I found my way into the story through slowly tracking Thettie's trip down Bad Mojo Lane and watching it mess with her head. After stepping over the covered up sidewalk crack she talks to a strange townie, she makes a spectacle of herself in the grocery store—one hard left turn of bad choices after another, again. At one point, she takes shelter in her son's boat with a mysterious one-eyed girl who joined the clan and is instrumental in bringing the Harpurs back to

WRITERS ON WRITING

Little Ridge. When I created this subterranean scene in the belly of the boat, I made sure to make the light unreliable, the rocking of the boat nauseatingly symbolic, the whole thing rendered as a trapped and breathless I AM.

Throughout the scene, I try to make Thettie increasingly uncomfortable, and to use setting to set up her growing estrangement from her son, what he's become, and especially from the truth of what she is trying not to see: if the one-eyed girl is the door, then Thettie must be the key.

4: It's all in the angles.

Go back to one of your favorite fictional worlds and have a look at the point of view through which the setting is described. Images on the page, no less than images on the screen, are always conveyed through angles—extreme close-ups, lots of Dutch angles, high crane shots. The famous zoom-in-pan-out shot we love in horror cinema? That comes from words on the page rendered to convey subjective vertigo. In my novel, I have two narrators: Thettie, and her lover Lee. Lee is a scientist and his movement through the world is narrated through slippery "long shot" language. But it is a distance that he can't sustain, no matter how hard he tries:

> *The land sloped steeply down to the rocky beach, past an ancient maple where a frayed rope swing hung from black branches, the wooden seat above the fist-sized knot splintered and warped. A memory of summer*

VOLUME 4

remained in the stillness of the foliage and a whisper of golden rod exhaled from the woods. A small orchard of peach and plum trees stood between his and the neighboring property, a twenty-six room sprawl which had belonged to Eli Zabriskie—a second son of one of Little Ridge's founding fathers. The Harpur woman outside the store seemed nervous.

The angles are up to you but they should be chosen with care, the way a cinematographer thinks about how best to convey the psychological/emotional state of the POV character. Just because you're telling the story in third person subjective, or first person, or parallel narrative, doesn't mean you can't play around with the angles, and you should.

5: Get bloody

Setting is the blood and guts of character splattered across the page.

Think of setting as a circulatory system, a medium for oxygen. What happens in the incremental development of character also happens in the development of atmosphere through setting—it slowly, platelet by platelet, deepens the conflict.

To change the metaphor, the best way to approach setting is in terms of the source-code more than the context. Setting is never just context. Your story question contains primary information—what if this happens—and secondary information—what if it happens this way at this time—but the latter, the secondary intel, is the medium for the former, much

WRITERS ON WRITING

as, to remix the metaphors again, blood is the medium for oxygen. Any superfluous detail in setting only serves to contaminate the medium, the blood-code of the story, and dilute its powers. Every element of setting in *The Haunting of Hill House*, including those sensory-deprived interior scenes where there is nothing but sourceless noise and fear, is there to advance Eleanor's haunting, up to the point where she merges with the house itself, and is, in the end, its haunting, too.

6: Secrets and lies.

Setting, to invoke Allison once again, 'is your character's secret place . . . setting is where the I goes.'

'I' emerges from character. What is at the heart of the conflict? Think about this in your own work. Hill House is Eleanor's secret place. It is the shame she has been running from, and *to*, her whole life. Similarly, in *Aletheia*, the crack in the sidewalk, reminds Thettie of her secret places—her lost innocence, bad choices, her forced exile at the edge of things. The lake is the secret place that she needs to return to. But she doesn't want to. Or vice versa. Setting is a site for this uncertainty between what everyone knows and what the 'I' sees.

So think, as you create your own worlds and return to your own secret places, about what the outer reveals and conceals about character, but only insofar as it escalates the plot. It's not so much what setting says about desire but about how it uses desire to move the story forward.

7: Smellarama!

VOLUME 4

There is no substitute for concrete sensual detail in setting. A hedge is never just a hedge, it's a poison Oleander hedge, or a fragrant Jasmine thicket, or a hedge bursting with hummingbirds. Showing your character, as a proxy of yourself, moving through the setting with no disjunctive similes or metaphors imposed from without, is the most effective form of telling us everything we need to know. Metaphors and other figurative styling, when it appears, must come from the mind and heart of the character. Are the falling snowflakes sharp as glass, or feathery as kisses? Is the sound the crackle, or the *cackle* of dry leaves?

Gustav Flaubert infamously noted that each paragraph of setting should invoke at least three senses. Your characters are in this world as independent constructs that may well exceed the limitations of your life and world view, but inasmuch as you can, you must try to inhabit them. To care as they do. To see, smell, feel, hear, taste and intuit, as they do. To care about what they know they have to lose or have already lost, because it is now, in a very real way, your care, too. And your loss. Their interaction with place occurs at the moment of its creation, and that wonder, that not-knowing, while deeply caring, is crucial to setting. Your character's world is as much an examination of your transforming subjectivity as it is of theirs. It has to be.

Think about this in your own work, and when you write and read widely as we all must, think about it in the settings that become you.

FINDING YOUR VOICE

LYNDA E. RUCKER

OF ALL THE skills that we must learn as writers, perhaps none are so elusive as the development of a voice. In fact, there's not even a consensus about what exactly "voice" means in fiction.

If you google "voice and style," you'll find a lot of blog posts discussing the difference in the two. I am not sure that pinpointing this particular difference is very useful, or rather, I think style is often an intrinsic part of storytelling that can't be separated from the substance of the work.

Because voice, at least for the purposes of my discussion here, encompasses everything about fiction from the words chosen to the rhythm of the prose to the kinds of details the writer chooses and the writer's worldview. Style is one element of voice, but writers can have styles that are similar to one another while still retaining unique voices. Different writers' voices result in similar stories being told in radically different ways in the same way that doing an activity with one person and then another person differs: because the person is different, the entire experience is different.

VOLUME 4

A strong voice is often what makes the difference between publication and rejection. Many aspiring writers go through a period in which they are getting encouraging personal rejections but can't quite seem to crack a good market. Many editors talk about getting stories that are technically competent but somehow lacking. Very often, that lack is voice.

That's not to say that once you develop a voice, you'll never get rejected—far from it, as plenty of established writers can tell you! But developing a voice is one of the higher-level skills you'll need to get in place before you can begin to consistently sell fiction.

A few months ago, I was asked by another writer, Chris Kelso, to write a brief contribution for his site "A Word to the Wise" in which he asks authors what advice they would give to aspiring writers. One of the points I made in my response was that (and I quote myself) you have to follow your own vision wherever it takes you. Essentially, what I meant was that you must find your voice. In fact, I would say that from an artistic standpoint, finding your voice is the most critical aspect of becoming a writer.

In the first half of this piece, I'm going to be talking about voice in a general way. In the second half, I'm going to discuss voice more specifically in the context of writing horror fiction.

So, How *Do* You Find Your Voice?

I'm a writer who took a long time to find my voice.

I have said before that I began writing from the moment I could hold a pencil, and it's true; I have scraps of stories started before the age of six. Yet for a

WRITERS ON WRITING

long time, I struggled with developing a voice that was not an imitation of some other writer's. I have juvenilia in which my characters talk like the ones in the British children's fantasy fiction that I adored; there are later, terrible, embarrassing stories from adulthood in which I was clearly making wild stabs at imitating favourite or even not-so-favourite writers, maybe just the author whose stories kept cropping up in the last few anthologies or small press zines of the 1990s that so many writers cut their teeth on—or appeared in for a few years and then vanished from the scene. I wanted so badly to be published that voice-wise, I was a bit like a kid who is desperately trying to find a clique to accept them.

You see, finding a voice is about finding your identity, and the process of doing so is much like being a teenager again, trying on and discarding different "yous" until you uncover the "you" that was there all along. It's the same with writing. And you face similar obstacles as you seek your voice:

- thinking you have nothing to say
- thinking your interests are weird or pointless
- thinking no one else will be able to connect with what matters most to you

A long time ago, I read something from another writer—I don't remember who or where—to the effect that those things that are most personal to us, the things that we try hardest to hide from others, that we believe isolate us the most, are invariably what other people respond to: *I thought I was the only one!* The irony in finding your voice is that it is a process both

VOLUME 4

of realizing how unique you are and that you aren't actually as special as you imagine yourself to be. In other words, no one can write the stories that you can write in the way that you can write them, but you would be surprised at how many people will connect with your stories when you are as honest and true as you know how to be.

At its best, the incredibly isolating work of writing can simultaneously be some of the least isolating work in the world. There is really no feeling like the one I get from a message or email from someone discussing one of my stories in a way that makes me think *they got it!* You suddenly feel so much less alone in the world. And that is all because you have allowed your true voice to come through and speak.

So, How *Do* You Find Your Voice, Part Deux?

The above is the underpinning of seeking and finding your voice, but how do you go about doing so in a practical sense? Here are some tips.

Write a lot. There's no substitute for this one. I hate that frequently-repeated-it-like-it's-scientific figure from Malcolm Gladwell about "10,000 hours to mastery," but there is one valuable takeaway from it, and it's that you need to write a lot to get to the point where you are any good. I'm not going to say you *should* write every day or you *should* take any particular approach—and more on those *shoulds* in a moment—but you are going to have to write a lot more than you probably imagine, and a lot more than a handful of stories.

WRITERS ON WRITING

Write about everything. People used to (and still do sometimes) keep something called a commonplace book. This is a book that is somewhere between a journal and a scrapbook that contains quotes and ideas and observations and sketches and anything else that you want to remember or that catches your eye. Or you may just want to keep a journal. Do it on a computer if you're more comfortable with that than pen and paper (but give pen and paper a shot, especially a nice notebook and a nice pen, and see if you are surprised by what you manage to shake loose working in a different medium). Write about your past. Write about your present. Write about things that surprise and infuriate you. Write about things you don't want anyone to know about you. These are all the kinds of things that will eventually make up your unique voice. Nobody has lived the life you have or had the experiences you have.

Read widely, in and out of the genre. But don't just read. Listen to music, look at art, watch movies, talk to people, and think about the world.

Learn from other artists' voices, and then move on. I've said artists here and not just writers because plenty of us are as influenced by other artistic mediums as we are by writers. For example, for a long time, I wanted to write stories that were like Tom Waits songs or David Lynch movies. Eventually, I realized that nobody but Tom Waits and David Lynch could tell those stories, but I had my own stories to tell.

But in the early days, it's okay to imitate. Hey, it worked for Ramsey Campbell, whose Lovecraftian

VOLUME 4

fiction famously caught the eye of August Derleth when Campbell was still just a teenager. Of course, it was Derleth's suggestion that Campbell take that inspiration and make it his own, which resulted in Campbell's moving the location of those stories from Lovecraft's New England to a partly-real, partly-invented Severn Valley in the U.K, that made those stories unique.

Ruminate on your obsessions. Do you love stories about plants, clocks, time travel, urban settings, giant killer bugs, haunted houses, home invasions? Are you in love with Southern Gothics or gothic gothics or hardboiled crime mixed with horror? Whatever your passions are and however odd or overdone they may seem to be, embrace them.

Ignore the should. Okay, there are plenty of shoulds you need to pay attention to. You should avoid haranguing editors or other writers. You should always work to improve your understanding of grammar, language and structure. But shoulds that are someone else's arbitrary rules for how you should arrange your writing life, such as "You should write every day" or "You should/shouldn't outline" can be ignored. Also, too many *shoulds* are one of the best ways to stifle your unique voice.

What Does All This Have to Do With Horror?

Ultimately, finding your voice is a similar process regardless of what genre you are working in. However, looking at a few horror writers with distinct voices can help illuminate the role of voice in horror.

WRITERS ON WRITING

Let's start with a writer most of us are familiar with and who has a strong voice: Stephen King. When I think of Stephen King's voice, here are some of the things that come to mind:

- populist
- plain-spoken
- small rural towns, and ordinary people who can be as bad as monsters
- faith in the common man, despite the above
- families
- blue-collar settings and characters
- an omniscient narrator who ominously informs the reader of future events such as a characters' impending death
- the use of italics for emphasis
- turning ordinary items and places—laundromats! trucks—into objects or locations of terror

That's just off the top of my head. Of the items on the list, I would say it is the first six in particular that account for King's wide appeal among not just people who don't normally read horror but among people who don't reach much at all. King's voice is so distinctive that even when he made an effort to hide under the Richard Bachman pseudonym, a reader eventually became suspicious and tracked down the man himself.

Keeping in mind that voice encompasses worldview, another distinctive element of King's fiction is a strong sense of morality and a belief in good versus evil. The good guys may not always win in a King story, and evil may sometimes wear the face of

VOLUME 4

goodness, but there is little doubt about the existence of the two in a clear dichotomy.

H.P. Lovecraft is another horror writer whose work is enormously popular. However, he is in almost complete contrast to King: his characters are anything but populist, and while the frequency of his use of dense and archaic prose is often exaggerated, many readers do find it distancing and alienating. In further contrast to King, Lovecraft posits a universe without morality. Perhaps the real triumph of Lovecraft's voice is in his explication of a universe in which human beings are simply insignificant. It is the power of this vision that has resulted in Lovecraft's growing influence across the decades—almost as though he looked into the future and anticipated the "God is dead" ethos that would preoccupy the Western world in the latter half of the twentieth century that he so despised. We see here that in many ways, voice is also akin to vision, and it is Lovecraft's vision that has survived, in games, in movies, and in many other aspects of pop culture, even for those who dislike his prose.

When thinking about voice, it might be instructive as well to consider and contrast the writings of Thomas Ligotti to the first season of the American television program *True Detective*. Writer and creator Nick Pileggi drew heavily on the writings and philosophy of Ligotti, who spent much of his career as a cult writer—his recent Penguin rereleases notwithstanding. Pileggi found a way to take that voice and transform it into something that was far more palatable to mainstream audiences without losing its essential bleakness. Within a more traditional storytelling structure that

WRITERS ON WRITING

includes a sense of narrative movement and plot—albeit a convoluted one—Pileggi developed a very popular season of television. It is an interesting exercise in examining voice to ask where, in *True Detective*, do the voices of Ligotti and Pileggi intersect and where do they diverge?

Anne Rice is yet another horror writer with a strong voice. As with King and Lovecraft, the mere mention of her name conjures a certain mood, setting, set of characters and assumptions and themes. Rice draws on the genre's Gothic, romantic, and decadent roots for her stories set in lush locales and often featuring new takes on old tropes of vampires and witches.

For a look at a writer of dark fiction whose style has changed over time but whose voice has remained consistent, compare the early work of Caitlin R. Kiernan to her more recent writing of the last few years. A style that used to be much more dense and that experimented more with wordplay became more straightforward and stripped down; Kiernan's powerful voice still shines through, however, and her work continues to challenge form, structure, and other traditional elements of narrative storytelling even if her prose style may appear these days to be ostensibly more conventional at a glance.

The Last Word

Recently, I attended a reading and Q&A by the British writer M. John Harrison in which a question was asked about his work across various genres including space opera, fantasy, horror, and something

VOLUME 4

approaching quasi-realism. Harrison pointed out that while he might range across any number of genres, his voice remains consistent throughout, and so a reader picking up an M. John Harrison novel is always going to get an M. John Harrison story whether that story is set on a spaceship in some far-flung future, an imaginary fantasy landscape or a grim urban street in present-day England.

In a way, voice is like one of those medical conditions for which there is no definitive test but is only diagnosed by the process of elimination. It is almost easier to say what it is not than to say what it is—it is not genre, it is not style; it is something unmistakable and unique to any writer who is working at the top of their craft.

Beginning writers are often told *you are not your stories*, in an effort to soften the blows of critique and rejection: you are not your flawed plots, your thinly realized characters, your hit-and-miss prose. You are, however, your voice: it is the most distinctive and original aspect of your writing, and simultaneously your most vulnerable and powerful tool. Cultivate your voice and you will create lasting stories that will resonate with readers long after they have reached the final pages.

If you'd like to read more of Crystal Lake's non-fiction and On Writing books, be sure to take a look at these titles:

Horror 101: The Way Forward—a comprehensive overview of the Horror fiction genre and career opportunities available to established and aspiring authors, including Jack Ketchum, Graham Masterton, Edward Lee, Lisa Morton, Ellen Datlow, Ramsey Campbell, and many more.

Horror 201: The Silver Scream Vol.1 and *Vol.2*—A must read for anyone interested in the horror film industry. Includes interviews and essays by Wes Craven, John Carpenter, George A. Romero, Mick Garris, and dozens more. Now available in paperback, as well.

Modern Mythmakers: 35 interviews with Horror and Science Fiction Writers and Filmmakers by Michael McCarty—Ever wanted to hang out with legends like Ray Bradbury, Richard Matheson, and Dean Koontz? *Modern Mythmakers* is your chance to hear fun anecdotes and career advice from authors and filmmakers like Forrest J. Ackerman, Ray Bradbury, Ramsey Campbell, John Carpenter, Dan Curtis, Elvira, Neil Gaiman, Mick Garris, Laurell K. Hamilton, Jack Ketchum, Dean Koontz, Graham Masterton, Richard Matheson, John Russo, William F. Nolan, John Saul, Peter Straub, and many more.

If you'd like to read some fiction by some of the authors in this omnibus, we recommend the following:

Tales from The Lake Vol.3 anthology—Dive into the deep end of the lake with 19 tales of terror, selected by Monique Snyman. Including short stories by Mark Allan Gunnells, Kate Jonez, Kenneth W. Cain, and many more.

Gutted: Beautiful Horror Stories anthology—an anthology of dark fiction that explores the beauty at the very heart of darkness. Featuring horror's most celebrated voices: Clive Barker, Neil Gaiman, Ramsey Campbell, Paul Tremblay, John F.D. Taff, Lisa Mannetti, Damien Angelica Walters, Josh Malerman, Christopher Coake, Mercedes M. Yardley, Brian Kirk, Stephanie M. Wytovich, Amanda Gowin, Richard Thomas, Maria Alexander, and Kevin Lucia.

Run to Ground by Jasper Bark—Jim Mcleod is running from his responsibilities as a father, hiding out from his pregnant girlfriend and working as a groundskeeper in a rural graveyard. Throw in some ancient monsters and folklore, and you'll have Jim running for live through this folk horror graveyard.

The Final Cut by Jasper Bark—Follow the misfortunes of two indie filmmakers in their quest to fund their breakthrough movie by borrowing money from one dangerous underground figure in order to buy a large quantity of cocaine from a different but equally dangerous underground figure. They will learn that while some stories capture the imagination, others will be the death of you.

Blackwater Val by William Gorman—a Supernatural Suspense Thriller/Horror/Coming of age novel: A widower, traveling with his dead wife's ashes and his six-year-old psychic daughter Katie in tow, returns to his haunted birthplace to execute his dead wife's final wish. But something isn't quite right in the Val.

Devourer of Souls by Kevin Lucia—In Kevin Lucia's latest installment of his growing Clifton Heights mythos, Sheriff Chris Baker and Father Ward meet for a Saturday morning breakfast at The Skylark Dinner to once again commiserate over the weird and terrifying secrets surrounding their town.

Tales from The Lake Vol.2 anthology—Beneath this lake you'll find nothing but mystery and suspense, horror and dread. Not to mention death and misery—tales to share around the campfire or living room floor from the likes of Ramsey Campbell, Jack Ketchum, and Edward Lee.

Pretty Little Dead Girls: A Novel of Murder and Whimsy by Mercedes M. Yardley—Bryony Adams is destined to be murdered, but fortunately Fate has terrible marksmanship. In order to survive, she must run as far and as fast as she can. After arriving in Seattle, Bryony befriends a tortured musician, a market fish-thrower, and a starry-eyed hero who is secretly a serial killer bent on fulfilling Bryony's dark destiny.

Apocalyptic Montessa and Nuclear Lulu: A Tale of Atomic Love by Mercedes M. Yardley—Montessa Tovar is walking home alone when she is abducted by Lu, a serial killer with unusual talents and a grudge against the world. But in time, the victim becomes the executioner as 'Apocalyptic' Montessa and her doomed 'Nuclear' Lulu crisscross the country in a bloody firestorm of revenge. HER MAMA ALWAYS SAID SHE WAS SPECIAL. HIS DADDY CALLED HIM A DEMON. BUT EVEN MONSTERS CAN FALL IN LOVE.

Eidolon Avenue: The First Feast by Jonathan Winn—where the secretly guilty go to die. All thrown into their own private hell as every cruel choice, every deadly mistake, every drop of spilled blood is remembered, resurrected and relived to feed the ancient evil that lives on Eidolon Avenue.

Flowers in a Dumpster by Mark Allan Gunnells—The world is full of beauty and mystery. In these 17 tales, Gunnells will take you on a journey through landscapes of light and darkness, rapture and agony, hope and fear. Let Gunnells guide you through these landscapes where magnificence and decay co-exist side by side. Come pick a bouquet from these Flowers in a Dumpster.

Nameless: The Darkness Comes by Mercedes M. Yardley—Luna Masterson sees demons. She has been dealing with the demonic all her life, so when her brother gets tangled up with a demon named Sparkles, 'Luna the Lunatic' rolls in on her motorcycle to save the day. Armed with the ability to harm demons, her scathing sarcasm, and a hefty chip on her shoulder, Luna gathers the most unusual of allies, teaming up with a green-eyed heroin addict and a snarky demon 'of some import.' After all, outcasts of a feather should stick together . . . even until the end.

Little Dead Red by Mercedes M. Yardley—The Wolf

is roaming the city, and he must be stopped. In this modern day retelling of Little Red Riding Hood, the wolf takes to the city streets to capture his prey, but the hunter is close behind him. With Grim Marie on the prowl, the hunter becomes the hunted.

The Outsiders Lovecraftian shared-world anthology—They'll do anything to protect their way of life. Anything. Welcome to Priory, a small gated community in the UK, where the only thing worse than an ancient monster is the group worshipping it. Is that which slithers below true evil, or does evil reside in the people of Priory? Includes stories by Stephen Bacon, James Everington, Rosanne Rabinowitz, V.H. Leslie, and Gary Fry.

Tales from The Lake Vol.1 anthology—Remember those dark and scary nights spent telling ghost stories and other campfire stories? With the *Tales from The Lake* horror anthologies, you can relive some of those memories by reading the best Dark Fiction stories around. Includes Dark Fiction stories and poems by horror greats such as Graham Masterton, Bev Vincent, Tim Curran, Tim Waggoner, Elizabeth Massie, and many more. Be sure to check out our website for future *Tales from The Lake* volumes.

For the Night is Dark anthology—Darkness, our most primitive fear since shadows first moved. Includes stories by Crystal Lake Publishing alumni like Gary McMahon, William Meikle, Jasper Bark, Tonia Brown, Blaze McRob, Daniel I Russell, Kevin Lucia, Armand Rosamilia, Ray Cluley, and many more.

Through a Mirror, Darkly by Kevin Lucia—Are there truths within the books we read? What if the book delves into the lives of the very town you live in? People you know? Or thought you knew. These are the questions a bookstore owner face when a mysterious book shows up.

Things Slip Through by Kevin Lucia—When a child mysteriously disappears from a small town and even his mother seems indifferent, it's time for the new sheriff to step in.

Sleeper(s) by Paul Kane—An entire city falls asleep, and when Doctor Andrew Strauss and the army move in to investigate, the sleepers stand up to defend a single woman as a cohesive group, and mind. As Strauss' covert past and foretold future clash, the twisted fairytale truth behind this event will leave you breathless.

Tricks, Mischief and Mayhem by Daniel I. Russell— Tricks, Mischief and Mayhem. These are not just some of the themes lurking in this tome of horror, but the names of three mischievous carnival clowns. Along with them you'll meet some of Australia's most popular monsters and legends, along with a popular cast of ghosts, demons, and zombies. Hell, there are more than a few stories portraying nature fighting back.

Stuck On You and Other Prime Cuts by Jasper Bark—A word of caution gentle reader, these tales will take you places you've never been before and may never dare revisit. They'll whisper truths so twisted you can only face them in the darkest hours of the night. They'll unlock desires so decadent you'll never wash their taint from your flesh.

Stuck On You by Jasper Bark—Cheating husband Ricardo could never keep it in his pants, and now it's stuck in the worst possible place. His Mexican road trip becomes a nightmare straight out of urban legend when he agrees to take the wrong woman back over the border. A bolt of lightning sees him fused to his fellow cheater on a detour into the backwoods. Now he's fighting wild beasts and raw nature just to stay alive in this dark comedy romance that blends erotic horror with black humour and extreme splatter.

Or check out other Crystal Lake Publishing books for your Dark Fiction, Horror, Suspense, and Thriller needs.

BIOGRAPHIES

Hal Bodner is a Bram Stoker Award nominated author, best known for his best selling gay vampire novel, Bite Club and the lupine sequel, *The Trouble with Hairy*. He tells people he was born in East Philadelphia because so few people know where Cherry Hill, New Jersey is located. The first person he ever saw was the doctor who delivered him, C. Everett Koop, the future US Surgeon General. Thus, from birth Hal was ironically destined to become a heavy smoker—a habit he greatly misses. He moved to West Hollywood in the 1980s and has rarely left the city limits since. In fact, he is so WeHo-centric that he cannot find his way around Beverly Hills—the next town over. In a burst of over optimism, he bought a six bedroom mansion in Highland Park, a supposedly up-and-coming area of East Los Angeles. After three years of watching the street gangs doing drug deals in his back yard, he fled back to WeHo. During his sojourn in East L.A., he was protected from the harm because of his habit of chasing his escaped pet peacock down Figueroa Boulevard at night, dressed in his fluffy bathrobe and fuzzy Cthulu slippers while yelling "Apollo! Apollo! Come back!" None of the gang members would shoot him; they were laughing too hard. His various professions have included stints as an entertainment lawyer, a scheduler for a 976 sex telephone line, a theater reviewer and the personal assistant to a television star. For several years, he owned Heavy Petting, a pet boutique where movie stars bought gold-plated water dishes and designer wardrobes for their Chihuahuas and Pomeranians. In the erotic paranormal romance genre—which he refers to as "supernatural smut"—he is best known for having written In Flesh and Stone and For Love of the Dead. His comic gay super hero trilogy will hopefully debut shortly with Fabulous in Tights to be followed by A Study in Spandex. He has recently agreed to write a series of mystery novellas featuring a gay detective and his Watsonian sidekick, who is the madam of a bordello. Hal married a man roughly half his age who had no idea that Liza Minnelli and Judy Garland were related. In consequence, he has discovered that the use of hair dye is rarely an adequate substitute for Viagra.

J.S. Breukelaar is the author of the novels, *American Monster* (Lazy Fascist Press) *Aletheia* (forthcoming from Crystal Lake Publishing), and the collection, *War Wounds*, (forthcoming from Omnium Gatherum). She is columnist and instructor and LitReactor and Gotham Writers Workshop and elsewhere. Her short fiction has appeared, or will, in publications including Gamut, Lightspeed, Lamplight, Nightmare, Dark Fuse, Juked, Prick of the Spindle, Opium, Go(b)et Magazine, Women Writing the Weird, Volumes I and II, and States of Terror Vol. II. An ex-pat New Yorker, she lives in Sydney with her family, and online at www.thelivingsuitcase.com.

Born and raised in a small harbor town in the south of Ireland, **Kealan Patrick Burke** knew from a very early age that he was going to be a horror writer. The combination of an ancient locale, a horror-loving mother, and a family full of storytellers, made it inevitable that he would end up telling stories for a living. Since those formative years, he has written five novels, over a hundred short stories, six collections, and edited four acclaimed anthologies. In 2004, he was honored with the Bram Stoker Award for his novella The Turtle Boy.

Kealan has worked as a waiter, a drama teacher, a mapmaker, a security guard, an assembly-line worker at Apple Computers, a salesman (for a day), a bartender, landscape gardener, vocalist in a grunge band, curriculum content editor, fiction editor at Gothic.net, and, most recently, a fraud investigator.

When not writing, Kealan designs book covers through his company Elderlemon Design.

A movie based on his short story "Peekers" is currently in development as a major motion picture.

Kenneth W. Cain is the author of the Saga of I trilogy, *United States of The Dead*, acclaimed short story collections *These Old Tales* and *Fresh Cut Tales*, and the forthcoming collection *Embers*. He lives with his wife and children in Eastern Pennsylvania. Find out more at kennethwcain.com

Dave-Brendon de Burgh wanted to be an artist and speak French, but Fate saved him and pointed him in the direction of writing. He's a bookseller, co-parent to three wonderful Pekingese 'kids', reads Speculative Fiction voraciously, and is the luckiest guy in the world because he has a blonde, blue-eyed woman in his life who supports his need to write and be crazy.

He lives in Pretoria, South Africa, and when he's not writing he's probably secretly laughing at cognitively challenged bookstore-customers. He's on Blogger, Twitter, Wordpress, Facebook and Instagram, and is also a paranormal investigator with Phoenix Paranormal SA.

Theresa Derwin was born and bred in Birmingham and her career has been pretty varied; from Warehouse Packer, then bar work, to being a crap waitress then swiftly into retail, Admin, Professional Student and dosser until finally entering the Civil Service in 1999. She left the service in 2012 to pursue a career as a writer.

Theresa writes humorous fiction including SF, Urban Fantasy & Horror.She also writes a number of book reviews and at her site www.terror-tree.co.uk Her collection of short stories, *Monsters Anonymous*, was released from Anarchy Books Sept 2012. She was Publishing Director for Fringeworks Ltd, took over KWP in 2013 selling it to Great British Horror 2015. She has had over twenty short stories published in various anthologies since then, has a collection of Christmas themed stories *Season's Creepings* Sept 2015 and her novella *God's Vengeance* is due out with Crystal Lake Publishing 2016.

She has loved horror, fantasy and SF all her life, thanks to her father who raised her on 1950s Sci-Fi Universal Monsters, tango and popcorn. Her love of the bizarre, (including her Dad) remains constant, to this day. She also owes a great debt to Rog Peyton from the BSFG who introduced her to alternative fiction at the tender the age of 14.

You can follow Theresa on Twitter @BarbarellaFem or find out more about her work at www.theresa-derwin.co.uk

Steve Diamond is the author of the YA Horror/Paranormal Thriller novel, RESIDUE. He is a Hugo Nominated author who has written for Baen, Ragnarok Publications, Privateer Press, Gallant Knight Games, and numerous other small publications. He also founded the Hugo Nominated review site, Elitist Book Reviews, and is the co-founder of Vault Books.

Nerine Dorman is an author, editor, designer, musician and gamer, who spends far too much time moving text and picture boxes around on-screen. She also freely admits to having impure thoughts about Dorian Pavus. You're welcome to stalk her on Twitter at nerinedorman.

Ben Eads lives within the semi-tropical suburbs of Central Florida. A true horror writer by heart, he wrote his first story at the tender age of ten. The look on the teacher's face when she read it was priceless. However, his classmates loved it! Ben has had short stories published in various magazines and anthologies. When he isn't writing, he dabbles in martial arts, philosophy and specializes in I.T. security. He's always looking to find new ways to infect reader's imaginations. Ben blames Arthur Machen, H.P. Lovecraft, Jorge Luis Borges, J.G. Ballard, Philip K. Dick, and Stephen King for his addiction, and his need to push the envelope of fiction. His horror novella, *Cracked Sky* was published by Omnium Gatherum, January 2015.

James Everington mainly writes dark, supernatural fiction, although he occasionally takes a break and writes dark, non-supernatural fiction. His second collection of such tales, *Falling Over*, is out now from Infinity Plus and he has had work published in *The Outsiders* (Crystal Lake), *Supernatural Tales*, *Morpheus Tales* and *Little Visible Delight* (Omnium Gatherum), amongst others.

Oh and he drinks Guinness, if anyone's asking. You

can find out what James is currently up to at his Scattershot Writing site.

Patrick Freivald is an author, high school teacher (physics, robotics, American Sign Language), and beekeeper. He lives in Western New York with his beautiful wife, two birds, three dogs, too many cats, and several million stinging insects. A member of the HWA and ITW, he's always had a soft spot for slavering monsters of all kinds.

He is the author of *Twice Shy*, Bram Stoker Award®-nominated *Special Dead*, *Blood List* (with his twin brother Phil), the Matt Rowley novels including Bram Stoker Award®-nominated novels *Jade Sky* and *Black Tide* as well as *Jade Gods*, a growing legion of short stories, and the *Jade Sky* graphic novella (with Joe McKinney) in Dark Discoveries magazine. There will be more.

William Gorman grew up listening to ghost stories and dark fantastical yarns from his grandfather—a magician and former 'mentalist' during the last great, fading days of vaudeville. He's had short fiction published in *Nightmares*, *Thin Ice*, *Severed Tales*, *The Midnight Shambler*, *Nightside*, and *The Rockford Review*. His first book, a collection of local myths and legends titled *Ghost Whispers*, came out in 2005 and spawned the highly popular Haunted Rockford tours and cemetery walks now operating in his Illinois hometown. His first novel, *Blackwater Val*, was published in April of 2016.

He now lives in the Ohio Valley with his Lady of the Manor, Suzanne, and their German shepherd Gabby, and is currently hard at work on his next novel and a new collection of macabre tales.

Mark Allan Gunnells loves to tell stories. He has since he was a kid, penning one-page tales that were Twilight Zone knockoffs. He likes to think he has gotten a little better since then. He has been lucky enough to work with some wonderful publishers. He loves reader feedback, and above all he loves telling stories. He lives in Greer, SC, with his fiance Craig A. Metcalf.

Sheldon Higdon has had numerous publications in various magazines and anthologies such as *Rue Morgue Magazine, Portland Magazine, Shroud Magazine, Shock Totem 4.5: Holiday Tales of the Macabre and Twisted, Madhouse* anthology, and *Death, Be Not Proud* anthology, to name a few. He is also an award-winning screenwriter.
www.sheldonhigdon.com @sheldonhigdon.

Brian Hodge is one of those people who always has to be making something. So far, he's made 10 novels, and is working on two more, as well as 120 shorter works and 4 full-length collections. His first collection, *The Convulsion Factory*, was ranked by critic Stanley Wiater among the 113 best books of modern horror.

He lives in Colorado, where he also likes to make music and photographs; loves everything about organic gardening except the thieving squirrels; and trains in Krav Maga and kickboxing, which are of no use at all against the squirrels.

His most recent releases include the novella *In the Negative Spaces* (half of a shared book called *Dark City*), and an updated edition of his early post-apocalyptic epic, *Dark Advent*.

Connect through his web site (www.brianhodge.net) or Facebook (www.facebook.com/brianhodgewriter).

Jonathan Janz grew up between a dark forest and a graveyard, which explains everything. Brian Keene named his debut novel *The Sorrows* "the best horror novel of 2012." The Library Journal deemed his follow-up, *House of Skin*, "reminiscent of Shirley Jackson's *The Haunting of Hill House* and Peter Straub's *Ghost Story*."

2013 saw the publication of his novel of vampirism and demonic possession *The Darkest Lullaby*, as well as his serialized horror novel *Savage Species*. Of *Savage Species* Publishers Weekly said, "Fans of old-school splatterpunk horror—Janz cites Richard Laymon as an influence, and it shows—will find much to relish." Jonathan's Kindle Worlds novel *Bloodshot: Kingdom of Shadows* marked his first foray into the superhero/action genre.

Jack Ketchum called his vampire western *Dust Devils* a "Rousing-good weird western," and his sequel to *The Sorrows* (*Castle of Sorrows*) was selected one of 2014's top three novels by Pod of Horror. 2015 saw the release of *The Nightmare Girl*, which prompted Pod of Horror to call Jonathan "Horror's Next Big Thing." His newest releases are *Wolf Land*, which Publishers Weekly called "gruesome yet entertaining gorefest" with "an impressive and bloody climax," and *Children of the Dark*, which garnered a starred Booklist review. He has also written four novellas (*Exorcist Road*, *The Clearing of Travis Coble*, *Old Order*, and *Witching Hour Theatre*) and several short stories.

His primary interests are his wonderful wife and his three amazing children, and though he realizes that every author's wife and children are wonderful and amazing, in this case the cliché happens to be true. You can learn more about Jonathan at www.jonathanjanz.com. You can also find him on Facebook, via @jonathanjanz on Twitter, on Instagram (jonathanjanz) or on his Goodreads and Amazon author pages.

Paul Kane is the award-winning, bestselling author and editor of over fifty books—including the *Arrowhead* trilogy (gathered together in the sell out *Hooded Man* omnibus, revolving around a post-apocalyptic version of Robin Hood), *The Butterfly Man and Other Stories*, *Hellbound Hearts* and *The Mammoth Book of Body Horror*. His non-fiction books include *The Hellraiser Films and Their Legacy* and *Voices in the Dark*, and his genre journalism has appeared in the likes of *SFX*, *Rue Morgue* and *DeathRay*. He has been a Guest at Alt.Fiction five times, was a Guest at the first SFX Weekender, at Thought Bubble in 2011, Derbyshire Literary Festival and Off the Shelf in 2012, Monster Mash and Event Horizon in 2013, Edge-Lit in 2014, plus HorrorCon, HorrorFest and Grimm Up North in 2015, as well as being a panellist at FantasyCon and the World Fantasy Convention. His work has been optioned and adapted for the big and small screen, including for US network television, plus his latest novels are *Lunar* (set to be turned into a feature film) and the Y.A. story *The Rainbow Man* (as P.B. Kane), with the sequel to *RED—Blood RED*—forthcoming from SST Publications. He lives in Derbyshire, UK, with his wife **Marie O'Regan**, his family and a black cat called Mina. Find out more at his site www.shadow-writer.co.uk which has featured Guest Writers such as Stephen King, Neil Gaiman, Charlaine Harris, Dean Koontz and Guillermo del Toro.

Todd Keisling is the author of the bestselling horror series *Ugly Little Things*, as well as the novels *A Life Transparent* and *The Liminal Man* (a 2013 Indie Book Award Finalist). He lives with his wife and son somewhere near Reading, Pennsylvania. He still has a day job, he's awkward and weird, and if you were to live next door to him, your grass would probably die.

Jack Ketchum is the pseudonym for a former actor, singer, teacher, literary agent, lumber salesman, and soda jerk—a former flower child and baby boomer who figures that in 1956 Elvis, dinosaurs and horror probably saved his life. His first novel, *Off Season*, prompted the *Village Voice* to publicly scold its publisher in print for publishing violent pornography. He personally disagrees but is perfectly happy to let you decide for yourself. His short story *The Box* won a 1994 Bram Stoker Award from the HWA, his story *Gone* won again in 2000—and in 2003 he won Stokers for both best collection for *Peaceable Kingdom* and best long fiction for *Closing Time*. He has written over twenty novels and novellas, the latest of which are *The Woman* and *I'm Not Sam*, both written with director Lucky McKee. Five of his books have been filmed to date—*The Girl Next Door, The Lost, Red, Offspring* and *The Woman*, the last of which won him and McKee the Best Screenplay Award at the prestigious Sitges Film Festival in Spain. His stories are collected in *The Exit At Toledo Blade Boulevard, Broken on the Wheel of Sex, Sleep Disorder* (with Edward Lee), *Peaceable Kingdom* and *Closing Time and Other Stories*. His novella *The Crossings* was cited by Stephen King in his speech at the 2003 National Book Awards. In 2011 he was elected Grand Master by the World Horror Convention.

Michael Knost is a Bram Stoker Award®-winning editor and author of science fiction, fantasy, horror, and supernatural thrillers. He has written in various genres and helmed several anthologies. His *Writers Workshop of Horror* won the 2009 Bram Stoker Award® in England for superior achievement in non-fiction. His critically acclaimed *Writers Workshop of Science Fiction & Fantasy* is an Amazon #1 bestseller. His novel, *Return of the Mothman* was a finalist for the Bram Stoker Award® for superior achievement in first novel. His *Author's Guide to Marketing with Teeth* was a finalist for the Bram Stoker Award® for superior achievement in non-fiction. Michael has taught writing classes and workshops at several colleges, conventions, and online, and currently resides in Chapmanville, West Virginia with his wife, daughter, and a zombie goldfish. To find out more, visit www.MichaelKnost.com.

Kevin Lucia is the Reviews Editor for Cemetery Dance Magazine. His short fiction has appeared in several anthologies, and he is the author of Hiram Grange & The Chosen One, the short story collection *Things Slip Through*, the novella duet *Devourer of Souls* and the novella quartet *Through A Mirror, Darkly*. He's currently finishing his Creative Writing Masters Degree at Binghamton University, he teaches high school English, and lives in Castle Creek, New York with his wife and children. Visit him at: www.kevinlucia.com or add him on Facebook at either www.facebook.com/kblucia or www.facebook.com/authorkevinlucia.

Doug Murano is an author and editor who lives somewhere between Mount Rushmore and the mighty

Missouri River. A proud South Dakota native, he earned his Master of Arts in English Literature (creative writing track) at The University of South Dakota. He is the co-editor of the best-selling and critically acclaimed small-town Lovecraftian horror anthology, *Shadows Over Main Street, Gutted: Beautiful Horror Stories* and the forthcoming *Shadows Over Main Street, Volume 2*.

An Affiliate Member of the Horror Writers Association, he was the organization's promotions and social media coordinator from 2013-15, served as the communications chair for the 2014 World Horror Convention in Portland, Oregon, and has served as a jurist for the Bram Stoker Awards. He is a recipient of the Horror Writers Association's Richard Laymon President's Award for Service.

Follow him on Twitter: @muranofiction.

Joe Mynhardt is a two-time Bram Stoker Award nominated South African publisher and editor.

Joe is the owner of Crystal Lake Publishing (Publisher of the Year in the 2013 This Is Horror Awards), which he started in August, 2012. Since then he's published and edited short stories, novellas, interviews and essays by the likes of Neil Gaiman, Clive Barker, Ramsey Campbell, Jack Ketchum, Graham Masterton, Adam Nevill, Lisa Morton, Elizabeth Massie, Joe McKinney, Edward Lee, Wes Craven, John Carpenter, George A. Romero, Mick Garris, and hundreds more.

Just like Crystal Lake Publishing, Joe believes in reaching out to all authors, new and experienced, and being a beacon of friendship and guidance in the Dark Fiction field.

Joe's influences stretch from Poe, Doyle and

Lovecraft to King, Connolly and Gaiman. His collection of short stories, *Lost in the Dark*, is available through Amazon. You can read more about Joe and Crystal Lake Publishing at www.crystallakepub.com or find him on Facebook.

Joe is also an Associate member of the HWA.

Lynda E. Rucker has sold more than 30 short stories to various magazines and anthologies including *F&SF, Nightmare Magazine, The Year's Best Horror, The Mammoth Book of Best New Horror, The Year's Best Horror and Dark Fantasy, Supernatural Tales,* and *Postscripts* among others and has had a short play produced as part of an anthology of horror plays on London's West End. She won the 2015 Shirley Jackson Award for Best Short Story and is a regular columnist for UK horror magazine *Black Static*. Her first collection, *The Moon Will Look Strange*, was released in 2013 from Karōshi Books, and her second, *You'll Know When You Get There*, was published by Ireland's Swan River Press in 2016.

Australian Shadows Award finalist **Daniel I. Russell** has been featured in publications such as *The Zombie Feed* from Apex, Pseudopod and *Andromeda Spaceways Inflight Magazine #43*. Author of *Samhane, Come into Darkness, Critique, Mother's Boys, The Collector* and *Tricks, Mischief and Mayhem*, Daniel is also the former vice-president of the Australian Horror Writers' Association and was a special guest editor of Midnight Echo.

Lucy A. Snyder is a four-time Bram Stoker Award-winning writer and the author of the novels *Spellbent, Shotgun Sorceress*, and *Switchblade Goddess*. She also authored the nonfiction book *Shooting Yourself in the Head for Fun and Profit: A Writer's Survival Guide* and the story collections *While the Black Stars Burn, Soft Apocalypses, Orchid Carousals, Sparks and Shadows,* and *Installing Linux on a Dead Badger*. She lives in Columbus, Ohio and is a mentor in Seton Hill University's MFA program in Writing Popular Fiction. You can learn more about her at www.lucysnyder.com and you can follow her on Twitter at @LucyASnyder.

Monique Snyman lives in Pretoria, South Africa with an adorable Chihuahua that keeps her company and a bloodthirsty lawyer who keeps her sane. She is a full-time author, part-time editor and in-between reviewer of all things entertaining. Her short fiction has been published in a number of small press anthologies, the *Charming Incantations* Series is published by Rainstorm Press, and she's working hard on a couple of other novels in her spare time

Shirley Jackson Award finalist **Tim Waggoner** has published over thirty novels and three short story collections of dark fiction. He teaches creative writing at Sinclair Community College and in Seton Hill University's MFA in Writing Popular Fiction program. His most recent novels are *The Way of All Flesh* and *Dream Stalkers*. You can find him on the web at www.timwaggoner.com.

Jonathan Winn is a screenwriter as well as the author of *Eidolon Avenue: The First Feast* (Crystal Lake Publishing, Jan 2016), the full-length novels *Martuk . . . the Holy* (A Highlight of the Year, 2012 Papyrus Independent Fiction Awards), *Martuk . . . the*

Holy: Proseuche (Top Twenty Horror Novels of 2014, Preditors & Editors Readers Poll), the upcoming *Martuk . . . the Holy: Shayateen* (Summer 2016) and *The Martuk Series*, an ongoing collection of short fiction inspired by *Martuk . . .*

In addition to his work in *Horror 201: The Silver Scream* and *Writers on Writing, Vol. 2*, Jonathan's award-winning short story *Forever Dark* can also be seen in Crystal Lake's *Tales from the Lake, Vol. 2*.

Stephanie M. Wytovich is an instructor by day and a horror writer by night. She is the Poetry Editor for Raw Dog Screaming Press, an adjunct at Western Connecticut State University, and a book reviewer for Nameless Magazine. She is a member of the Science Fiction Poetry Association, an active member of the Horror Writers Association, and a graduate of Seton Hill University's MFA program for Writing Popular Fiction. Her Bram Stoker Award-nominated poetry collections, Hysteria: A Collection of Madness, Mourning Jewelry, An Exorcism of Angels, and Brothel earned their home with Raw Dog Screaming Press, and her debut novel, The Eighth, is simmering in sin with Dark Regions Press. Follow Wytovich at stephaniewytovich.blogspot.com and on twitter @JustAfterSunset.

Mercedes M. Yardley is a dark fantasist who wears red lipstick and poisonous flowers in her hair. She writes short stories, nonfiction, novellas, and novels. She is the author of *Beautiful Sorrows, Apocalyptic Montessa and Nuclear Lulu: A Tale of Atomic Love, Nameless, Little Dead Red*, and her latest release, *Pretty Little Dead Girls: A Novel of Murder and Whimsy*, from Ragnarok Publications. Mercedes lives and works in Sin City, and you can reach her at www.mercedesyardley.com.

Hi, readers. It makes our day to know you reached the end of our book. Thank you so much. This is why we do what we do every single day.

Whether you found the book good or great, we'd love to hear what you thought. Please take a moment to leave a review on Amazon, Goodreads, or anywhere else readers visit. Reviews go a long way to helping a book sell, and will help us to continue publishing quality books.

Thank you again for taking the time to journey with Crystal Lake Publishing.

We are also on . . .

Website
http://www.crystallakepub.com/

Books
http://www.crystallakepub.com/book-table/

Blog
http://www.crystallakepub.com/blog-2/

Newsletter
http://eepurl.com/xfuKP

Instagram
https://www.instagram.com/crystal_lake_publishing/

Patreon
https://www.patreon.com/CLP

YouTube
https://www.youtube.com/c/CrystalLakePublishing

Twitter
https://twitter.com/crystallakepub

Facebook page
https://www.facebook.com/Crystallakepublishing/

Tales from The Lake Anthologies Facebook page
https://www.facebook.com/Talesfromthelake/

Writers on Writing Facebook page
https://www.facebook.com/WritersOnWritingSeries/

Beneath the Lake Videocast Facebook page
https://www.facebook.com/BeneathTheLake/

Google+
https://plus.google.com/u/1/107478350897139952572

Pinterest
https://za.pinterest.com/crystallakepub/

Tumblr
https://www.tumblr.com/blog/crystal-lake-publishing

We'd love to hear from you.

With unmatched success since 2012, Crystal Lake Publishing has quickly become one of the world's leading indie publishers of Mystery, Thriller, and Suspense books with a Dark Fiction edge.

Crystal Lake Publishing puts integrity, honor and respect at the forefront of our operations.

We strive for each book and outreach program that's launched to not only entertain and touch or comment on issues that affect our readers, but also to strengthen and support the Dark Fiction field and its authors.

Not only do we publish authors who are legends in the field and as hardworking as us, but we look for men and women who care about their readers and fellow human beings. We only publish the very best Dark Fiction, and look forward to launching many new careers.

We strive to know each and every one of our readers, while building personal relationships with our authors, reviewers, bloggers, pod-casters, bookstores and libraries.

Crystal Lake Publishing is and will always be a beacon of what passion and dedication, combined with overwhelming teamwork and respect, can accomplish: Unique fiction you can't find anywhere else.

We do not just publish books, we present you worlds within your world, doors within your mind, from talented authors who sacrifice so much for a moment of your time.

This is what we believe in. What we stand for. This will be our legacy.

Welcome to Crystal Lake Publishing.

We hope you enjoyed this title. If so, we'd be grateful if you could leave a review on your blog or any of the other websites and outlets open to book reviews. Reviews are like gold to writers and publishers, since word-of-mouth is and will always be the best way to market a great book. And remember to keep an eye out for more of our books.

THANK YOU FOR PURCHASING THIS BOOK

www.ingramcontent.com/pod-product-compliance
Lightning Source LLC
Chambersburg PA
CBHW070047080526
44586CB00013B/947